HUMAN CONFLICT
AN ATTITUDINAL PSYCHOLOGY MODEL

Attitude
+Behaviour
+Contact
+Differences
+Societal views
+Responses

G. A. Mohr, PhD
R.S. Mohr & P.E. Mohr

HUMAN CONFLICT
AN ATTITUDINAL
PSYCHOLOGY MODEL

G. A. MOHR, PhD
R.S. MOHR & P.E. MOHR

G. A. Mohr, R.S. Mohr & P.E. Mohr
Human Conflict
An Attitudinal Psychology Model

TRI

(Transworld Research & Innovation)
9 Hampstead Drive
Hoppers Crossing VIC 3029
AUSTRALIA

TABLE OF CONTENTS

PREFACE

Human history is dominated by tales of war and other conflict. It has been estimated that in the period 1820 to 1990 there were at least 100 wars involving at least two nations. In the last century there were two world wars, the second killing 60 million people, mostly civilians. In the period 1946 to 1990 there were more than 100 wars in 60 countries or territories, killing another 16 million, mostly civilians.

The four chapters that make up Part 1 of this book give an overview of man's long history of conflict.

The six chapters of Part 2 discuss the psychology of human conflict, beginning in Chapter 5 with some of the theory behind the advertising and propaganda used to brainwash the masses into following lousy leaders into needless wars.

In Chapters 6 and & 7 the psychology and measurement of attitudes is discussed, including the information integration model of attitude formation, the theory of reasoned action, the Guttman scalogram, and Bogardus' social distance scale.

Chapter 8 is devoted to discussion of the contact hypothesis and its application to ethnic conflict, and Chapter 9 to the important role hierarchies play in allowing ambitious people with type A personalities to satisfy their ambitions by fair means and foul.

The final chapter of Part 2 (Chapter 9) introduces the Attitudinal Model of Conflict in which a person or group's overall attitude to another group is assessed as a summation of five parts, each with its own multi-item assessment.

The 13 chapters of Part 3 discuss the many areas in which human conflict occurs, beginning with areas of individual conflict such as marital conflict and bullying in schools and the workplace. Chapter 14 includes discussion of mass shootings which have been a major concern in the USA in the last decade or two. Following chapters discuss tribal, territorial, imperial, religious, ethnic, societal, and political conflict. The last three chapters discuss the two World Wars of the last century, modern terrorism, and revolution.

The first chapter of Part 4 of the book expands discussion of the Attitudinal Model of Conflict.

The next two chapters discuss democracy and socialism, and the decline of the Western empires at a time when the 21st century is often referred to as "The Asian Century."

The penultimate chapter points out the frightening prospects of nuclear and biological warfare, whilst the final chapter suggests many things we can do to reduce future conflict, with particular emphasis on our improving our inter-group attitudes and communication and directing all our efforts at tackling the many problems that threaten our very survival, including our grossly excessive population, resource depletion, and climate change.

I hope the book will make people more aware of man's disastrous history of conflict and of how to reduce hostility and conflict at every level of society so that we can focus on improving our survival prospects as a species.

I hope too that the world will one day see *real democracy* as I describe it in the final chapter, my having run for party preselection at both state and federal levels having helped me envision some of the electoral procedures required.

Finally, thanks again to Amazon-Kindle for their efficient publication process.

Geoff Mohr   2018

Chapter 1

TRIBAL HOMO SAPIENS

Tribalism is the strongest force in the world today.
Vine Deloria, U.S. Native American leader,
Custer Died for Your Sins: An Indian Manifesto (1969), ch. 11.

Introduction

Humans are animals, of course, but simply with an enlarged cerebral cortex to store the semantic memory needed for our advanced languages. Nevertheless, we evolved from animal origins and, therefore, possess the same physical and behavioural characteristics as most of the larger land-based animal species.

Physically, we eat, we sleep, we defecate, and so forth. Behaviourally, besides our language, which we take so long to learn in infancy, we make various other communicative noises, we still encourage the despicable alpha-male phenomenon (for example in such animalistic sports as rugby), our male sports stars still bare and beat their chests after victory, just as apes might do, and, of course, we have a sorry history of conflict ranging from interpersonal conflict to world wars.

Indeed, our history of wars and other disasters is such that we might, indeed, wonder whether we are not, perhaps, in many ways the most stupid of animals.

Evolution of tribal man

Chimpanzees, with which we share circa 96% of the same genes, are sociable animals that live in groups of 20 to 60, forming into subgroups of adults (male and female), all-male groups and groups of mothers and offspring. African gorillas also live in bisexual groups of between 2 to 30 but which do not comprise smaller subgroups.

The best known studies of chimpanzees were conducted by Jane Goodall and associates in the Gombe National Park on the edge of Lake Tanganyika in Tanzania (Goodall, 1971).

Ultimately, Goodall was quite disillusioned to find that *tribes* of chimps were led by an alpha male and would occasionally have small wars with neighbouring tribes, these resuming at intervals over periods of many years. She concluded that they were all too much like humans!

Comparisons of blood proteins and the DNA of the African great apes with that of humans indicates that the line leading to modern people did not split off from that of chimpanzees and gorillas until comparatively late in evolution, perhaps 6 million to 8 million years ago.

Fossils of the first *hominines,* the *australopithecines*, dating to 5 million years ago have been discovered. This genus seems to have become extinct about 1.5 million years ago, but before doing so one of seven species of australopithecines, *Australopithecus africanus*, evolved into the genus *Homo* between 1.5 and 2 million years ago.

The earliest evidence of stone tools comes from sites in Africa dated to about 2.5 million years ago. These tools seem to be associated with all hominine species.

Around 1.7 to 1.9 million years ago two new species of large brained, small-toothed hominines emerged, *Homo ergaster* in Africa and *Homo erectus* in Asia.

Later *H. erectus* skulls possess brain sizes in the range of 1100 to 1300 cc (67.1 to 79.3 cu in), within the size variation of *Homo sapiens*.

A number of archaeological sites dating from the time of *Homo erectus* reveal a greater sophistication in tool making than was found at earlier sites. Evidence found at the cave site of "Peking Man" in northern China, suggests that *Homo erectus* used fire.

The remains of the foundations of an oval structure built by a *Homo erectus* group were found at the Terra-Amata site in France, and within this structure, there was a fireplace (Weiss and Mann, 1978).

The *Homo* species spread widely and by 350,000 years ago planned hunting, fire making, wearing of clothes, and probably burial rituals, were well established.

Between 200,000 and 300,000 years ago, *Homo sapiens* evolved.

The Neanderthals or *Homo sapiens neanderthalensis* had similar DNA to modern man and occupied parts of Europe and the Middle East as early as 120,000 years ago. They lived only in family groups, the men being hunter-gatherers to feed the family.

The Neanderthals left cave paintings that were an important evolutionary advance. These often depicted a simple activity, perhaps a precursor to the highly pictorial hieroglyphic script of the ancient Egyptians (Egerton-Eastwick, 1896).

Though Neanderthals had 10% larger brains than modern man has, there is some evidence that the part of the cerebral cortex devoted to language and thinking in modern man was underdeveloped in Neanderthal man, casting some doubt on whether Neanderthal man was capable of modern spoken language.

Thought by some to be a different evolutionary branch, the Neanderthals disappeared from the fossil record about 30,000 years ago.

Differing in appearance, modern humans or *Homo sapiens sapiens* evolved in southern Africa or the Middle East perhaps 90,000 to 200,000 years ago and 70,000 years ago began to spread to all parts of the world, reaching Europe about 40,000 years ago, soon outnumbering, perhaps interbreeding with, and finally supplanting the local, earlier *Homo sapiens* populations.

Like chimpanzees, Homo sapiens sapiens formed tribes and there is evidence of religion, recorded events and art dating from 30,000 to 40,000 years ago implying the advanced language and ethics required for the ordering of social groups.

Evolution of religion

Around the same time Homo sapiens developed cave art, about 100,000 years ago, he would have developed language and, eventually some form of 'pictorial' communication which eventually evolved into hieroglyphic script, then cuneiform script, and finally the symbolic writing we now use.

Typically, each tribe had a leader, a religion, and a common language and culture.

The first forms of religion involved such beliefs and practices as:

(a) *Animism*, belief that plants, inanimate objects and natural phenomena had souls or spirits.

(b) *Polytheism,* belief in multiple Gods, sometimes attributing certain acts of nature to each.

(c) *Ancestor Worship* teaching that a tribe's people were descended from a common ancestor.

(d) *Immortality* or belief that the dead live on as spirits, promises of immortality to the faithful still being amongst the 'blackmail' tactics preachers use today.

Eventually these religions evolved into the *monotheism* that dominates the world today.

Thus, at the outset it was the tribal elders who passed on tribal beliefs from one generation to another, a situation that still exists amongst a few primitive people today. Along the way *shamans* or 'witch doctors' claiming some special connection with the spirits appeared, along with religious rites and ceremonies.

In groups of hunter-gatherers, just as with many other species of animals, the 'dominant' males were, of course, responsible for protection of the group from external threats which, just as with chimpanzees, often took the form of other 'tribes' or groups.

At the same time, however, the supposedly wiser elders still indoctrinated the young into religion and had considerable influence, if not control, over the 'dominant males.' Their weapons for control ranged from rhetoric to dire threats of a vengeful spirit or God.

Thus, from the ancient Greeks through to the middle ages a study of *rhetoric* was considered important because of its use to bullshit people into doing as political and religious leaders wished. Francis Bacon (1561 - 1626), for example, studied Elizabethan logic and rhetoric at Cambridge University for two years, leaving at the age of 14 (note that people got married at this sort of age then).

Conflict

No doubt there was occasional conflict within the family groups that Homo sapiens lived in, perhaps, for example, over decisions about where to search and hunt for food.

Indeed, such arguments may have led to conflict over who leadership of the group should be trusted to.

There may, of course, have also been occasional conflict with other family groups over territorial issues or, in effect, 'hunting and searching rights' in certain areas which more than one group lived near.

Once tribes were established, questions of leadership may have become more important. No doubt the stronger males were likely to be chosen as leaders in both regular hunting and occasional conflicts between neighbouring tribes.

Indeed, tribal conflicts are 'war' and, of course, some American Indians still ceremonially perpetuate the practice of covering their faces with 'war paint' that traditionally preceded a tribal conflict.

In addition, the elders would often, at least, have had some influence, whilst their role in passing on tribal folklore would certainly have involved tales of conflicts past with other tribes and thus encouraged acceptance and continuance of such conflicts.

In addition, tribal witch doctors or shamans would have had considerable influence, their superstitious view of things no doubt causing other tribes to be considered 'heathen' and viewed with suspicion, if not hostility.

Thus they increased the 'differences' between their tribe and others, an important factor in ethnic conflict which is further discussed in Chapters 8 and 10.

Indeed, it was often supposed that the Neanderthals were wiped out by invading Homo sapiens sapiens from the South, but is now believed that, in fact, the two closely related species interbred and thus those of us with European lineage have some Neanderthal DNA.

No doubt the invaders also killed a great many Neanderthals as well, perhaps mostly the more threatening males. In other words, in war kill the men and rape the women, something that has not changed since then in the brutality of war.

Conclusion

Primitive man was not far different from modern man, having large groups sometimes in conflict, supposedly stronger leaders to lead or dictate those conflicts, religious leaders to create ethnic differences to encourage mistrust and tribal conflict, and elders to keep alive and thus help continue a history of conflict.

An example of the latter today, some people call one of the major Australian TV channels 'The Hitler Channel' because it so often airs documentaries about Hitler and his associates to keep us reminded of one of the greatest villains in relatively recent history, and keep us mentally prepared to blindly accept the political propaganda and bullshit that will precede the next war some of us are ordered to participate in.

Thus, when we saw repeated pictures of Saddam Hussein holding a rifle in the media in the months before the post 9/11 US invasion of Iraq, we knew that the US would go to war with that country, however mistakenly. As usual, they did far more harm than good and, in effect, lost because, of course, they certainly didn't win anything but lost a great deal of money yet again, as they did in Vietnam and Korea.

The US also lost WW2 (to Joseph Stalin) but made a great deal of money using Lend Lease to sell badly needed weapons to several countries including England, France, the Netherlands, and Russia.

Finally, and farcically, humans still perpetuate the absurd tribal practices of sports with a conflict connotation, for example shooting, archery, and rugby (do as told and charge the enemy as in the trench warfare of WW1).

Primitive tribal man did likewise but with spears and perhaps knives and rocks.

Modern man, thanks to advanced technology, has far more brutal weapons and thus could be argued to have become far more brutal, just one factor in our 'reverse evolution' discussed in a recent book (Mohr, 2012b).

1. Tribal Homo Sapiens

Chapter 2

THE AGRICULTURAL REVOLUTION & CITY-STATES

Clearly, then, the city is not a concrete jungle, it is a human zoo.
Desmond Morris, *The Human Zoo* (1969), Introduction.

The Agricultural Revolution

About 12,000 years ago the Agricultural Revolution, in part enabled by development of primitive forms of permanent housing, led to the growth of human societies from small tribes to those of settlements of hundreds and eventually, as farming became more productive, thousands of people.

More efficient farming allowed more specialization, for example millers, bakers and weavers. In these growing societies religion became increasingly important as a means of imparting ethics and standards.

These larger societies now had houses and farms to defend, however, so that the need for stronger males for territorial defence grew and with it the influence that their leaders had upon society. This may have led to the appearance of leaders of towns or regions involving a few nearby towns and, eventually, monarchs.

In some societies, however, priest-kings emerged, but generally 'church' and 'state' have remained, ostensibly at least, separate entities to this day, both doing their utmost to control their societies.

In the rest of society the mercantile infrastructure of the consumer society that we have today began to evolve with open air markets largely giving way to shops and barter systems giving way to currency.

Regular armies

With towns and surrounding farms to defend from intrusion and theft of agricultural products, the task of defence would have fallen into the hands of ordinary local citizens, particularly the outlying farmers whose fields were most vulnerable to intrusion.

Eventually, as towns grew in size, and the occupations of the citizens in them continued to diversify, small citizen territorial armies may have been formed on an occasional basis to protect towns and their surrounding farms.

Ultimately, however, increasingly powerful leaders formed regular armies, their power increasing with each conquest during which, no doubt, they were able to seize valuables and slaves from captured towns.

Mesopotamia

Mesopotamia, the area between the Tigris and the Euphrates, was conventionally divided in two: Upper Mesopotamia, the home of the Assyrians, extending from Baghdad to eastern Turkey, and Lower Mesopotamia.

Sumer, the part of Lower Mesopotamia between Babylon and the Persian Gulf, was the place where the world's first urban civilization evolved. Eridu, Ur and Uruk were amongst the greatest Sumerian city-states dating as far back as 4000BC.

Political primacy passed from one city and its kingly dynasty to another, for example the Alkadians (first under Sargon I circa 2350BC), the Amorites (whose laws, codified by Hammurabi circa 1792-1750BC, have biblical parallels), and the Assyrians, with interludes by the Hittites, Kassites, and Mitannia (World Almanac, 1998).

Surviving art forms date from 2500BC, and include stone statues of Gudea and coloured bas-reliefs.

Gudea, the fourth ruler of the Sumerian dynasty of Lagash, ruled from circa 2144 to 2124BC. Lagash was a powerful city-state on the present-day site of Telloh near the Persian Gulf in southern Iraq. Gudea built 15 temples in Girsu, an administrative centre of Lagash, including the massive temple Eninnu which was devoted to the city god Ningursu. Gudea had military victories over the nearby settlements of Anshan and Elam.

Later came Babylonia, the region in Lower Mesopotamia around the ancient city of Babylon, around which was centred two extensive but short-lived empires (Chambers, 1993).

The first was created by the Amorite King Hammurabi (c. 1795 – 1750BC) and covered the whole of Mesopotamia but was destroyed by the Hittites circa 1595BC. The second resulted from the Babylonian overthrow of Assyria in 612BC and under its greatest monarch, Nebuchadnezzar (605 - 562BC), it stretched as far east as the Mediterranean. It was conquered by Persia in 539 – 538BC.

Egypt

Agricultural villages along the Nile were unified by 3300BC into two kingdoms, Upper and Lower Egypt, which were unified circa 3100BC by the pharaoh Menes. Hieroglyphic writing appeared by 3200 BC and a bureaucracy supervised construction of canals and monuments, construction of the first pyramids beginning circa 2700BC.

A powerful priesthood in Memphis served a hierarchical order of gods, including totemistic animals, and believed in the afterlife.

Control over Nubia to the south was gained from 2600BC. After a period of dominance by semetic Hyksos from Asia (1700 – 1550BC), the New Kingdom established an empire in Syria. Egypt became increasingly embroiled in Asiatic wars and was conquered by Persia in 525BC (World Almanac, 1998).

India

Between 3000 and 1500BC urban civilization with an as yet undeciphered writing system stretched across the Indus Valley and along the Arabian Sea, and the entire region may have been ruled as a single state.

The cities of Harappa and Mohenjo-Daro in Pakistan were geometrically well-planned with underground sewers and large granaries.

Religious life mainly derived from fertility cults and Indus civilization was destroyed by Aryan invaders from the north-west, speaking an Indo-European language from which most languages in Pakistan, north India and Bangladesh derive. Led by a warrior aristocracy the Aryans spread east and south, bringing their sky gods, elaborate Brahman rituals, and the roots of the caste system.

Greece

On Crete, the Bronze Age Minoan civilization emerged circa 2500BC, reaching its peak in 1500BC, the economy prospering by seaborne commerce.

Mycenae and other cities in mainland Greece and Asia Minor such as Troy preserved Minoan culture until circa 1200BC. Cretan Linear A script (c. 2000 – 1700BC) remains undeciphered but Linear B script (c. 1300 – 1200BC) records an early Greek dialect.

Sparta, in the south Peloponnesus, was one of the leading city-states of ancient Greece, having expanded its power by subjugating the neighbouring Laconians and Messenians as serfs. Government was oligarchic and led by two hereditary kings whose duties were primarily military and religious.

The revolt of Messenia in 650BC led to military and social reforms aimed at preventing further uprisings. By the 6th century BC Sparta was the greatest military power in Greece, its leadership of the Peloponnesian League helping it defeat Athens in the Peloponnesian War of 431 – 404BC.

Thereafter Sparta's military power declined and was never to be revived after defeat by the Thebans at the Battle of Leuctra in 371BC (Chambers, 1993).

China

North and south-east China had long had Neolithic cultures when the Shang dynasty (c. 1523BC) formed the first large political state in which a writing system with 2,000 characters was in use. Shang kings called themselves Sons of Heaven, and presided over cults of human and animal sacrifice to ancestors and nature gods.

The Chang dynasty, which started circa 1027BC, expanded the area of the Sons of Heaven's dominion, but feudal states still had most temporal power.

The Americas

Circa 1500 BC Olmecs settled on the Gulf of Mexico and developed the first civilization in the Western hemisphere. Temple cities dated from 1200BC and a crude calendar and writing system existed. Olmec religion, based on a jaguar god, and Olmec art forms are said to have influenced all later Central American cultures.

Rome

Legend has it that Rome, the greatest city-state in history, was founded in 753BC by Romulus and Remus, the twin sons of Rhea Silvia, a vestal virgin and daughter of Numitor, king of Alba Longa, a nearby City in ancient Latium. Alba Longa was founded by Ascanius, son of the Trojan leader Aeneas, who was founder and first king of Alba Longa.

Romulus was the first of 7 kings in Rome's 'regal period' from 753 to 510BC. The king, or rex, was chosen by the Senate, or Council of Elders, from the ranks of the patricians, who constituted the *populus*, or people, whose dependants (often slaves), known as clients or the plebs, had no political rights.

The king called out the populus for war and led the army himself. He was the supreme judge in civil and criminal suits and the Senate gave its advice only when the king chose to ask for it.

Later in the regal period, when the plebs had been allowed to acquire property and wealth, both patrician and plebeian property holders were compelled to serve in the army, their rank depending upon their wealth.

Over time, of course, Rome grew in power, ultimately forging a great empire covering much of the globe, as will be discussed in Chapter 4.

Conclusions

In the early city-states, their growing societies and the organizations within them, especially the army and the church, took on hierarchical forms and the main weapons of control ranged from verbal persuasion to threats throughout a chain of command to see that the rest of the population towed the line.

Unfortunately, however, the ambitious, aggressive, and assertive people who literally fight their way to leadership positions through impatience, stupidity and deceit have done far more harm than good and our unending history of conflict and war attests to this.

In the early city-states these wasteful leaders required grand residences and temples to be built, had large numbers of domestic slaves, and organized large armies of soldiers.

As we have seen throughout history, these armies were used all too often, often for little or no good reason, and some attempt to bring a little science to the understanding of mankind's seemingly endless history of conflict is made in following chapters of this book.

2. THE AGRICULTURAL REVOLUTION & CITY-STATES

Chapter 3

MONARCHY & OLIGARCHY

*In all ages, hypocrites, called priests, have put crowns
upon the heads of thieves, called kings.*
Robert G. Ingersoll, *Prose-Poems and Selections* (1884).

They that are discontented under *monarchy,* call it *tyranny;*
and they that are displeased with *aristocracy,* call it *oligarchy;*
so also, they which find themselves grieved under a *democracy,*
call it *anarchy,* which signifies a want of government;
and yet I think no man believes, that want of government,
is any new kind of government.
Thomas Hobbes, *Leviathan* (1651), pt. 2, ch. 1.

Introduction

Throughout history man has had many kinds of leadership, some of the historically most common forms of leadership or government having been:

1. Autocracy is government by a single individual and WordWeb 6 defines autocrat as: *A cruel and oppressive dictator.* The Concise Oxford Dictionary (edn 9) defines dictator as: *1 a ruler with (often usurped) unrestricted authority.*

2. Representative democracy is government by a collection of freely elected representatives of the people. In direct democracy the public participates directly in government, as in some ancient Greek city-states.

3. Fascism, according to Encyclopaedia Britannica Ready Reference 2003, is: *a philosophy of government that stresses the primacy and glory of the state, unquestioning obedience to its leader, subordination of the individual will to the state's authority, and harsh suppression of dissent.*

4. Monarchy is government led by a monarch, the Concise Oxford Dictionary (edn 9) defining monarch as: *a sovereign with the title of king, queen, emperor, empress, or the equivalent.* To this list *pharaoh* may be added for the case of ancient Egypt.

WordWeb 6 defines monarchy as: *An autocracy governed by a monarch who usually inherits the authority.*

5. Oligarchy is defined by Encyclopaedia Britannica Ready Reference 2003 as: *Rule by the few, often seen as having self-serving ends,* adding that: *Aristotle used the term pejoratively for unjust rule by bad men.*

Here the 'few' is unspecified in nature and more specific terms are:

(a) Aristocracy, according to the Concise Oxford Dictionary (edn 9) is:

1 a the highest class in society; the nobility.
  b the nobility as a ruling class.
2 a government by the nobility or a privileged group.
  b a state governed in this way.

(b) Plutocracy is defined by the Concise Oxford as:

1 a government by the wealthy.
  b a state governed in this way.
2 a wealthy elite or ruling class.

5. Theocracy is defined by Encyclopaedia Britannica Ready Reference 2003 as: *Government by those regarded as divinely guided. The government's leaders may be clergy, or that state's legal system may be based on religious laws. Theocratic rule was a constant of early civilizations. The enlightenment marked the end of theocracy in most Western countries. Present-day examples include Saudi Arabia, Iran, Afghanistan, and the Vatican.*

6. Totalitarianism is defined by the Concise Oxford as: **adj.** *of or relating to a centralized dictatorial form of government requiring complete subservience to the State.*

In relatively early history there were sometimes Priest-Kings, this being a form of theocracy relating back to the tribal witch doctors and shamans of primitive man.

Whatever form of leadership, however, mankind has throughout history continued to suffer dreadful spates of conflict and war, and almost invariably the blame for this must lie with the leaders for, of course, common man struggling to provide for his family, has little or no spare resources. To despicable leaders, however, the common working man is a *resource* to be used at their whim should they, yet again, find reason to engage in yet another war.

The Greek and Roman empires and war

As noted in Chapter 2, man's early civilizations were invariably at war, the early Greek and Roman Empires being perhaps the best examples as in these the king had the exclusive power to call the populace out to war.

As discussed in Chapter 4, Alexander the Great, regarded by many as one of the greatest generals in history, was almost always fighting one war or another in seeking to expand his empire.

There are few better examples of the absurd and underhand politics of war than that of Cleopatra's dealings with Rome. To save Egypt from annexation by Rome she bore a son to Julius Caesar, who supported her claim to the throne against her brother in 47BC. Mark Antony, by whom she had three children, restored to her portions of the old Ptolemaic Empire and gave their joint offspring parts of the Roman East in 34BC.

Eventually Marc Antony fell into disfavour in Rome and his and Cleopatra's combined forces suffered defeats by those of Octavius, he and later Cleopatra both committing suicide in 30BC.

The mighty Roman Empire always had trouble holding its borders in the West which lasted from 31BC to 476AD, but it lasted to 1453 in the East as the Byzantine Empire when the eastern capital Constantinople fell to the Ottoman Turks. The long history of conflict associated with both the Greek and Roman empires is detailed in Chapter 4.

Europe's mad monarchs

Early man's tribes were led by chiefs, defined by the Concise Oxford Dictionary (edn 9) as: *1 a a leader or ruler. b the head of a tribe, clan, etc.*

Originally man's tribal leaders were the bravest, strongest and smartest. With monarchy came the establishment of hereditary thrones which, thanks to the premature demise of the monarch, were often occupied by children who were advised by often untrustworthy people.

Worse still, many royal families married their own cousins and sometimes even their own sisters or brothers, perhaps seeking to ensure that they married royalty. The result was the odd half-witted monarch thanks to genetic defects.

The bottom line is, as Joy Masoff points out, that through history there have been many "cruddy kings, stupid shahs, evil emperors, and flat-out crazy Caesars" (Massof, 2006). Thus in the time of Henry Tudor "one thing kings did back then was go to war. France and England were always at each other's throats" (Massof, 2006).

After a brief alliance with Francis, the French king, Henry signed a treaty with Charles V, ruler of the Holy Roman Empire which included what is now Germany, Switzerland, Hungary, Austria, and the Netherlands. Within a month England and France were at war and kept at it on and off for the next 200 years.

Indeed, for hundreds of years, some part of Europe has, more often than not been at war with another, culminating in WW1 and WW2, whilst more recently we saw war in the former Yugoslavia.

China

In 221BC, the king of Qin proclaimed himself Shihuangdi, or First Emperor of the Qin dynasty (221-206BC). The name China is derived from this dynasty (Encarta, 1999).

The First Emperor welded a loose configuration of quasi-feudal states into an administratively centralized and culturally unified empire. The hereditary aristocracies were abolished and their territories divided into provinces governed by bureaucrats appointed by the emperor.

The Qin capital, near the present-day city of Xi'an, became the first seat of imperial China. A standardized system of written characters was adopted, and its use was made compulsory throughout the empire.

The First Emperor also attempted to push the perimeter of Chinese civilization far beyond the outer boundaries of the Zhou dynasty (c. 1027-256BC), his armies marching south to the delta of the Red River, in what is now Vietnam. In the southwest the realm was extended to include most of the present-day provinces of Yunnan, Guizhou, and Sichuan. In the northwest his conquests reached as far as Lanzhou in present-day Gansu Province. In the northeast part of what today is Korea was added to the empire.

The centre of Chinese civilization, however, remained in the Huang He valley. Aside from the unification and expansion of China, the best-known achievement of the Qin was the completion of earthen fortifications that centuries later came to be known as the Great Wall.

The foreign conquests of the Qin and the wall building and other public works cost a great many lives and drained the public coffers.

The increasing burden of taxation, military service, and forced labour caused resentment against the Qin rule amongst the common people and finally rebellion resulted in the establishment of the Earlier Han Dynasty (206BC – 8AD) and by the middle of the 2nd century BC almost all Han territory was under direct imperial rule.

The Han established Confucianism as the official ideology, incorporating ideas from many other philosophical schools into it. In staffing the bureaucracy the Han emperors followed the Confucian principle of appointing men on the basis of merit rather than birth and written examinations were used to find the best people. In the late 2nd century BC an imperial university was established, in which prospective bureaucrats were trained in the five classics of the Confucian school (Encarta, 1999).

The power of the Earlier Han peaked under Emperor Wu Ti's reign (from 140 to 87 BC) and almost all of what today constitutes China was brought under imperial rule.

The short-lived Hsin Dynasty (AD 9-23) followed after a period of discontent. This was followed by the Later Han (25-220) which suffered considerable internal disunity and external rebellion from religious sects.

The Han Empire began to disintegrate as large landholding families established their own private armies. Finally, in 220 the son of Ts'ao Ts'ao seized the throne and established the Wei dynasty (220-264).

Soon other leaders with dynastic claims established three other kingdoms in regions of China and these waged incessant warfare against one another.

Many other dynasties were to follow but, typical of man's history, disunity and conflict reappeared periodically.

The Re-established Empire reunited China during the Sui dynasty (589-618). The brief Sui reign was a time of great activity. The Great Wall was repaired at an enormous cost in human life. A canal system, which later formed the Grand Canal, was built to carry the rich agricultural produce of the Yangtze delta to Luoyang and the north.

Under Sui rule Chinese control was reasserted over northern Vietnam and, to a limited degree, over the Central Asian tribes to the north and west. A prolonged and costly campaign against a kingdom in southern Manchuria and northern Korea, however, ended in defeat. With its prestige seriously tarnished and its population impoverished, the Sui dynasty fell in 618 to domestic rebels led by Li Yuan.

Founded by Li Yuan, the Tang dynasty (618-907) was an era of strength and brilliance unprecedented in the history of Chinese civilization. Its system of civil service examinations for recruitment of the bureaucracy was so well refined that its basic form survived into the 20th century. Under the Tang, Chinese influence was extended over Korea, southern Manchuria, and northern Vietnam. In the west, by means of alliances with Central Asian tribes, the Tang controlled the Tarim Pendi and eventually made their influence felt as far afield as present-day Afghanistan (Encarta, 1999).

Oligarchy

A democracy exits whenever those who are free and are not well-off, being in the majority, are in sovereign control of government, an oligarchy when control lies with the rich and better born. Aristotle, *The Politics* (343 BC).

The administration of the Roman Empire was largely oligarchical, the Senate being comprised of the wealthiest men in Rome who elected the emperor and charged him with the task of extending and defending the empire.

Indeed, from man's earliest tribal days there has always been a tendency for the strongest and thence more powerful to control the affairs of a tribe, town, city, or nation. Thus European kingdoms usually established an aristocracy to govern them, with the king as the head of state, an example being England's House of Lords.

In more recent times both the UK and USA are strongly oligarchical, a good example being the Trilateral Commission funded by David Rockefeller in the 1970s.

In 1975 it held a meeting of multinational corporate executives to consider the "excess of democracy" afflicting advanced capitalist countries and to "rationalize the US economy through capitalist dominated planning and in conjunction with other leading capitalist nations to reassert US authority on a world scale" (Crough et al., 1980).

In both the USA and UK big business largely runs the government, particularly their massive arms industries, the world's two biggest (Thomas, 2007).

Indeed, as discussed in Chapter 25, it was the fears of big business in the UK and US that led to the immensely prolonged and costly Cold War against the USSR, the immense stockpiles of nuclear and biochemical weapons, for example, helping to keep the barons of the arms industry filthy rich.

Conclusion

The Greek and Roman Empires were, it seems, at war as often as not, the same applying to some of the European states and empires of the last millennium, particularly England.

For over a thousand years China too had conflict as often as not, much of it a result of internal dissent, and its empire did not expand a great deal compared to that of Rome at its peak.

In much of this history one is tempted to associate the territorial ambitions of leaders with those of alpha males in the animal kingdom, and no better example of this might have been Alexander the Great (see Chapter 4).

Today still we still suffer bad and/or mad leaders and the oligarchies usually associated with them.

A case in point is the President of the USA who is chief of the army and has the sole power to kick start a nuclear war at the push of a button.

Indeed, no doubt influenced by the Rockefellers et al., the USA is still busy trying to be the 'world's only superpower' and exert that power, a history of mistaken and lost wars growing with every decade and including Korea, Vietnam, Iraq and now Afghanistan and resulting in the death of circa 10 million innocent civilians, a result even Hitler would not have dreamed of.

There is nothing very democratic about this.

We elect people with party power behind them, that being funded by large handouts from big business and the public purse. We do not elect the party leaders, however, and nor do we have any real say in policy.

Worse still, what little firm policy parties announce before an election is as likely as not to be changed within a few years, a good example being Australia's Prime Minister John Howard announcing before an election in the 1990s that he would never introduce a GST. Re-elected, he did just that within a few years.

As for war, normal adult people with families to care for want peace and enough money to get by on without too much suffering. Most of them dare not even dream of the prosperity that bullshit artist politicians so often talk of.

More importantly, normal sane people do not want to fight wars sometimes thousands of miles away from their homes, wars which, as discussed in Chapter 26, only send their nations broke in the end in any case.

As we have already seen in only 3 chapters of this book, it seems that wars are usually in the interests of lousy leaders and their oligarchies rather than the populace, and this needs change. Indeed, it seems that this practice became something of a habit for national leaders thousands of years ago, one that to a large extent, at least, remains to the present day. What we need is for warring leaders to kill each other and leave it at that!

3. Monarchy & Oligarchy

Chapter 4

EMPIRE BUILDING

An empire founded by war has to maintain itself by war.
Baron Montesquieu, Considérations sur les causes de la grandeur
des Romains, et de leur dècadence (1734), ch. 8.

The Empires of Athens and Macedon

The first known European empires resulted from the unification of city-states in Greece to deal with invading Persians who were turned back in 480BC at the land battle of Thermopylae and the naval battle of Salamis. From 478BC the alliance was centred in Athens but the empire collapsed in the Peloponnesian Wars of 431-404BC when some of the city states rebelled against Athenian rule (Cowie et al., 1994).

Alexander ascended to the Macedonian throne in 336BC when his father was assassinated. A student of Aristotle, he quickly executed domestic opponents, quickly restored Macedonian rule to a rebellious Thessaly, and was elected by a congress of state at Corinth.

In 335BC he led a successful campaign against defecting Thracians, reaching as far as the Danube River.

On return to Greece he crushed threatening Illyrians in just a week. Then he took the revolting city of Thebes by storm, razed it, and took the 8,000 survivors prisoner as slaves.

In 334BC he went to war with Persia with an army of 35,000 Macedonians and Greeks and defeated an army of 40,000 Persians and Greek *hoplites* (mercenaries), legend having it that he lost only 110 men in the process. After this battle all the states of Asia Minor submitted to his authority.

In 333BC he defeated what legend has it was a huge Persian army led by Darius at Issus in northeastern Syria, but Darius escaped, leaving his family behind.

After a 7 month siege he captured the strongly fortified seaport of Tyre, moving on to Gaza and then Egypt, gaining control of the entire eastern Mediterranean coastline.

In 332BC he founded the city of Alexandria at the mouth of the Nile River. Soon afterward Cyrene, the capital of the ancient North African kingdom of Cyrenaica, submitted to Alexander and he then extended his dominion to Carthaginian territory.

After a spell in Egypt he headed northward again towards Babylon with an army of 40,000 infantry and 7,000 cavalry. Crossing the Euphrates and Tigris he defeated another huge army led by Darius at the battle of Gaugamela on Oct. 1st, 331BC. Again Darius fled but was eventually assassinated by two of his generals.

Babylon surrendered after Gaugamela, and the city of Sûsa with its enormous treasures was soon conquered.

Then, in midwinter, Alexander forced his way to the Persian capital Persepolis and plundered and burned it, completing his destruction of the ancient Persian Empire.

Alexander's domain now extended along and beyond the southern shores of the Caspian Sea, including modern Afghanistan and Baluchistan, and northward into Central Asia. It took Alexander only three years, from the spring of 330BC to the spring of 327BC, to master this vast area.

In order to complete his conquest of the remnants of the Persian Empire, which had once included part of western India, Alexander crossed the Indus River in 326BC, and invaded the Punjab but then the Macedonians rebelled and refused to go further.

Alexander then constructed a fleet and passed down the Indus, reaching its mouth in September 325BC. The fleet then sailed to the Persian Gulf. With his army, he returned overland across the desert to Media. Shortages of food and water caused severe losses and hardship among his troops.

Alexander then spent about a year organizing his dominions and completing a survey of the Persian Gulf in preparation for further conquests but in June 323BC he contracted a fever and died, willing his empire "to the strongest," a testament that led to conflicts for 50 years.

The Roman Empire

The powerful city state of Rome's 'regal period' (753 - 510BC) was briefly outlined in Chapter 2.

In the period 510 – 264BC there were many administrative and social changes, the senate including both patricians and plebeians and electing two consuls as leaders with only a one-year term.

Rome had acquired leadership of Latium before the end of the regal period. Now the military policy became more aggressive and, assisted by their allies, the Romans fought wars against the Etruscans, the Volscians, and the Aequians. In 390BC the Romans were defeated by the Gauls at Allia and Rome was captured and burned.

Nevertheless, Rome continued to overtake Etruria and by the middle of the 4th century BC all southern Etruria was kept in check by Roman garrisons and denationalized by an influx of Roman colonists. Eventually the whole country was assimilated by the Romans circa 200BC (Encarta, 1999).

Victories over the Volscians, the Latins, and the Hernicans gave the Romans control of central Italy and brought them into conflict with the Samnites of southern Italy, who were defeated in a series of three wars, extending from 343 to 290BC. A revolt of the Latins and Volscians was put down and resistance elsewhere was also eventually overcome.

Circa 270BC the Romans completed their conquest of southern Italy and thus gained control of the entire peninsula as far north as the Arno and Rubicon rivers.

In 264BC Rome engaged in struggle with Carthage, the foremost maritime power in the world at that time, for control over the Mediterranean Sea.

In the First Punic War (264-261BC) Rome gained its first foreign possession, the Carthaginian part of Sicily, and Sardinia and Corsica were annexed soon after this.

Carthage responded by taking over part of Spain and using it as a military base.

In the Second Punic War (218 – 201BC) Hannibal crossed the alps and invaded Italy from the north and ravaged it for years but was recalled to fight Scipio Africanus, the Roman general who had invaded Carthage, and who defeated Hannibal at Zama in 202BC. Rome forced Carthage to cede Spain and its Mediterranean islands and pay a huge indemnity.

In the Third Punic War (149-146BC) the Romans, led by Scipio the Younger, captured the city of Carthage, razed it to the ground, and sold the surviving inhabitants into slavery.

Meanwhile, in the preceding years Rome had increased its holdings in Europe, Asia Minor and Greece.

After two wars with Macedonia, it was made a province in 146BC.

A series of Spanish campaigns ended with the capture of Numantia in 133 BC. In the same year Attalus III of Pergamum (in what is now western Turkey) died, ceding his kingdom to Rome, and soon after this the territory was formed into the province of Asia (Encarta, 1999).

By now Rome's power had spread from the Italian Peninsula to cover much of the world.

From 133 to 27BC there was much internal conflict as wealthy families sought to increase their power. In that period, however, Rome continued to gain more territory in Africa, Gaul and Northern Italy.

In 67BC Julius Caesar began to rise to prominence as leader of the popular party, becoming consul in 59BC. Given extensive military commands competition between he and other leaders led to a five-year civil war from which Caesar emerged victorious.

Conflict with his remaining political opponent, Pompey, continued for some time, however, but Caesar finally defeated him and was made dictator for life in 45BC, only to be assassinated a year later.

Further battles for control of Rome ensued, Octavian eventually becoming undisputed ruler of the Empire in 29BC.

The following 200 years were prosperous and Rome's empire expanded considerably, extending as far as Britain where in 122 Hadrian ordered construction of the wall named after him.

The years 193-476 were those of the decline and fall of the Western Roman Empire but Rome's influence continued from 330 until 1453 in the East as the Byzantine Empire when the eastern capital Constantinople fell to the Ottoman Turks.

The Vikings

The Vikings were pagan pirates, traders and settlers who between the late 8c and the mid-11c conquered and colonized large parts of Britain (Dublin, est. 831), Normandy (settled 911), and Russia (8c – 11c).

They also attacked Spain, Morocco and Italy; traded with Byzantium, Persia and India; and discovered and occupied Iceland (874) and Greenland (986). They also reached the coast of North America circa 1000 and led by Duke William of Normandy conquered England in 1066 (Chambers, 1993; World Almanac, 1998).

The Islamic Empire

The Islamic Empire that emerged in the 7th century AD derived its cohesion from a religious belief. Early in the 8th century BC Muslim forces occupied Spain and threatened France, being repulsed at Tours only 300 km from Paris (Cowie et al., 1994).

The Ottoman Empire was a dynastic state centred in what is now Turkey. It was founded circa 1300 in Asia Minor. Ottoman forces entered Europe in 1345, conquered Constantinople in 1453, and by 1520 controlled most of south-eastern Europe, including part of Hungary, the Middle East, and North Africa.

From this peak the Ottoman Empire was eroded by the ambitions of Russia and Austria in south-east Europe, the ambitions of France, Britain and Italy in North Africa, and the emergence of the Balkan nations.

By the early 1900s the Ottoman Empire only controlled Asia Minor (the Anatolia region of present-day Turkey) and parts of the Balkans and the Middle East.

The empire lost further territory during WW1 and was occupied by Allied troops until 1922. These were driven out by nationalist forces and the Republic of Turkey was proclaimed in 1923 (Chambers, 1993; Encarta, 1999).

The Aztecs and Incas

By 1519 the Aztecs had built a Meso-American empire with its capital in Tenochtitlán (founded 1325) the centre of a cult requiring enormous levels of human sacrifice

Most of the civilized areas of South America were ruled by the centralized Inca Empire (1476 – 1534) which extended from Ecuador to NW Argentina.

The Spanish Empire

Besets by revolts, the Aztec and Inca Empires fell to gold-seeking Spanish forces based in the Antilles and Panama, Cortez taking Mexico (1519-21), and Pizarro taking Peru (1532-35) and founding its capital Lima.

From these centres land and sea expeditions claimed most of North and South America for Spain, most Indians being reduced to poverty whilst their cultures were destroyed by Christian missionaries and the new upper class of whites and mixed racial ancestry mestizos (World Almanac, 1998).

Spain overtook Portugal in 1580 but a national uprising began in 1640. This soon gained French naval and military support. In 1660 the marriage of Catherine of Braganza to Charles II of England ensured British help. After repeated failures by the Spanish to subdue the rebellion the Treaty of Lisbon (Feb. 1668) restored Portugal's independence.

The Spanish-American Wars of Independence (1810 – 1826) involved Venezuela, New Granada, Quito, Argentina, Chile and Peru. Peru was liberated in 1824 and the last Spanish garrisons surrendered to the patriots in 1826.

After the Spanish-American War of 1898 Spain lost the final remnants of its empire, Cuba, Puerto Rico and the Philippines, to the USA, signalling the emergence of the USA as an imperial power. The 'Disaster of 1898' triggered a protracted internal crisis that culminated in the fall of the monarchy in 1931 (Chambers, 1993).

The Portuguese Empire

The Portuguese reached Brazil by 1500 and settled after 1530. Portuguese explorers established a commercial empire in the Indian Ocean based on trade and war, rather than on taking large amounts of land and dominating its people. At first they had little competition because the Chinese called their fleets home and Indian and Arab ships did not carry guns.

By the early 16th century the Portuguese had established a string of strategic bases, including Hormuz at the tip of the Persian Gulf, Goa on the west coast of India, and the Straits of Molucca, the gateway between the Indian Ocean and the China Sea. From these bases the Portuguese controlled the sea-trade of the entire region and dominated the slave trade in the 16th century.

When larger European nations arrived in the area, however, Portuguese naval supremacy vanished.

The Dutch Empire

The urban Calvinist provinces of the northern Netherlands rebelled in 1568 against Hapsburg Spain and founded an oligarchic mercantile republic. After Spain absorbed Portugal in 1580, the Dutch seized Portuguese possessions and created a vast but generally short-lived empire in Brazil, the Antilles, Africa, India, Ceylon, Malacca, Indonesia and Taiwan.

Belgium gained its independence from the Netherlands in April 1839 after a revolution in 1830, followed by successful Dutch retaliation in 1831, and then an armed standoff and bitter negotiations for several years.

The French Empire

France founded permanent colonies in Canada (1608), the Caribbean (1626) and India (1674).

France's coastal blockade of Europe failed to neutralize Britain and Napoleon's 1812 invasion of Russia was a disaster. After his exile at Elba in 1814 his armies were defeated at Waterloo in 1815 by British and Prussian troops.

At the Congress of Vienna (Sept. 1814 – June 1815), the monarchs and princes of Europe revised their boundaries, Prussia making gains in Saxony and the Ruhr, Austria in Illyria and Venetia, Russia in Poland and Finland.

British conquest of Dutch and French colonies (South Africa, Ceylon and Mauritius) was recognized and France retained its expanded 1792 borders. This settlement gave Europe 50 years of peace.

After World War 2 former French colonies were reclassified as departments of France or overseas territories, most of which rapidly gained their independence in the following two decades.

China

The Great Wall of China was begun using 300,000 troops in 221BC during the Qin dynasty to repel attacks from northern nomads. It was improved during the Han (202BC – 220AD) and the Ming dynasties (1368 – 1644) and stretches 2150 miles from the Yellow Sea to the central Asian desert.

The Manchu invaded from the north-east in 1644 and created the Qing dynasty (1644 – 1912). This expanded Chinese control to its greatest extent in central and south-east Asia and established cautious diplomatic and trade contacts with Europe. It was overthrown by revolution.

Russia

Under Peter I (r 1682 – 1727) and Catherine II (r 1762 - 1796) Russia's borders continued to expand in all directions and trade and cultural contact with the West increased from the new Baltic Sea capital of St Petersburg (est. 1703).

Alaska was a Russian colony for 126 years until sold to the USA in 1867.

In 1898 Russia leased Port Arthur from China with the intention of making it the base of Russian naval power in the Pacific. Russia poured troops into Manchuria during the Boxer Uprising in 1900 but, faced with the Anglo-Japanese alliance of 1902, promised to leave Chinese territory.

The promise was not kept and in June 1903 Japan proposed an agreement with Russia recognizing Japan's interests in Korea and Russia's in Manchuria, and insuring the integrity of China and Korea.

Russia refused and on of February 8, 1904, the Japanese navy launched a surprise attack on Port Arthur and blockaded the damaged Russian fleet.

Hostilities continued for several months and, after Russian defeats at Shenyang and Tsushima, on September 5, 1905, the Treaty of Portsmouth was signed. Russia surrendered its lease to Liaoyang and Port Arthur, ceded the southern half of Sakhalin, evacuated Manchuria, and recognized Korea as a Japanese sphere of influence (Encarta, 1999).

African colonies

After 1880 the vast African interior was rapidly colonized by European nations and West African Muslim kingdoms (Fulani), Arab slave traders (Zanzibar) and Bantu confederations (Zulu) were subdued. Only Christian Ethiopia, which defeated Italy in 1896, and Liberia, resisted the invasion successfully.

The major beneficiaries were France (West Africa) and England ('Cape to Cape and the Boer War, 1899 – 1902).

The slave trade

The African and Caribbean colonies of several European nations developed a plantation economy where sugarcane, tobacco, cotton, coffee, rice, indigo and lumber were grown commercially by slaves.

The Portuguese dominated the slave trade in the 16th century, the Dutch in the early 17th, whilst the late 17th century was a period of intense competition between these two nations and the French, British, Danes and Swedes.

The trade peaked in the second half of the 18th century from which point the East African slave trade become predominant.

The British formally abolished the slave trade in 1807, and the institution of slavery in 1833. Then Britain formed Royal Navy anti-slavery squadrons on the west and east coasts of Africa.

The best estimates are that from circa 1650 to 1850 circa 12.5 million slaves were transported to work in the New World, this keeping the African population static for over two centuries (Chambers, 1993).

The Austro-Hungarian Empire

An agreement between the Habsburg Emperor of Austria, Francis Joseph I, and the Magyar rulers of the kingdom of Hungary, created the Austro-Hungarian Empire in 1867. The empire extended over more than 675,000 sq km in central Europe, and included Austria, Hungary, Slovakia, and the Czech Republic, as well as parts of present-day Poland, Romania, Italy, Slovenia, Croatia, Bosnia and Herzegovina, and the Federal Republic of Yugoslavia.

Austria-Hungary was regarded as a great European power along with France, Germany, Russia, and Britain, but the empire was ultimately destroyed by defeat in World War 1 (Encarta, 1999).

Hitler's Third Reich

Adolf Hitler rose from humble beginnings to leadership of the National Socialist German Worker's Party, or Nazi party, becoming Chancellor of Germany in 1933.

An ethnic German born in Austria, Hitler set about unifying Germany and Austria to form an empire he named *The Third Reich* by external pressure, eventually ordering his army to march into Austria, proclaiming the official union of Austria and Germany on March 12th 1938.

In 1936 he established the Rome-Berlin 'axis' with Mussolini, pursuing an aggressive foreign policy which resulted in Czechoslovakia ceding ethnic German parts of the country, particularly *The Sudetenland* in the west.

In March 1938 Hitler's forces occupied most of Czechoslovakia, breaking the Munich Pact.

Next they annexed part of Lithuania.

Offering Stalin a share of any conquests in Eastern Europe, on August 23rd 1939 Hitler signed a pact with the USSR ensuring that it would not stand in his way.

The invasion of Poland began on September 1st 1939, causing Britain and France to declare war on Germany and beginning World War 2.

Much of the terrible history of that war is well known, particularly the mass murder of millions of Jews by the Nazis, a process aided by IBM's German subsidiary Demohag, which collected data on Jewish families in Germany, and Du Pont, which made the Zyklon B gas used to kill them.

Like Napoleon before him, Hitler made the mistake of taking on Russia, the turning point being the prolonged Battle of Stalingrad during which the Russians dropped tularemia on the German Panzer divisions, the first large scale use of biological warfare in history.

The war was finally ended with the nuclear bombing of Hiroshima (Aug. 6) and Nagasaki (Aug. 9) in 1945.

The British Empire

British privateers such as Drake (1540 – 96) challenged Spanish control of the New World, establishing the North American colonies of Jamestown (1607) and Plymouth (1620), and penetrated Asian trade routes, taking Madras in 1639.

Britain founded colonies in the Caribbean and North America in the 17th century, losing the American colonies after the American War of Independence (1775 – 1783).

Much of India was conquered (1757 – 1857) and islands and trading posts were acquired from Aden to Hong Kong.

Settlements were established in Canada, Australia, New Zealand and the Cape in South Africa, each of which became 'dominions' in 1910.

Towards the end of the 19th century other 'dependent territories' were established in Africa such as Rhodesia.

In addition Britain also had an 'informal empire' over which it had considerable industrial and commercial influence, including parts of South America, the Middle East, the Persian Gulf and China.

After WW1 Britain, heavily in debt, could not control its extensive empire and the dominions gained effective independence in 1931.

After WW2 Britain had run up huge debts, much of this to the USA via lend-lease, and India gained independence in 1947, most of the rest of the empire was decolonized in the 1960s, whilst Rhodesia became independent in 1980.

The USA

After losing the Crimean war (1853 – 1856) against the British and French the Russian government thought it could no longer afford an American colony. Thus, in 1867 Alaska was sold to the USA for $7.2 million.

By winning the Spanish-American War of 1898 the USA gained control of Cuba, Puerto Rico and the Philippines.

Hawaii was also annexed by the USA in 1898.

Involved in allied victories in WW1 and WW2 the USA continued to grow in economic strength, power and influence to the point that the 20th century was called by many "The American Century."

Conclusions

According to Cowie et al. (1994): *The oldest and most repeated justification for imperial activity was the Christian mission to go into the world and preach the Gospel, bringing salvation to the 'heathen'. Early imperialist activities by the Spanish and Portuguese carried the pope's blessing for this endeavour.*

Rudyard Kipling extolled the virtues of such imperialism as being a responsibility:

> *Take up the White Man's burden -*
> *Send forth the best ye breed -*
> *Go, bind your sons to exile*
> *To serve your captive's need;*
> *To wait in heavy harness,*
> *On fluttered fold and wild -*
> *Your new-caught, sullen peoples,*
> *Half-devil and half-child.*

R. Kipling, *Rudyard Kipling's Verse*, Inclusive edition. Hodder & Stoughton, London (1949) pp 371-372.

Indeed, Baden Powell, creator of the Boy Scouts movement, originally considered calling it *Young Knights of the Empire*, a good example of the imperialist and warmongering spirit of the UK at the time.

As noted in Chapter 1, early tribal man was influenced by religious superstitions which allowed leaders to declare other tribes 'heathen' and justify conflict.

According to World Almanac 1998, the notions of Kipling's "white man's burden" or a "civilizing mission" justified the European conquests of Africa.

The quotation that opens this chapter rings very true in the pages that follow it. That is, empire building requires war, in turn provoking opposition and thence further war.

Thus conflict seems to be a human habit, as with almost all other animal species (particularly if you call eating other animals a hostile act), and war comes with organization into misguided groups.

The difference with humans is that we are led like lemmings into one disaster after another by bullshit spouted by lousy leaders (Mohr, 2012a).

All too often these lousy leaders are none too clever, whilst some are quite clearly crazy, for example:

[1] Alexander the Great considered himself divine.

{2] Early in his reign Nero had a rival poisoned. In 59 he had his mother killed because she had criticized his mistress, who he later married, then killing his ex-wife. His second wife he kicked to death and then married another woman after killing her husband.

After a plot against Nero, 18 of 41 Romans implicated in it perished, including his former tutor Seneca.

Eventually the Senate declared Nero a public enemy and he committed suicide.

[3] Some think Hitler contracted syphilis from a Jewish prostitute in WW1, in part explaining his hostility to the Jews (in addition to the centuries old prejudice against their proclivity for running pawnshops, banks etc.). Syphilis was relatively untreatable without antibiotics and Hitler was no doubt psychotic, a symptom of tertiary syphilis.

Part of the problem with lousy leaders may be Mohr's Law of Hierarchy (see Chapter 9), that is, they do little real work, and thus have plenty of time to dream up stupid, if not disastrous ideas.

Another is that all too often government is oligarchical, never truer than today in such countries as the USA and UK where powerful industrialists, most notably in the arms industry, have great influence on policy.

Some effort to suggest solutions to our ongoing problems of overpopulation, bad government, and war will be made in the final chapter of this book.

4. Empire Building

PART 2
THE PSYCHOLOGY
OF CONFLICT

Chapter 5

ADVERTISING & PROPAGANDA

The chief customers of the public house today are the elderly and middle-aged men. Unless you can attract the younger generation to take the place of the older men, there is no doubt that we shall have to face a steadily falling consumption ..... if we begin advertising in the press we shall see that the continuance of our advertising is contingent upon the fact that we get educational support as well in the same papers. In that way it is wonderful how you can educate public opinion, generally, without making it too obvious that there is a public campaign behind it all ...
Sir Edgar Saunders, Director of the Brewers' Society,
Birmingham, 1930 (Sargent, 1979).

In wartime, truth is so precious that she should always be attended by a bodyguard of lies.
Winston Churchill, said to Stalin,
The Second World War (1948-53).

Introduction

The first quotation above is a good example of the social effect of advertising, here the objective being to ensure that men, en masse, keep drinking beer.

We, the authors, often picture a street in an industrial suburb of an English city with a long row of small rented terrace houses on each side. In these the worker-slaves live and work in a factory at one end of the street.

At the end of the day they go to the pub at the other end of the street to spend a good part of their meagre earnings. The owner of the factory, on the other hand, probably owns the pub too, and he drives home to his mansion on 'the right side of the tracks' after work where dinner and fine wine is served by a maid.

These days, of course, advertising has become absurdly ubiquitous and it only remains to connect automatic advertising messages to the button you press to flush the toilet.

Thus, not only do the boys and men drink beer or bourbon and coke, the girls drink pink vodka cruisers, the ladies drink wine, and poor people drink the cheapest cask wine. In other words just about everybody drinks booze.

Just about everybody eats junk food too and junk food restaurants cluster at prominent corner locations throughout our major cities, reminiscent of how churches were once amongst the few prominent buildings in typical suburbs.

Politicians, of course, use increasing amounts of advertising before elections, along with a good deal of propaganda to promote the political party they represent.

Wordweb 6 dictionary's entry for propaganda is:

1. *Information that is spread for the purpose of promoting some cause.*
"The propaganda brainwashed many people."

As with priests coming from on high from a pulpit, politicians do likewise from prominent lecterns, all too often in history decrying some opponent in another country and ultimately urging the already brainwashed, beer drinking young men to go to war.

The purpose of advertising

Nowadays there are massive media and advertising industries devoted to turning us into consumer zombies.

The main objectives of ads, in approximate order of priority, are to:
1. Make the brand name familiar.
2. To give the brand a distinct image.
3. Attribute at least one key attribute to the brand.
4. Associate the product with certain usages.
5. To convince us that this brand is the best (for us).
6. To persuade us that we should buy the product.

To meet these objectives ads will involve:

slogans, demonstrations, comparisons, testimonials, and repetition.

Comparisons, of course, are usually of price, but sometimes also some sort of semi-official rating, for example safety ratings for cars.

By way of style, ad types include basic facts, 'mood', feel-good, social setting, slice-of-life, humour, fantasy, hard-sell, and anxiety/danger/risk.

An example of risk type ads are those for household insect sprays.

To make ads more appealing attractive female models, smooth talkers, or sports and movie stars are often used to promote products.

To give ads more authority statements by experts or organizations may be used to help persuade us.

To make purchase more imperative ads will scream of huge price reductions for a limited time, huge bargains for as little as two days only, and buy on the never-never deals with no interest for a year or two, if not longer.

In their efforts to get you in ads will go to ends which range from boring to extremely irritating, from dull and routine to the heights of excess and absurdity, from mere suggestion to downright pleading, and from slight desperation to screaming at us to buy the product.

More subtle are 'advertorials' of bought space in newspapers or conspicuous 'product placement' in movies.

For maximum tedium there are half-hour infomercials on afternoon or late night TV which sometimes repeat night after night, week after week, and year after year. In these and most other types of ads there are often trial offers, bonus products for quick purchase etcetera.

In monetary economic theory aggregate demand and aggregate supply are equated to obtain $MV = PQ$ where M is the amount of money in circulation, V is its velocity of circulation (in transactions per year), P is the price of goods in circulation, and Q is the quantity of goods in circulation per year.

Then if, for example, we increase Q we should advertise to ensure a corresponding increase in V or turnover. As the first author puts it, Mohr's First Law of Advertising is that we *'increase the velocity of bullshit in order to increase turnover.'*

One way of maintaining higher levels of production is through planned obsolescence of which there are three types (Packard, 1963):
[1] Quality: the product wears out in some planned manner.
[2] Function: a new product performs the function better.
[3] Desirability: the product is 'restyled', making the old version seem obsolete.

In the context of war [1] corresponds to a failed campaign, [2] to a new alternative plan, and [3] to restructuring of the forces to be used in the new plan. Then, of course, political leaders 'sell' the new plan to the public, whilst army leaders force it upon their troops.

Types of advertising

The main objectives of brand advertising and the various types of ads used to achieve them are summarized in the Table 5.1 (O'Guinn et al., 2006).

Table 5.1. Types of advertisement.

Objective	Type of advertisement
Promote brand recall	Repetition Slogans & jingles
Link a key attribute to the brand name	Unique selling proposition (USP)
Convince consumers to buy a product or service through high-engagement arguments	Reason-why ads Hard-sell ads Comparison ads Testimonials. Demonstration Advertorials. Infomercials
Instil brand preference	Feel-good ads Humour ads Sexual-appeal ads.
Scare consumer into action	Fear-appeal ads
Change behaviour by inducing anxiety	Anxiety ads Social anxiety ads
Suggest a feeling or mood when product used	Transformational ads (for long term usage)
Situate the brand socially	Slice-of-life ads Light-fantasy ads Product placement (movies etc.) Short Internet films
Define the brand image	Ads relying mainly on images, not words or argument

In addition, manufacturers and retailers periodically advertise bargains and "buy now!" special deals.

Targeting advertising

Maslow defined two kinds of needs (Lindzey at al., 1978):

(a) *Basic needs* such as hunger, thirst, sex and security.

(b) *Metaneeds* such as achievement, beauty, goodness, justice, order and unity.

Maslow defines achievement as a basic need but the present authors prefer to classify it as a 'higher' or more human metaneed.

First, we must meet our basic or 'animal' needs. That done we can turn our attention to the higher 'human' metaneeds and thence Maslow's 'meaning of life' goal of 'self-actualization' as a human being.

These needs provide *primary goals* that may motivate us towards *secondary goals* such as money in order to achieve them.

Most of our basic needs are *intrinsic motivations* whereas most of our metaneeds are *learned goals.*

Advertising usually targets the metaneeds of your *ego.* A Coke ad, for example, is not designed to remind you that you may be thirsty. If so, you might rush to the fridge and grab whatever drink you can find to satisfy that thirst. No, a Coke ad makes it look 'cool' to drink Coke with your friends and being 'cool' is a metaneed! So next day a young boy will want to be 'cool' when hanging out with his friends so they will all drink Coke and act foolishly, just like the actors in some Coke and Pepsi ads

Here again we see the downside of advertising, namely that increasingly ambitious executives will stop at nothing to sell their product, even if it has to brainwash the young into acquiring both bad behaviour and bad teeth.

In marketing to children, of course, familiar cuddly looking cartoon figures are often displayed on packaging and used to speak the lines of TV ads. Here, however, ads usually target the *Id,* the basic 'animal' personality that has basic needs like hunger.

Young children tend to eat in smaller doses and often so that almost any time they are awake is a good one to put a picture of confectionery in front of them.

One of the best examples of brainwashing, however, is the use of *consumer panels* of children in marketing research. The children are often asked what they will say and do to persuade parents to buy them the product.

Finally, the extent to which children are exposed to advertising is incredible:

- - *"it is estimated that children between two and 11 years old may see over 20,000 advertisements in a year,"* (O'Guinn et al., 2006).

Advertising, therefore, will persuade someone in your family, even if it doesn't persuade you!

In marketing to adults well known sporting identities are often used to market such things as golf clubs, household appliances and cars and houses. Indeed, this was the basis of Mark McCormack's very successful IMG (McCormack, 1986) and one of his earliest clients was Greg Norman who, marketed as 'The Shark', was made out to be a much better golfer than he was, and made an awful lot of money from TV ads.

When politicians seek to prepare us for yet another war they appeal to our *basic need* of security by instilling fear of the party against whom war is being considered, 'fear type ads' being a common form of advertising, a common example being ads for insect sprays.

Persuasion or brainwashing?

Today advertising is so repetitive and effective in reducing us to consumer zombies that the results are comparable to those of classical conditioning of laboratory animals. In other words, it goes a little, if not a long way beyond just *persuasion.*

Colloquially, at least, most would agree that it would be fair to use the term *brainwashing* but, strictly speaking, this originated in connection with 'conversion' of American prisoners by the Communists during the Korean war in the early 1950s when The Three D's Method (debilitation, dread, dependency) was used in this context (Mohr, 2012a).

Sometimes referred to in psychology as *thought reform*, brainwashing is an extreme form of *social influence* aimed at changing a person's views without their consent and often against their will.

To this end brainwashing combines three approaches:

(a) The **coercive** or 'just do it' approach which is concerned only with *compliance* and not with your attitudes and beliefs.

(b) The **persuasion** or 'do it because it will make you feel good, happy, healthy or successful' approach.

(c) The group-based **education** or 'do it because it's right' approach which is much used for *propaganda* campaigns.

The 1999 Encyclopaedia Britannica describes brainwashing as **coercive persuasion**, noting its origins as a means of political indoctrination. It also notes that it is a *"colloquial term"* usually *"applied to any technique designed to manipulate human thought or action - -."*

The third edition of the American Heritage Dictionary of the English Language gives two definitions of brainwashing:

1. *Intensive, forcible indoctrination, usually political*
or religious, aimed at destroying a person's basic convictions
and attitudes and replacing them
with an alternative set of fixed beliefs.

2. *The application of a concentrated means of persuasion,*
such as an advertising campaign or repeated suggestion,
in order to develop a specific belief or motivation.

Indeed, most of us now associate brainwashing with persuasive advertising, political campaigns, mass media, and perhaps education.

In fact, media brainwashing is widespread, and it is a major concern for many people. Thus, a search for 'media brainwashing' on the Internet gives over 2 million results.

Just three examples of 'mass brainwashing' are:

[1] Claims that after WW1 psychological warfare research at the Tavistock Centre in London resulted in *"a theory of mass brainwashing, involving group experience, that could be used to alter the values of individuals, and through that induce, over time, changes in the axiomatic assumptions that govern society"* and that this work found application in both the UK and the US media (Wolfe, 1997).

US journalist Walter Lippmann was involved in Britain's WW1 'psywar' effort and was first to translate Sigmund Freud's work into English. In his 1922 book *Public Opinion* he wrote of the brainwashed masses:

". . the mass of absolutely illiterate, of feeble minded grossly neurotic, undernourished and frustrated individuals is very considerable, much more considerable, there is reason to think, than we generally suppose. Thus a wide popular appeal is circulated among persons who are mentally children or barbarians, whose lives are a morass of entanglements, people whose vitality is exhausted, shut-in people, and people whose experience has comprehended no factor in the problem under discussion."

[2] Hitler had a well-oiled propaganda machine led by Joseph Goebbels, head of the Ministry of Public Enlightenment and Propaganda. Goebbels banned four Berlin newspapers in 1935.

[3] Claims that, because it supposedly misled the public over the 2001 WTC attacks, the American news media *"is the largest, most expensive, mass-brainwashing machine ever assembled in human history. It is a machine that so completely brainwashes the nearly 300 million Americans, that the Nazis' infamous Propaganda Minister Josef Goebbels would be envious"* (Wolfe, 2001).

Some of this is a bit 'over the top' but, if we consider that advertising has reduced most of us to brainwashed zombies wearing uncomfortable if not ridiculous jeans and carrying a mobile phone in one hand and a drink bottle or cigarette in the other, then 'brainwashing' is a serious issue.

And make no mistake, it must certainly be fair to call today's high pressure TV and radio advertising brainwashing. After all, in line with the original brainwashing of POWs, the victims are seated in a room and screamed at for hours each day with up to 10 ads blaring at them in each of all too frequent ad breaks (make that up to 50 ads per ad break in Brazil, according to Cateora (1996)).

After all, 50+ years ago advertising made about half the adult population take up smoking, a downright unpleasant practice in reality. If advertising can do that then it can make us do just about anything short of eating shit.

For this reason, therefore, the term *brainwashing* is used frequently in connection with the increasingly ubiquitous, repetitive and persuasive advertising used today. It applies equally well, if not more so, to the propaganda put out by governments to justify their every action, including those involving war.

Conclusion

The extent to which man has been persuaded, one way or another, to adopt countless religions, periodically fight wars over them, and in modern times become mindless consumer zombies is regrettable.

We should all hope that we will never be subjected to *coercive persuasion* or *brainwashing* in its 'original' form but few of us would disagree that we are perhaps now subjected en masse to something far more subtle, far more effective and sometimes, at least, far more sinister and detrimental to both ourselves and, in turn, the world we live in.

Regardless of the politics of a country, however, politicians will always mislead the brainwashed public. Edward Suchman gave useful definitions of some of the tactics used to cover-up failures in policy (Davis, 1974):

[1] *Eye-wash:* deliberately selecting for evaluation only those aspects that 'look good' on the surface.
[2] *White-wash:* avoid any objective evaluation.
[3] *Submarine:* 'torpedo' the program.
[4] *Posture:* use evaluation as a 'gesture' only.
[5] *Postponement:* delay needed action by pretending to seek the 'facts'.

An example of this, perhaps, in Volume 1 of the book series *Yes Prime Minister,* Chapter 7 is entitled 'The Smokescreen" (Lynn & Jay, 1986). The chapter begins with discussion of cuts in defence spending to allow for cuts in income tax, presumably because the latter help garner votes.

Seeing this as difficult, the alternative idea of increasing revenue with huge taxes on smoking is had, but eventually dropped, by this time the issue of cuts in defence spending seemingly forgotten by the absent minded Jim Hacker and, presumably, the public also.

On the issue of propaganda, some people refer to Australia's SBS1 TV channel as "The Hitler Channel" because seemingly once or twice a week it screens a documentary about Hitler, the Nazis and WW2. This, it would seem to us, is British-made propaganda to remind people of their warmongering but defunct empire of the need for war whenever the government wishes it, how despotic any enemy is, and the glory of victory.

Similarly, we knew, once we saw repeated images of Sadam Hussein holding a rifle circa 2001, that war with his regime was imminent, such association of negative objects being an important tool in fear ads.

5. ADVERTISING & PROPAGANDA

Chapter 6

THE PSYCHOLOGY OF ATTITUDES

*However, most psychologists agree that attitudes have three main
components: a 'cognitive', or thought, component; an 'emotional'
component, including affective (arising from our emotions)
and evaluative (arising from our value judgments) aspects;
and a 'behavioral' component.*
Lindzey, Hall, and Thompson, *Psychology* (1978).

The psychology of attitudes

Attitude can be defined as 'psychological *tendency* expressed by *evaluating* a particular entity with some degree of favour or disfavour.'

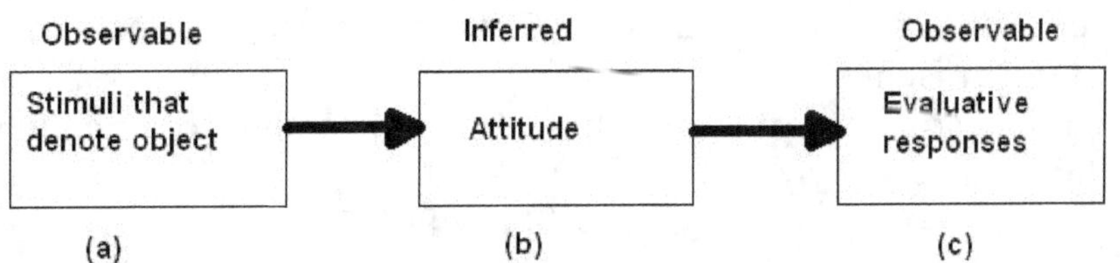

Figure 6.1. Psychological responses

Figure 6.1 illustrates the three types of response involved in attitudinal psychology. These are:
(1) *Cognitive response.* This response is that of recognition of, for example, a name, a picture or other stimulus.

(2) *Affective response.* This is a hypothetical construct and a latent variable. Here the sympathetic nervous system responds to (1) with feelings or emotions.

(3) *Behavioural response.* This is the outward expression of (2) and may be a positive, neutral or negative response of some degree or intensity involving some observable action.

In this context conservatism, environmentalism or racism are objects. Then when we label a person a conservative, environmentalist or racist we infer an attitudinal position. Such attitudes are evidenced and also developed by the 'CAB' mechanism illustrated in Figure 6.1.

Schemas are cognitive structures that represent a person's past experience in a stimulus domain by a higher order or abstract cognitive structure. Then attitude is a subset of such a schema.

Schemas have a selective effect on the remembering of information so that people have a better remembrance of stimuli that 'fit' their schemas, and also for those that 'oppose.' This same selectivity applies to the 'output' of information as well as its input.

Figure 6.2 illustrates McGuire's reception-yielding model of attitude formation (Eagly & Chaiken, 1993). Here 'reception' refers to comprehending a 'message', for example an advertisement.

This model postulates that the probability of attitude change is given by

$$P(C) = P(R) \times P(Y)$$

so that a maximum change is obtained where the reception and yielding curves intersect, as shown in Figure 6.2.

One application of this idea is to 'get them young' so that advertising companies target the young and naive before they have the maturity or 'consumer intelligence' to develop resistance. Indeed, the present authors hold that the horizontal axis in Fig. 6.2 should be labelled Consumer Intelligence.

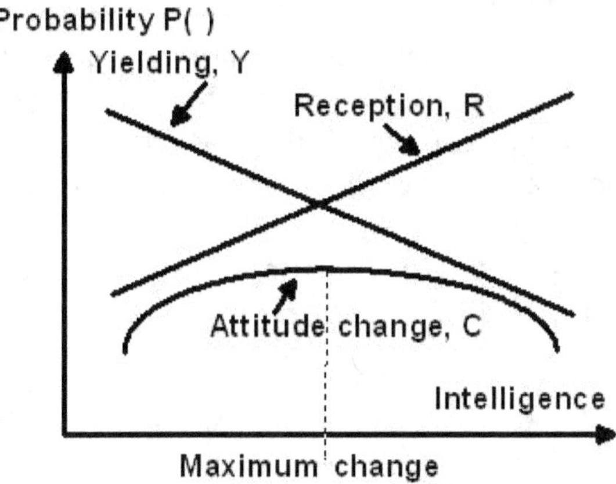

Figure 6.2. Probability of reception, yielding and attitude change.

One of the main motivations for advertising is that advertisements need only persuade some of the target audience and then imitative or 'social' learning ensures that many of the rest follow them.

Advertisements having achieved this, regular advertising reminds the audience of a product. Then in Figure 6.1 the 'C' response will be one of recognition of a brand, the 'A' response will be one of approval of it, and the 'B' response will be to make a mental note to buy it.

Figure 6.2 might also remind us that more intelligent, better educated, or simply older and wiser people tend to be less affected by advertising and propaganda. Indeed, often throughout history dictatorial and fascist regimes have locked up members of the intelligentsia willy-nilly without evidence as to whether the individuals imprisoned have openly opposed their regimes or not.

Learning curves

Learning curves emphasize that in advertising it is important to have sufficient repetitions of an ad to ensure adequate average learning by the audience.

Suppose the degree to which a person or group has learnt something or been conditioned is given by the probability $p = 0$ to 1, and p depends on n, the number of repetitions of the learning process.

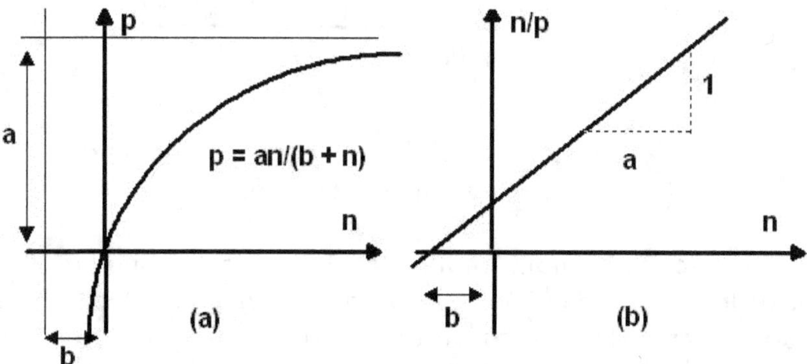

Figure 6.3. Mohr Plot for learning.

If we assume that the learning process is hyperbolic so that the degree of learning gradually increases towards 100% or the asymptote $p = a$ with $a = 1$, then this is represented by the hyperbola of Figure 6.3(a), the equation for which is $p = an/(b + n)$

This equation can easily be rearranged to give

$$n/p = (b + n)/a$$

so that if we plot n/p against n the straight line of Figure 6.3(b) is obtained and the magnitude of the intercept with the n axis $= -b$ whilst, of more interest, the inverse slope of the line equals the horizontal asymptote a of the hyperbola.

In experimental situations this plot is useful in testing whether results are indeed hyperbolic and, if so, estimating the 'ceiling' value towards which some variable is converging.

Applied to the memory of a single person we set $a = 1$ and a typical result might be $b = 3$, $n = 3$, giving $p = 0.5$, or 50% memory retention after three repetitions. Here p is either:

(a) How well an item is learnt. People's names might be a good example of this, and typically people often need about three repetitions of such things to remember them.

(b) How much of a 'block' of information is learnt. An example might be a list of names where, because of *interference,* words at the beginning (the *primacy effect*) and end (the *recency effect*) are remembered best.

For a slower learner, on the other hand, b might double to 6 so we need $n = 6$ to get $p = 0.5$ or 50% learning.

Applied to conditioning of the populace by advertising, p is the proportion of the population affected and larger values of the asymptote b which flatten the curve might occur when there are two or more competing advertisers in the market. In politics this highlights the advantage of dictatorship.

In education it perhaps highlights the importance of avoiding conflicting messages so that it is often best to learn one subject at a time.

The forgetting curves of Figure 6.4 also have important application in developing long-term marketing plans. Here curves A and B are for two messages and curve B* is the result after the second message is repeated.

Then, after time has elapsed after an advertisement its 'residual' effect depends upon both the *primacy,* or strength of the ad compared to others, and its *recency.* In Figure 6.4, after two weeks ad B* has greater recency than ad A, but less primacy, so that they have nearly equal effect.

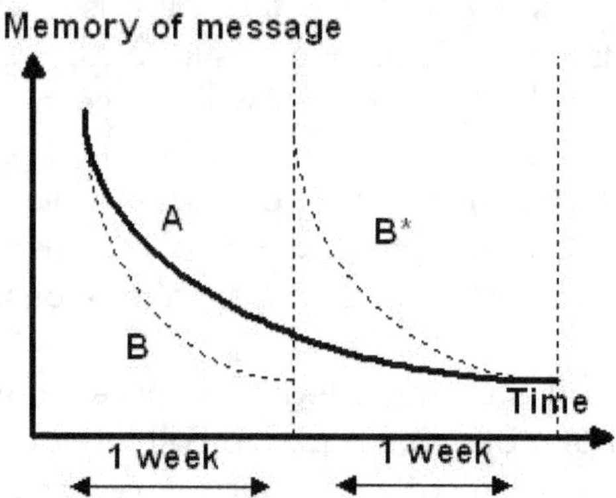

Figure 6.4. Forgetting curves.

Such repetition of ads will ensure long-term potentiation of the remembered message, an important objective (Vander et al., 1994). Correlation between retention and persuasion, however, is by no means guaranteed and ads can be tailored to these two ends.

How we are persuaded

Effective persuasion of people en masse involves several key factors including:

➤ Simple messages are more effective that complex ones and these should target the appropriate *segment* of the population.

➤ From early in our history we have been talked down to by tribal and religious leaders that pitch to us from 'on high.' Today, however, the pulpit has been largely replaced by the TV screen but effective ads still take the high ground by having an air of authority and confidence.

➤ Messages should be structured to ensure (Robertson, 1970):

    (1) *Cognitive response* to the message involving
      (a) *Awareness* of the product's existence.
      (b) *Knowledge* of the product's features.

(2) Positive *attitudinal response* to the message, that is
   (a) *Liking* of the product.
   (b) *Preference* for the product.

(3) The desired *behavioural response* to the message, that is
   (a) *Conviction* that the product is worth buying.
   (b) *Purchase* of the product.

➢ This *cognitive/attitudinal/behavioural* or 'CAB' approach to advertising is *conditioning,* where now an advertisement is a *stimulus,* comparable to Pavlov's classical experiments in which dogs were conditioned to salivate on hearing a bell (the conditioned response), having become accustomed to bell-ringing preceding the appearance of food, the original unconditioned response having been salivation on the appearance of food.

➢ The proportion of the target population that remembers a message increases with the number of repetitions and thus follows a *learning curve* such as that of Figure 6.3.

➢ Frequency of messages should be limited to avoid *advertising wearout*. The *three-hit theory* is that only 3 ads are needed to make consumers aware of a product, make them perceive its relevance to their needs, and inform them of its benefits, but it needs to be realized that more like a dozen ads will be needed to ensure that a substantial proportion of the population will see the ad.

➢ Consumer memory follows the *forgetting curves* of Figure 6.4 so that advertising campaigns must be periodically renewed.

➢ Appealing to people's secondary *psychological needs* such as achievement and beauty, rather than their primary and regular 'anything will do' *physical needs* such as hunger and thirst.

➤ Pitching messages at those with a lower 'consumer IQ' because high 'CIQ' increases likelihood of messages being understood but reduces likelihood of being influenced by them. This *reception-yielding* situation is illustrated in Figure 6.2, and the 'get them young' notion that this suggests is illustrated by the quotation that opens Chapter 5.

➤ Taking advantage of the fact that for brainwashed modern man his car and the brand of soft drink or beer he drinks is an important part of his *identity*. Similarly, for a woman the way she does her hair and makeup, and the way she dresses are part of her identity. Thus, just as we describe different species of animals by their appearance and habits, we view other people in the same way.

➤ We humans are suckers for anything new and effective advertising need not appeal to our higher instincts or the advancement of mankind. For example, supposedly civilized societies happily copied people their explorers thought 'savages' by taking up tobacco en masse. That our love of novelty has not 'raised' mankind but 'regressed' us is called *reverse evolution* (Mohr 2012a; Mohr & Fear, 2016; Mohr et al., 2018d).

➤ It is important to note that we are not simply persuaded as individuals, but also en masse or sociologically. The key to this is *imitative* and *social learning* so that just one or two of a particular group of people need to be persuaded to a buy product successfully and then it is certain that, one by one, others in the group may follow their lead.

➤ It is also important to note that we often *imprint* upon a particular type or group of people and adopt their behaviours and imprinting, imitative learning, and modelling are important modes of learning in childhood.

➤ Finally, our memories are 'hard wired.' That is, unless neurons are damaged physically, memories that have been stored in long-term memory are permanent. This is why it is we remember some of our earliest childhood experiences and why we find it so hard to give up some of our habits.

Message simplicity

Table 6.1. Effect of word-length & reading speed on recall.

No. of syllables in word	Reading speed (words per second)	% of words recalled correctly
1	2.3	90
2	2.1	80
3	1.9	70
4	1.87	56
5	1.53	42

Table 6.1 shows the relationship between word length, reading rate, and memory for words ranging in length from one to five syllables (Baddeley et al., 1975, 1990).

As expected, longer words reduce both reading speed and recall. Thus Table 6.1 suggests that, as might be expected, more persuasive messages will involve relatively short, simple words.

Table 6.2 shows that both complexity of message and mode of communication have an important effect on retention and attitude change. Here subjects were presented with an easy- or difficult-to-comprehend message that was presented in written, audiotaped, or videotaped form (Eagly & Chaiken, 1993).

The message concerned a dispute between a company and its union employees, the simple message using short sentences and simple vocabulary, the difficult version using relatively complex sentences and sophisticated vocabulary.

Retention of the simple message was quite high regardless of modality, yet attitude change was greatest with visual presentation. In contrast, for the complex message both retention and attitude change were greatest when it was written.

For both the simple and complex message short-answer items were recalled best, as expected.

Table 6.2. Effect of message type on attitude change.

	Easy message			Difficult Message		
	Written	Audio	Video	Written	Audio	Video
Attitude Change	2.94	3.75	4.78	4.73	2.32	3.02
# persuasive arguments recalled	2.45	2.21	2.17	2.29	1.74	1.67
# of short-answer items recalled	4.57	3.93	4.45	4.21	3.71	3.36
Perceived message difficulty	4.76	4.21	4.83	5.31	7.50	7.43

Repetition and quality of message are also, of course, important factors, and one study found that agreement with a high quality message with strong arguments was increased from one to three exposures, whereas agreement with a low quality message with weak arguments decreased with increased exposure (Eagly & Chaiken, 1993).

Association effects

Many studies have found that pairing 'new' objects with 'unconditioned stimulus objects' that routinely elicit positive or negative evaluations can produce a 'conditioned stimulus' effect for the 'new' objects.

A good example of this was repeated media presentation of a picture of Saddam Hussein in military dress and holding a rifle in the months preceding the US invasion of Iraq in 1972. After seeing this picture a few times the authors knew that invasion of Iraq was imminent.

According to McGuire (1968, 1969) fear's "cue" properties make one want to escape and avoid threatening material, thus interfering with message reception (see Figure 6.2).

On the other hand, the "drive" properties of fear should energize behavioural inclinations.

McGuire's implicit assumption that fearful or *anxious* recipients would tend to comply led him to propose that increased fear arousal should increase yielding to message content.

Group learning effects

Studies have found that with repeated exposure to stimuli the responses of groups of people become increasingly similar, whereas individual responses may have been considerably different initially (Eagly & Chaiken, 1993).

This is, of course, a result of 'social learning' by perhaps most members of the group on hearing a few more assertive and talkative members of the group express their responses.

Conclusions

The 'CAB' model of Figure 6.1 and the reception-yielding model of Figure 6.2 help us understand how people process messages and how their attitudes are influenced by them.

Repetition of messages is, of course, important for both retention and comprehension.

Simplicity and mode of presentation of messages are also important factors.

'Association' of both positive and negative objects and group effects also affect responses to messages.

In the case of propaganda about the need for war, the repeated use of pictures of Saddam Hussein holding a rifle referred to earlier was a good example of association with an 'uncontrolled stimulus' object to evoke a negative response.

Similarly, regular programs about Hitler at circa 6PM on Australia's SBS TV network led the authors to nickname SBS the "Hitler channel".

6. The Psychology of Attitudes

Chapter 7

ATTITUDE MEASUREMENT

The body of science described in this book could only have been developed in democratic societies, where attitudinal influence is the form of control that is most often relied upon.
Alice H. Eagly and Shelly Chaiken,
The Psychology of Attitudes (1993).

Information integration models

The information integration theory of attitude formation calculates the response to a series of stimuli *i* as

$$R = w_0\, s_0 + {}_{i=1}\Sigma^n\, w_i\, s_i \tag{7.1}$$

where w_i and s_i are respectively the weight and scale of a person's attitude to a set of *n* items of information, and w_0 and s_0 are the weight and scale value of the person's initial attitude (Eagly & Chaiken, 1993).

Here the scale value of information is its location on the evaluative dimension (e.g. how nice is the colour of --- ?), and the weight is the relative importance of the item or issue (e.g. how important is colour?).

Simple summation models such as that of Equation 7.1 emphasize the importance of using multiple 'selling points' in advertising.

If the sum of the weights is required to be one then the model becomes an averaging model, but averaging models are more generally expressed as

$$R = (w_0\, s_0 + {}_{i=1}\Sigma^n\, w_i\, s_i)/(w_0 + {}_{i=1}\Sigma^n\, w_i)$$

The initial attitude parameters w_0 and s_0 may in some instances, that of religion being perhaps the best example, represent 'intergenerational' attitudes acquired from a very early age from family and society at large.

Such initial attitudes, of course, may involve *prejudice*, for example ethnocentricity or racism, and, as history shows, such prejudices are often firmly rooted and perhaps could only be modelled by assigning them an exceptionally large weight.

More important in the modern consumer society, however, is social or imitative learning and in this context w_0 and s_0 represent initial attitude acquired by social learning from a peer or social group.

For example, a person believes that Christianity provides good moral codes (attribute 1) and that Christ did exist and provide a good exemplar of how we should live (attribute 2), but doubts that God really exists (attribute 3). Even if God did exist, however, in view of man's disastrous history he has a low evaluation of this last attribute, so that, using scales 0 to 10 for both w_i and s_i, he might thus rate Christianity as follows:

Attribute 0 (initial attitude): $w_0 = 5/10$, $s_0 = 5/10$
(i.e. 'halfway' values)

Attribute 1 (morality): $w_1 = 8/10$, $s_1 = 8/10$

Attribute 2 (good life model): $w_2 = 8/10$, $s_2 = 8/10$

Attribute 3 (God): $w_3 = 2/10$, $s_3 = 1/10$

giving a response score

$R = [(5 \times 5 + 8 \times 8 + 8 \times 8 + 2 \times 1)/100]/[(5 + 8 + 8 + 2)/10]$

$= [155/100]/[23/10] = 1.55/2.3 = 0.674$

whereas a 'middling importance/evaluation score' with 5/10 for both the weights and scale values for attributes 0-3 would give $1/2 = 0.5$.

In contrast to simple summation models such as Equation 7.1, averaging models emphasize the need to have a limited number of effective selling points in advertising.

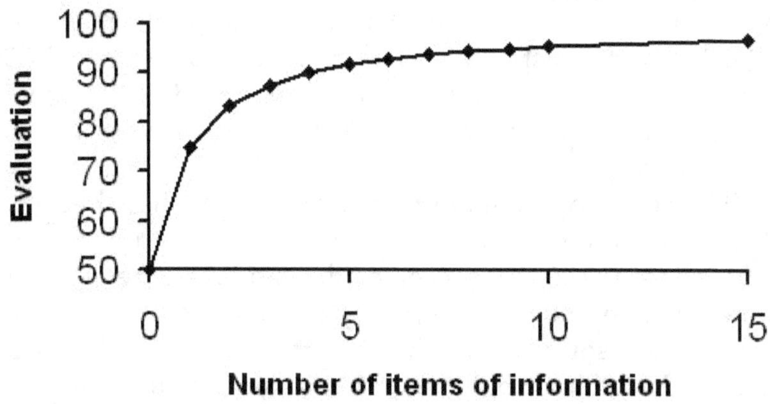

Figure 7.1. Theoretical set-size effect.

Set size effect can be demonstrated by assuming all weights = 1 and an initial attitude score of 50 on a scale of 0 to 100. Then if all further pieces of information have a score of 100 the resulting weighted average score for *k* additional attributes is

$R = (50 + 100k)/(1 + k)$

giving the values 50, 75, 83.3, 87.5, . . . for 0, 1, 2, 3, . . . pieces of information, resulting in the hyperbola converging towards the asymptote $R = 100$ shown in Fig. 7.1.

As might be expected, this hyperbolic result takes the same general shape as a learning curve. For advertising and other persuasive purposes it emphasizes that there is a diminishing return for each additional piece of information about a given subject, albeit with the simplifying assumption that every piece of information has the same weight (w_i).

The theory of reasoned action

Precursors to this theory were Dulany's propositions concerning *verbal operant conditioning* (Dulany, 1961, 1962). Then Fishbein suggested that attitudes influence behaviour by their influence on *intentions,* which are decisions to act in a particular way (Fishbein, 1967; Fishbein & Ajzen, 1975). Then, of course, attitudes are influenced by external influences such as imitative social learning, advertising and propaganda.

The class of attitudes considered in the theory of reasoned action is attitudes towards behaviours, not attitudes towards targets, and these enter the model as determinants of intention. The other determinant of intention, the *subjective norm*, is a person's belief whether others of whom he or she takes notice think that he or she should engage in a behaviour (Eagly & Chaiken, 1993).

Thus the model of behavioural intentions is:

$$B \text{ approx.} = BI = w_1 A_B + w_2 SN \tag{7.2}$$

where B is the behaviour, BI is the behavioural intention, A_B is the attitude toward the behaviour, SN is the subjective norm, and w_1 and w_2 are the empirical weights indicating the relative importance of the two terms.

Both the attitude and the subjective norm can be evaluated by the 'expectancy-value' summation process (Eagly & Chaiken, 1993), but the present authors prefer the information integration approach of Equation 7.1 because, rather than evaluate a person's attitude 'as it stands,' it gives some indication of how that attitude changes with the addition of further information.

The bottom line here is that by influencing people's attitudes one can in turn influence their behaviour, as Figure 6.1 clearly suggests. This is, of course, obvious, but Equation 7.2 does provide a means of evaluating behavioural intentions and, in turn, a means of better understanding how these are formed.

Guttman scaling

This approach gives stimulus-person scaling simultaneously and results in a matrix of data called the *Guttman scalogram* (Eagly & Chaiken, 1993).

As an example, imagine that we have five rods of from 5 to 7 feet in length (the exact lengths are not known). Then we ask each respondent to place a one in the Guttman scalogram matrix shown in Table 7.1 when they are taller than a particular rod. This raw data is then reorganized to give the result in Table 7.2.

Table 7.1. Guttman scalogram.

Persons	Stimuli (rods)				
	C	E	B	D	A
2*	1	1	1	1	0
4	0	1	0	1	0
3	1	1	0	1	0
6	0	0	0	0	0
5	0	1	0	0	0
1	1	1	1	1	1
* e.g. person 2 is taller than C, E, B, D but not A					

Table 7.2 is obtained by placing the column with least ones at the left, the column with the most ones at the right, and so on. Then the row with the maximum number of ones is placed at the top (this is for person '1' in our example and hence this is the tallest person) and that with the least ones is placed at the bottom.

The result is an upper diagonal matrix, as shown in Table 7.2, and this results in a score for each person shown on the right side in Table 7.2, this giving the ordinal ranking for each person.

Table 7.2. Reordered Guttman scalogram.

Persons	Stimuli (rods)					Score
	A	**B**	**C**	**D**	**E**	
1	1	1	1	1	1	5
2	0	1	1	1	1	4
3	0	0	1	1	1	3
4	0	0	0	1	1	2
5	0	0	0	0	1	1
6	0	0	0	0	0	0

The Guttman scalogram has the advantage that the degree to which the reordered response matrix is 'triangularized' gives an immediate indication of the reliability of a survey.

The preceding example of Guttman scaling was for physical stimuli, when a perfect upper triangular matrix resulted. Generally, however, this is not the case when attitudinal stimuli are considered. Attitudinal stimuli do not yield a perfect upper triangular matrix but it has been suggested that when about 90% of the non-zero entries do appear on or above the diagonal that this *coefficient of reproducibility* value is acceptable.

Guttman scaling is applicable to the Bogardus social stimulus scale, illustrated in Table 7.3, in which respondents are asked to judge how closely they would relate to people of various nationalities or races.

The behavioural intention items of the Bogardus scale are cumulative in nature and thus fit the requirements of a Guttman scale. Thus it is possible to assign scores to individuals (and thence groups by averaging) that indicate the social distances they are willing to permit for particular groups, and these scores then indicate which items on the scale are deemed acceptable and which not.

Table 7.3. Bogardus' social distance scale.

	Acceptance level					
	Would marry	As a friend	Would give a job	Allow as citizen	OK as visitor	No contact
Armenians						
Bulgarians						
Canadians						
etc.						

Likert scaling

Likert's *method of summated ratings* is the simplest method of attitude measurement and it is widely used in market research. In this approach a large pool of items which are chosen intuitively for their relevance to the attitude object is used.

These items usually consist of statements of belief but statements about behaviours or affective reactions can also be used.

Typically each item is presented to respondents in a multiple-choice format such as:

1. Strongly disagree.
2. Disagree.
3. Undecided.
4. Agree.
5. Strongly agree.

Then, for example, a survey on attitudes towards women might contain questions like:

(a) Swearing is more objectionable from a woman.

(b) Intoxication in women is worse than in men.

With scores from 1 - 5 given to each of perhaps a dozen or so such questions the total score is then obtained for each respondent.

Desirably an initial pool of items should be pilot tested on a group of people to eliminate ambiguous and non-discriminating items which tend to result in neutral responses. This can be done by examining the *item-total score correlations*, each of which correlates the respondents' scores on an item with their scores summed over all the items. Then a good item will have a positive correlation and generally better items have higher correlations.

Likert Scaling is widely used, for example to assess the response to political advertising campaigns.

Conclusions

The information integration method of measuring attitude is important because:

(1) Its initial $w_0 s_0$ term may include intergenerational prejudices.

(2) As shown in Figure 7.1, in averaged form it emphasizes how our attitudes may 'converge' as information is accumulated.

The theory of reasoned action then shows how behavioural intentions are established from:

(3) A person's own attitude to the behaviour.

(4) Their view of how others would expect them to behave.

It is easy to imagine that all of these considerations would have applied very well to a young man in England wondering whether he should heed the call to join the armed services when England declared war on Germany in 1939. Such a young man would have had:

(1) Prejudice learnt from his parents concerning WW1.

(2) A deluge of propaganda in the media would have engulfed him.

(3) Brought up as a typical boy to 'rough it' somewhat, play with toy guns, and play mindless "charge when I tell you" sports like rugby, the young man would be accustomed to the idea of fighting, whether in games or 'for real'.

(4) Finally, the young man would have been made to feel very guilty indeed if he had refused to fight for 'king and country.' Indeed, at many times in history, he might have been summarily executed or sent to jail for his refusal to fight.

Bogardus' social distance scale gives a simple and sound method of assessing the degree to which a person accepts, or rejects, those of another ethnic background.

Then the Guttman scalogram allows a score to be given to a person, or a group of people, that indicates their comparative ethnocentricity.

Finally, Likert scaling is a quick and easy way of assessing attitudes and is this widely used in marketing, political and other surveys.

7. Attitude Measurement

Chapter 8

THE CONTACT HYPOTHESIS

*The leading idea in the preceding discussion of ethnic conflict
was simply that contact produces ethnocentrism,
so that there is a positive correlation between the two variables
at the aggregate, or societal, level of analysis.
H. D. Forbes Ethnic Conflict,
Commerce, Culture, and the Contact Hypothesis (1997).*

*Two prisoners whose cells adjoin communicate with each other
by knocking on the wall. The wall is the thing which
separates them but is also their means of communication.
Simone Weil, Gravity and Grace, "Metaxu" (1947; tr. 1952).*

Contact hypothesis

According to Forbes (1997): "The most frequently quoted statement of the (contact) hypothesis, provided more than forty years ago by Gordon Allport, says that prejudice may be reduced by equal-status contact between majority and minority groups with common goals, especially when this contact is sanctioned by law or custom (Allport, 1954, p. 281)."

This simple idea that bringing people who are in conflict (or when one is bullying the other) together will bring mutual understanding and reduce conflict often failed dramatically when first tried in multi-racial schools in the USA.

In fact, to reduce conflict other conditions are required, including:

(1) Remove conflict, as well as tackling the factors that lead to it.

(2) Equal status so that neither party has advantages over the other.

(3) Positive contact that is conducive to friendly and productive interactions.

(4) Typical contact: the representatives of each party must be typical members of it so that positive perceptions are generalized to the rest of the population.

(5) Social norms supporting inter-group contact.

(6) Common goals, including that of reaching a common understanding.

(7) Working as a team to improve the situation, neither party being able to terminate the process.

(8) No competition between groups.

Given such conditions, reduction of conflict at a more 'local' level (for example, small scale ethnic conflict in a suburb) is usually possible, at least for substantial periods of time. Reducing international and religious conflict, however, is a much more difficult task, as all history shows.

The contact hypothesis and ethnocentricity

Forbes (1977) proposed that ethnocentricity of different ethnic groups tended to be increased by cultural differences and (presumed negative) contact between them, expressing the ethnocentrism within two groups A and B as

$$E_A = a_1\, C_T\, D_T \qquad\qquad\qquad (8.1a)$$
$$E_B = b_1\, C_T\, D_T \qquad\qquad\qquad (8.1b)$$

where:

a_1 and b_1 are assumed to be positive, and are measures of the latent tendency of each group to respond ethnocentrically to each other,

C_T is the amount of contact between the 2 groups at time T, and D_T is the magnitude of the cultural differences between the two groups at time T.

Forbes further proposed that the amount of contact and the cultural differences between the groups depended upon their proximity, incentives for contact such as trade, and upon the ethnocentrism of the groups, expressing this as

$$C_{T+1} = C_T (1 + g)/(1 + a_2 E_A + b_2 E_B) \tag{8.2}$$

$$D_{T+1} = D_T (1 + a_3 E_A + b_3 E_B)/(1 + h C_T) \tag{8.3}$$

where g is a factor that represents all the factors that determine growth or decline in contact other than the repulsive ethnocentrism and cultural differences of the two groups.

In Equations 8.2 and 8.3 ethnocentricity decreases contact and increases cultural differences, as might be expected.

The denominator of the last equation ensures that cultural differences are reduced by contact so long as h is positive (the normal situation).

Contact theory has obvious application in marketing, PR and other activities involving persuasion, for example,

[1] It emphasizes that attitude changes with contact or, in general, information transfer.

If contact is 'positive', however, rather than negative as has generally been the case throughout man's sorry history, then Equations 8.1 could be modified to reflect this by writing them in the form

$$E_{A,T+1} = E_{A,T} - a_1 C_T + a_4 D_T$$

where a_1 and a_4 are positive. Indeed, it might be hoped that the latter situation might be more likely in today's age of electronic communication and high speed travel. Moreover, it is in this situation that such equations might be applicable to advertising with $E = $ 'resistance'.

[2] It reminds us that ethnic or 'local' considerations are important in international marketing of a product.

[3] It reminds us of the importance of targeting advertising towards an appropriate demographic for a product, and that cultural differences exist between teenagers and their parents and, more so, their grandparents.

Proximity

People who live close together should tend to interact more frequently than those who live further apart, but they may not do so, and the difference between proximity and interaction is sometimes hard to differentiate.

A study in England found that white English people were more prejudiced against non-white immigrants who lived next door than those who lived further away (Schaefer, 1973).

An Italian study, however, found the opposite result. This showed a modest negative correlation between proximity and prejudice between 222 residents of Bologna against black immigrants living in the same neighbourhood (Kirchler & Zani, 1995).

It would appear, therefore, that in the English study the immigrants living next door were 'too close for comfort' and the occasional necessity for communication did more harm than good, perhaps involving cultural differences and language competency problems that made contact less than comfortable. With immigrants living only in the same neighbourhood, however, that gives an opportunity to get used to seeing them regularly without any requirement for communication.

From such studies Forbes (1997) concludes: "Contact in this sense seems to produce prejudice. But proximity to racial minorities or other immigrants at work seems to have the opposite effects: those with more contact show lower levels of racial and anti-immigrant prejudice."

This conclusion is in accord with some of the points listed in the first section of this chapter, for example (2) and (7).

Mere exposure research

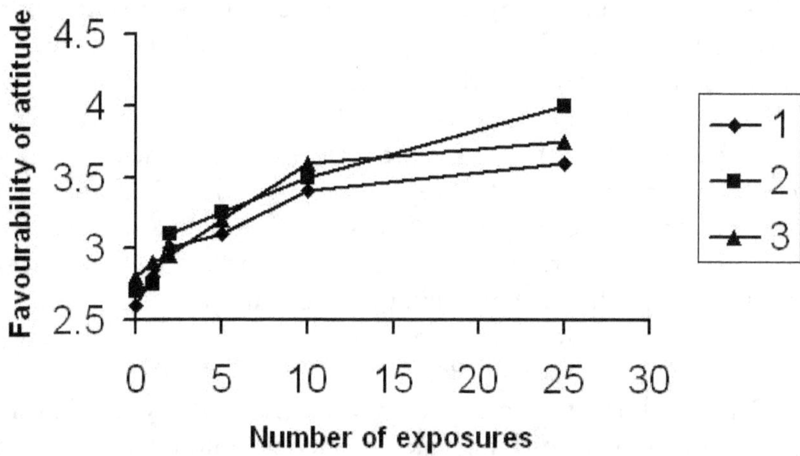

Figure 8.1. Increase in attitude favourability with increasing number of exposures to: 1. Turkish nonsense words. 2. Chinese-like characters. 3. Photographs of men.

Persuasion studies on message repetition usually focus on the effects of repeated exposure to *information* about attitude objects. In a classic monograph Zajonc dealt merely with the objects themselves (Zajonc, 1968). Figure 8.1 illustrates the increase in attitude favourability with repeated exposure to three types of stimuli, showing a somewhat asymptotic behaviour similar to that of learning curves.

This result is comparable to the set size effect seen in Figure. 7.1 insofar as increasing response is seen with increasing amounts of information, albeit repetition of the same information in the case of mere exposure.

It is also comparable, of course, to the learning curve of Figure 6.3.

One study found that the mere exposure effect reaches its maximum with 10-20 presentations, and others that longer series of exposures may eventually result in decreased liking. This latter result is comparable to the phenomenon of *advertising wearout* when excessive repetition of an advertisement has a negative effect.

Other studies of mere exposure, however, have yielded results more in line with the contact hypothesis. One found that college students repeatedly exposed to pictures of persons with different cultural backgrounds gave enhanced evaluations when their initial evaluation was positive, whereas they gave decreased evaluations when their initial evaluation was negative (Perlman & Oskamp, 1971).

This finding was also supported by a research finding that people who did not like abstract paintings on initial viewing showed increased dislike with frequent further exposure (Brickman et al., 1972).

Conclusions

The conditions for positive and productive contact suggested in the first section of this chapter may prove helpful in resolving conflicts at a more 'local' level, for example relatively minor disputes and conflicts in schools, workplaces and suburbs.

Reducing conflict between nations with a history of hostility, however, is much more difficult.

Religious differences, of course, are often a major factor, current examples of ongoing conflict being between:

(1) Shiites and Sunnis in Iraq and elsewhere.

(2) Israelis and Palestinians.

(3) Muslims and the West, particularly the US and its allies.

As for the effect of proximity, there is no doubt that throughout history this has been a major factor in conflict, for example:

(1) Conflict between neighbouring tribes, just as has also been observed with chimps.

(2) Conflict between nearby city states as the first nation states evolved.

(3) Conflict between neighbouring countries as empires evolved.

(4) Conflict between empires and other regions as empires sought to expand.

Finally, mere exposure research does show that with increasing exposure to 'foreign' material we do become increasingly accustomed to it, even if we do not understand it.

As the world increasingly integrates economically and, to a lesser extent socially, we can only hope that the world's different peoples and cultures will become more accustomed to one another, if not integrate to some extent. If so, there will surely be less conflict than hitherto.

With our population already greatly excessive, and with resource depletion and environmental degradation increasing, however, our prospects of survival for the long term are diminishing, and there is a likelihood of increasing conflict for fast disappearing resources (Mohr, 2012b; Mohr et al., 2018a).

8. The Contact Hypothesis

Chapter 9

HIERARCHICAL ORGANIZATIONS

All inequality that has no special utility to justify it is injustice.
Jeremy Bentham, Supply Without Burthen or Escheat Vice Taxation,
Jeremy Bentham's Economic Writings (W. Stark, ed., 1952).

*All wars are planned by old men
in council rooms apart.*
Grantland Rice, *Two Sides of War* (1955).

The Peter Principle

Dr Laurence Peter drew on his experiences in the education sector to try and explain why we always seem to have lousy leaders (Peter & Hull, 1969). The result was his celebrated *Peter Principle:*

IN A HIERARCHY EVERY EMPLOYEE TENDS TO RISE
TO HIS OWN LEVEL OF INCOMPETENCE.

In other words, *the sour cream rises.*

A corollary is: *In time every post tends to be occupied by an employee who is incompetent to carry out his duties.*

In his often tongue-in-cheek book Peter gives a few excellent historical examples of his celebrated principle, including:

(a) Socrates was a brilliant philosopher but a lousy defence attorney.

(b) Hitler was a brilliant politician but a lousy general.

Mohr's Law of Hierarchies

This can illustrated by the small (hierarchical) DC network shown in Figure 9.1 which can be modelled as a DC network using a simple Finite Element Method program (Mohr, 1992, 2012a).

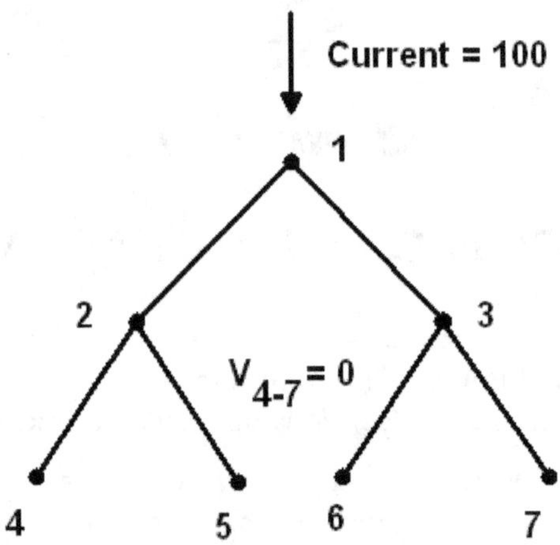

Figure 9.1. Hierarchical network.

At node 1 we have the pyramid building and lunatic 'boss' and a current 'load' of 100 is input. This is done by specifying the voltage at node 1 as 100, this being equivalent to adding a 'load' to the network.

Then zero datum voltage is specified at nodes 4-7 and unit resistance is given to all 6 elements so that the results from the program are:

Voltage 75 at node 1.

Voltage 25 at nodes 2 and 3.

Zero voltage at nodes 4 to 7.

Currents 50 in the top two elements and 25 in the rest.

This illustrates what the 'econobabble' of economists and politicians calls 'the trickledown effect', that is, the boss of this very small hierarchy has 3 times the voltage (or power, money and status) of his subordinates (the front line managers) one rung below. The workers at the bottom have no status at all.

If we add a further bottom row of 8 nodes in Figure 9.1 then now the 'voltage hierarchy' is 87.5, 37.5, 12.5, 0 so that the boss now does 7 times as well as the 'front line managers' on the row above the bottom row.

Then if we add a further fifth row of 16 nodes the voltage hierarchy is 93.75, 43.75, 18.75, 6.25, 0 and the boss does 15 times as well as the front line managers and infinitely better than the workers at the bottom!

The latter 'voltage hierarchy' is the fundamental principle of modern management, leading to Mohr's Law of Hierarchies (Mohr 2018b):

In hierarchical organizations the amount of real material-producing work people do is inversely proportional to their rank or level in the organization.

The amount of compensation they receive, however, is proportional to their level, sometimes to an exponential degree.

For such people their earnings might be expressed as an exponential function:

$$\$ = C\exp(kR)$$

where $\$$ = salary, R = rank, and C and k are constants.

This, of course, is not fair at all.

In ancient times philosophers felt that nobody should be paid more than about 10 or 20 times as much as anybody else, and even that is a great difference, of course, but it might be justified in the case of an elected national leader who must be able to present a strong, powerful image and might have only a relatively short term in office.

In the case of big biz, however, things have got out of hand and remuneration of CEOs is often tens of millions, on top of which they get huge share issues as annual bonuses, huge 'golden handshakes' when they retire, and gigantic 'golden parachutes' then the company collapses.

To add insult to the injury of poverty the worker-slaves endure 'top-down one-way' (TDOW) communication as they did all through their long years at school, in other words, they are treated like shit.

It is not always this way, however, as shown by the counter-example of modern movie and sports stars, in those businesses also the people who do the actual work. The trouble is that they are doing what is at school called play, not work, so that they make zillions more than the poor peasants who work on farms, in factories or on building sites to produce what is essential to human life is not fair at all either.

So those posters we recall seeing from the USSR decades ago which picture the workers as heroic perhaps make some sense. Then, of course, the hammer and sickle on their flag was also symbolic of the importance of the workers.

So the bottom line is that we have to create fairer societies which have real or *direct democracy* and leaders who 'check their ego at the door' (Marcum et al.). In these greed, hunger and famine, war and other evils will not be tolerated by the people.

Power corrupts

As figure 9.1 illustrates, the higher up you are in a hierarchy the more 'power' you have, which might be stated symbolically as:

$$P = C\,R^n$$

where P = power, R = rank, and C and n are constants.

Assuming the value of n is 2 then when one is twice as high in the hierarchy one has four times as much power.

Then, as we all know, power corrupts, and it is this that is one of the major factors in mankind's endless history of conflict.

As noted in the previous section, salaries may increase exponentially in hierarchical organizations and this result can be related to Mohr's Law of Capitalism which is the exponential growth law of money (\$) with time (T)

$$d(\$)/d(T) = c_1(\text{activity}) \quad \text{where} \quad \text{activity} = c_2\,\$$$

Here the rate at which money is made is proportional to the rate of business activity, this in turn proportional to the amount of money available to fund this activity.

Combining the two constants above as $k = c_1 c_2$ we have

$$d(\$)/d(T) = k\$ \quad \text{where } k \text{ is the } \textit{growth factor.}$$

where \$ = money made. This is *separable* which means that it can be integrated in the form

$$\text{Integral } [\, d(\$)/\$ \,] = \text{Integral } [\, k\,d(T) \,]$$

giving, with the inclusion of the initial values, the exponential growth law

$$\$/\$_0 = \exp[k(T - T_0]$$

If, for example, the growth factor is 10% per year, that is $k = 0.1$, then over 10 years we obtain the growth ratio $\$/\$_0 = 2.7$, so that we have nearly *tripled* our money.

The only real beneficiaries, however, are those higher in the hierarchy. The workers at the bottom who do all the *real work* (sitting and raving at sometimes boozy board meetings is not hard work) can't usually save any money and thus are slaves to all intents and purposes.

This is an intolerable situation and the CEOs who earn 'megabucks' are, of course, corrupt, and such corruption has always sown the seeds of discontent that have always, sooner or later, ended up as revolutions.

Thus it has been said the socialism tends to be ruled by a single dictator, but capitalism by a multiplicity of petty dictators:

> *Capitalism tends to produce a multiplicity of petty dictators each in command of his own little business kingdom. State Socialism tends to produce a single, centralized totalitarian dictatorship, wielding absolute authority . . . through a hierarchy of bureaucratic agents.*
> Aldous Huxley, *Ends and Means* (1937).

Politicians too are often corrupt, of course, often being found to take bribes from big business.

Monarchs and dictators, of course, have nearly always been the greediest of all. Not only do they help themselves to plenty of money and live in grand palaces, but throughout history their hunger for power and thence territorial gain has led to one war after another.

How hierarchies operate

Hierarchies operate through a chain of command, leaders meeting with a chosen few top-level executives responsible for overseeing the various operations of the organization. In the case of government, for example, there are ministers for defence, treasury, education, health, and so forth.

In each of these areas there is a permanent and hierarchical bureaucratic department with several levels of seniority ranging from head of the organization and department heads to front-line managers who manage teams of workers.

Through the whole chain of command there is an implicit level of intimidation and fear that usually makes sure that everybody does as they are told. At the front line, however, things often get ridiculous, for example the traditional screaming of army sergeants at their miserable subordinates.

It is through such bullying and intimidation, of course, that soldiers are brainwashed into following orders without question or delay, essentially becoming expendable slaves to satisfy the whims of their leaders. Don't worry about 'executive stress,' therefore, worry about 'slave-stress.'

Indeed, our many sports with a relationship to conflict, for example absurd rugby with its 'charge at the enemy' no matter what the risk of injury, or archery and rifle shooting, all relate to our historical predilection for conflict.

Throughout hierarchies there is, of course, ambition to rise, often leading to a good deal of competitive behaviour, much of it often downright dishonest and unfair. In politics, for example, plenty of 'backstabbing' goes on day in and day out.

This corresponds quite closely, perhaps, with the alpha-male behaviour seen in several animal species, notably our close relatives, gorillas.

The result is, of course, that those who end up as leaders may well be the most rotten people in the organization and, indeed, historically in both government and business this has always proved to be the case to some extent at least. That is, leaders are always greedy and bossy to some extent at least, but often they are exceptionally so.

The problem is that, being people who have proved themselves good at the 'rat race', they tend to be the worst leaders, exactly in accordance with the Peter Principle.

Not only that, power not only corrupts, it makes people vain, self-centred, neurotic, obsessive, and, basically, mad. Here we must hasten to note Mohr's 10th Law, that is, that things such as madness must be judged on a scale of 1 to 10, not merely as a true-or-false judgment.

Furthermore, we like to make the important distinction between *bad mad* (depression etc.) and *sad mad* (Mohr, 2012c, 2018), and all too often political leaders have been bad mad, for example Nero and Hitler (see Chapter 4).

Conflicts in society

Societies have a hierarchical structure, of course, English society, for example, still being regarded as having an upper class (the rich), a middle class, and a lower class of the poorest people.

Throughout history the oppressed people in the lower classes have often become discontented and revolted, an example in ancient times being the revolt of the slaves led by Spartacus, examples in more recent times being the Russian and Cuban revolutions.

On a smaller scale, in modern so-called democratic societies unions are often in dispute with companies and sometimes governments over grievances over pay and conditions, occasionally this leading to conflict. In extreme cases, indeed, national strikes sometimes occur, often resulting in the army being called out to quell the violence that often occurs during these.

In society there are many other organizations with special causes, for examples The Green and Gay movements, and such organizations often organize large demonstrations that sometimes result in conflict with police called to attend them.

Terrorist organizations

When external parties initiate conflict with cities or nations, of course, things happen on a grand scale.

Sometimes, indeed, the initial conflict may be on a very small scale yet result in a massive response, the assassination of Archduke Ferdinand of Austria being one of the causes of World War 1.

Terrorism, of course, has always been a weapon of revolutionaries, WordWeb 6 defining terrorism as:

The calculated use of violence (or the threat of violence) against civilians in order to attain goals that are political or religious or ideological in nature; this is done through intimidation or coercion or instilling fear.

Modern examples spring readily to mind, particularly the decades of conflict in Ireland between Protestants and Catholics, and the IRA's (established in 1919) decades of paramilitary operations aimed at ending British influence in Northern Ireland.

Currently, however, Muslim terrorism affects many countries still, the al-Qa'ida organization being the best known Muslim terrorist group.

In such groups hidden leaders like Osama Bin Laden operated through a hierarchical structure beginning with a couple of trusted 'lieutenants' (Kawahiri and Zawahiri in al-Qa'ida in the 1990s) and ranging through to those in command of training camps and those selected to lead particular teams for larger scale attacks such as the 9/11 attacks in the USA.

Here, as always, the second quotation that heads this chapter rings true, Bin Laden being in hiding in Afghanistan when the 9/11 operation was carried out, and George Bush being far away in Washington when he responded by taking over Iraq.

Conclusions

It requires hierarchies, whether monarchical, democratic, or socialist, to organize and carry out large scale conflicts. This is, of course, because large scale conflict or war requires many people and thus both leaders and 'sub-leaders' to organize and control them.

It is thus leaders, or groups of leaders, who start major conflicts.

In so-called democratic societies such leaders may be much influenced by wealthy industrialists, particularly those in the arms industry who stand to profit greatly by war.

Within hierarchical organizations, of course, there is also conflict, particularly over the 'rat race' involved in rising in the hierarchy.

Indeed, it may more often than not be that ambitious, driven people are psychopathic, the pathology of their condition involving lying, cheating, aggressiveness, and bullying to get to the top.

Given power, it seems, they become psychotic with dreams of greater wealth and power and thus superiority. Alexander the Great, for example, began to think that he must be divine.

The bottom line, however, is that it is generally loony leaders, whether of terrorist organizations or nations, that start conflicts. Then, often without any real attempt at negotiation or *communication* of any kind, equally misguided leaders affected by the initial conflict respond militarily and the situation escalates into war.

As noted in Chapter 8, as well as 'bad contacts', cultural differences are often also a factor in conflict, and how such factors combine to affect our attitudes, and those of our leaders, is discussed in the following chapter.

Chapter 10

THE PSYCHOLOGY OF CONFLICT

*It is disturbing to see that still today, even in the most
advanced countries, in large sections of human society,
aggressiveness is praised as a virtue - or at least as a valuable
asset - and it is constantly advertised in the motion pictures and on
television. We need - more than anything else -
to educate people to tolerance and gentility.*
Carlo Cipolla, *The Economic History of World Population* (1974).

An attitudinal model of conflict

In this, the final chapter of the six that make up Part 2 of this book, some of the key ideas of those five preceding chapters are drawn together to form a very simple 'first approximation' formula for assessing the potential for conflict between a person or group assessed and another person or group. The basic formula takes the form:

$$A^* = A + xB + yC + zD \qquad\qquad (10.1)$$

where A^* = current 'overall' attitude,
A = initial or 'basic' attitude (based on 'known history'),
B = attitudes towards behaviours of the second party,
C = contact history between the two parties,
D = degree of difference between the parties considered,
and x, y, z are scaling factors that indicate the relative importance of the terms and here these will be assumed unity for simplicity.

Equation 10.1 can, of course, be used to assess the attitude of both parties involved in the assessment.

Here attitude is assessed in the same way as attitude is measured by the information integration model of Equation 7.1 but for simplicity only scale values (but not weights) will be given to a small set of items in measuring A.

Similarly, only scale values are used in assessing B, C and D. These extra terms add a great deal to the 'basic' A assessment to give a 'picture' of the 'overall' attitude.

Example application

As an example of application of the simple model of Equation 10.1 the attitude of a typical individual towards a hypothetical terrorist organization 'HTO' is considered.

To assess this only five items are assessed by simple questions for the initial attitude, behavioural, contact and difference terms in Equation 10.1. Assessment is similar to that used for the 'five-factor' model of personality (Larsen & Buss, 2002) and uses five possible scores:

+2 = strongly like/very similar etc.
+1 = like/similar etc.
0 = neutral
-1 = dislike/different etc.
-2 = strongly dislike/very different etc.

Table 10.1 gives an example assessment for a hypothetical individual.

Here total scores less than -30 are 'very negative', -10 to -20 'negative', -10 to +10 are moderate, +10 to +20 'positive', and more than +20 'very positive'.

Thus the results of Table 10.1 are 'negative', the total of -22 indicating a considerable degree of disapproval. It is only very negative scores of less than -30 that might be a cause for concern if they were obtained for a significant percentage of a population.

Table 10.1. Person's hypothetical attitude towards 'HTO'.

SCORE:	-2	-1	0	1	2
A, initial/basic attitude	Dislike/Like				
The people			0		
Their government(s)		-1			
How they look		-1			
What they say	-2				
What they do	-2				
B, group behaviour	Dislike/Like				
Sectarian conflict		-1			
Negative rhetoric		-1			
'Pushing' their religion	-2				
Threats	-2				
Terrorism	-2				
C, contact history	Uncomfortable/Comfortable				
See on TV			0		
See on street			0		
Close to		-1			
Talk to		-1			
Socialize	-2				
D, differences	Different/Similar				
Language		-1			
Economic				1	
Culture		-1			
Religion	-2				
History		-1			
TOTAL SCORE, A*:	-22				

Weighting factors can be assigned to items in Table 10.1 to reflect differing importance associated with them, for example the 9th and 10th items might have weights >1.

Effect of Societal views

The effect of the views of society on individuals and groups can be included in Eqn 10.1 by adding an extra term comparable to the inclusion of 'social norms' in Eqn 7.2:

$$A^{**} = A^* + fS = A + xB + yC + zD + fS$$

where *f is a scaling factor* here assumed = 1 for simplicity, and the factors *x, y, z* are also assumed =1 so that:

$$A^{**} = A + B + C + D + S \qquad (10.2)$$

and *S* is the person or group's assessment of the attitude or 'position' of society, society here including the media, politicians, religious leaders, the public, friends and family.

Then measurement of *S* is done in the same way as for *A, B, C* and *D* in Table 10.1.

Table 10.2. Person's assessment of society's attitude.

SCORE:	-2	-1	0	1	2
S, perceived society view		Negative/Positive			
TV/radio/papers		-1			
Politicians			0		
Religious leaders		-1			
The public		-1			
Friends & family		-1			
TOTAL SCORE:			-4		

For the views of a typical person regarding society's attitude towards 'HTO' the result might be that shown in Table 10.2. Adding this result to that of Table 10.1 the aggregate score is -26, a 'negative' overall result.

A 'very negative' score would be less than -30, so the combined result of Tables 10.1 and 10.2 (i.e. -26) for an individual or a group is not of concern but worth taking some notice of.

Responses to conflict

When the group, attitudes towards which are sought, is in some form of dispute or conflict, whether this be economic, concerning mistreatment of a few people, or armed conflict on any scale, the attitudes concerning what measures should be taken against the group can also be measured in like fashion to Table 10.1.

Table 10.3. Attitudes towards measures against group.

SCORE:	0	1	2	3	4
	Level of support for action				
Government condemns					4
Cut diplomatic ties				3	
Trade embargo			2		
Public demonstrations				3	
UN sanctions		1			
War	0				-
TOTAL SCORE:	13				

Table 10.3 shows an example of such an assessment for a hypothetical individual concerning his or her views towards HTO's terrorism around the world. The total score is $R = 13$ out of a possible 24, perhaps a 'fail' mark by way of assessment of the group in question, but not an extremely bad score. Total scores of close to 20, on the other hand, would indicate very strong feelings of which, perhaps, considerable notice should be taken should they be found to apply to a significant number of people.

The results of Tables 10.1 – 10.3 can be combined as:

$$A^{***} = A + B + C + D + S - (R - 12)$$

with the last term adjusted to allow for its different scale of measurement, giving $A^{***} = -27$ for the present example case. When the results of Table 10.3 are included, those of Table 28.1 should also be added for 'balance.'

Other factors affecting attitudes & conflict

[1] Hierarchical influences.

These include the influence of strongly hierarchical organizations that have very great influence on society and its individual people, some of these being:

(a) Governments of any type, whether they be monarchies or dictatorships have considerable influence on the populace by way of propaganda and enforceable laws, for example those of conscription.

(b) Political parties. Even when they are not in government, supporters of political parties are often considerably influenced by their views.

(c) Religions. These, of course, have had great influence throughout history but have less influence in the West now, whilst in contrast Muslim sects still have great influence on many of the world's 1.5 billion Muslims.

(d) TV, radio and print media also tend to come from 'on high' and also have considerable influence.

[2] Social norms.

Social norms have a great influence on the thinking of individuals and groups within any society, for example the wearing of scarves, veils and burkas by Muslim women is still very widely practiced.

The structure of society has also been an important factor. Fairly soon after the Agricultural Revolution and the formation of man's first permanent towns and farms the first small armies would have been formed to defend them, at first only temporarily.

Indeed, with the diversification of occupations that the Agricultural Revolution brought, permanent armies were one eventual result, notably in the Rome and its empire, for example. Then, of course, given the availability of armies, there has always been a tendency to use them sooner or later, most obviously as the 'external police force' to deal with external problems, albeit a very large force all too often in history.

[3] Economic factors.

Economic considerations have often been the cause of human conflict, for example competition for resources, a good historical example being the Spanish Empire's enthusiastic search for gold in the Americas.

Man has always been inventing new tools and weapons, particularly since the Industrial Revolution. Now the arms industries have become massive and are able to considerably influence government policy in many countries whose economies have suffered a steep decline in their manufacturing industries in recent decades (Sampson, 1977; Thomas, 2006).

An example of the absurdity of it all, the CIA knew that chemical weapons were pouring into Iraq from Chile and South Africa in the 1980s. Cardoen industries in Santiago, for example, sent its chemical weapons, and the German-made artillery 'cups' or shells to contain them, to Iraq (Ben-Menashe, 1992). Then, the US later condemned Iraq for using these weapons on the Kurds and used this as an excuse for their first invasion of Iraq early in 1991.

[4] Growing populations.

Even as far back as early man's troglodyte days it is not hard to imagine an extended family group growing to the point at which a second cave was needed.

Similarly, when man had towns and then cities these too grew in size, needing ever more space and, more importantly, resources, particularly food.

This, coupled with man's habit of exploration, which no doubt dates back to his hunter-gatherer days and thence the hunt for food, has led man to engage in conflict with neighbouring populations.

Conflicts may have arisen simply out of the suspicion that the sight of strangers aroused when they suddenly appeared. Perhaps, for example, a spear might be thrown to scare them away. Then, of course, there might be retaliation and thus conflict.

As man's population continued to increase, of course, the tendency for migration and thence conflict must have increased, for example people leaving crowded and disease-ridden cities in Europe to colonize the 'New World' from the 16th to 19th centuries.

[5] Proximity.

For tribal man, as with his chimpanzee relatives, proximity was a key factor in regular tribal conflicts.

Indeed, until only about two thousand years ago, human conflicts were only between neighbouring cities, regions, or countries. With the building of ships capable of sailing hundreds of miles, however, came the ability to explore more widely, and human conflict began to occur over greater distances and on a greater scale.

As described in Part 1 of this book, eventually ships travelled even greater distances and great empires were built, notably the Roman Empire and the Spanish and British Empires.

As noted in a section of Chapter 8, proximity also affects people's attitudes as does contact which, of course, is facilitated by proximity, the more 'negative' the contact the more negative the attitude formed.

[6] Competitiveness.

In the Roman Empire, for example, there was a competitiveness in its governments, an obvious drive that made it wish to become 'bigger and grander' and go out and conquer other lands to achieve that end.

This obsession with competition runs all through the history and cultures of Homo sapiens, an example being our obsession with sport, or any kind of competition even if it is called a 'game.' It seems fundamentally related to the alpha-male behaviour of several other animal species.

Man, however, takes the alpha-male issue to absurd lengths, for example the original Olympic Games in Ancient Greece being conducted in the nude and, indeed, it seems to be returning slowly towards that situation now.

Equally, man has often indulged in war without good reason, usually because some loony leader and his acolytes want to 'beat' some other foe.

Conclusions

The simple formula of Equation 10.1 combines the measurement techniques of attitudinal psychology with the concepts of the contact hypothesis to assess the attitudes of individuals and groups of people to other groups of people. The point of this exercise is that, when the attitude of one group to another is very negative, then conflict between the groups is, of course, more likely.

The attitudes of leaders are of particular importance, as it is these that may lead to conflict and war. The attitudes of leaders will, of course, be influenced by many of the same factors and stimuli that affect the public.

There are many other factors that affect modern human conflict. For example, particularly in modern times, alliances between nations have played a part in many wars, World War 1 and World War 2 being notable examples.

One difficulty is that, if two groups of 4 nations are allied, then a single nation attacking some part of another may quickly result in 8 nations being at war. In other words, the larger the parties involved, the bigger the conflict.

One fear for the future, therefore, is the increasing power of such huge nations as China and India, and also of the 1.5 billion Muslims around the world. The numbers involved here are an order of magnitude greater than those involved in the two world wars of the last century and war between any of these three entities and another of perhaps similar size could well be the war to end all wars.

Chapter 11

THE WAR OF THE SEXES

When I asked female viewers and readers what they got out of raunch culture, I heard - - - They wanted to be one of the guys"; *they hoped to be experienced "like a man." Going to strip clubs or talking about porn stars was a way of showing themselves and the men around them that they weren't "prissy little women" or "girly-girls." Besides, they told me, to regard this bacchanal as problematic would be old-school and uncool.*
Ariel Levy, *Female Chauvinist Pigs, Women and the Rise of Raunch Culture*, Schwartz Publishing, Melbourne 2005.

At the same time, British writer Julie Burchill came out in The Sunday Times – after having left her husband for a woman and then left that woman for her brother - -.
Elizabeth Wurtzel, *Bitch, In Praise of Difficult Women*, Quartet Books, London 1998.

Introduction

In the chapters of Part 3 of this book the penultimate or last section of each chapter will summarize the relevance of each of the items of Equations 10.1 and 10.2, that is, A, B, C, D and S, respectively 'initial attitudes', behaviours, contact history, differences, and societal views.

In that way some consistency will be given to discussion of each of the areas of 'application' discussed in Part 3.

It should also help show that the ideas and concepts of Part 2, the 'theory' part of the book, do indeed have wide application.

A brief history of the War of the Sexes

Over two hundred years ago the seeds of the feminist movement were sown in Europe:

A king is always a king – and a woman always a woman:
his authority and her sex ever stand
between them and rational discourse.
Mary Wollstonecraft, mother of Mary Shelley,
A Vindication of the Rights of Woman (1792).

In the USA the First Women's Rights Convention was held in New York in 1848 and declared that all men and women are created equal.

It took some time, but women eventually gained 'the vote' in the West at least, and subsequently they were given, in principle at least, equal pay for equal work.

One of the books that helped inspire the modern Fem Lib movement was Simone de Beauvoir's *Le Deuxieme Sex* (1949) which appeared translated into English as *The Second Sex* in 1953.

Fem Lib really began to have an impact by the 1970s, however, in part thanks to the Germaine Greer's *The Female Eunuch* (1970), a deliberately 'over the top' at times book. For example, in the chapter "Loathing and Disgust" she says:

Is it too much to ask that women be spared the daily struggle for superhuman beauty in order to offer it to the caresses of a subhumanly ugly mate?

Being deliberately controversial the book was a success but Greer has continued with her often excessive bias to this day. Indeed, recently the first author remarked to a woman at Oxford University Press that Greer might be a "bitch" and the OUP woman swiftly replied: *"I wholeheartedly agree with you."*

Nevertheless, a high proportion of women in the West are very supportive of the feminist movement which continues to seek a better deal for women.

The many differences between men & women

We are sometimes inclined to think that there are more differences between men and women than there are between different races. The many differences include:

{1] Physical differences.

Men are usually larger and have more muscle. To allow greater physical activity men have coarser skin with more sweat glands to assist use of their larger muscle mass.

Women, on the other hand have more adipose tissue, some of it stored in the breasts for the mothering function. This greater amount of fat storage also allows the average woman to survive about four months without food, whereas the average male can only survive about a month before his body begins to shut down, blindness being one of the first results.

A larger, more muscled hunter, of course, is not as calming a sight as a smaller, weaker, and 'softer' woman so that, when they are in their prime, at least, women tend to be more attractive. Indeed, in modern society they go to a great deal of trouble and expense to look nice.

[2] Chemical differences.

There are, of course, many metabolic differences between men and women. For example, to help cope with their larger amounts of adipose tissue women have higher HDL levels to assist in reverse cholesterol transport. For similar reasons they can also tolerate higher homocysteine levels without ill-effects.

Hormones are a major difference, men having higher testosterone levels and women higher levels of oestrogens, the female sex hormones. Levels of sex hormones peak in the late teens, of course, and then slowly decline.

[3] The maternal instinct.

MRI scans of mothers' brains show that they do indeed have a maternal instinct. Is it passed on in the female genes in some animal species, or is it a learnt trait, or does this seemingly powerful instinct come, like intelligence, from both *nature* and *nurture*?

The maternal instinct, however, is a powerful caring and bonding instinct that men do not have, of course, though they may also have a strong 'protective instinct' for their children.

[4] Sociological differences.

In all human societies we have traditionally developed different roles and behaviours for men and women.

Men, being bigger and stronger, and not tied down with children, have usually been the hunters and the warriors, comparable roles, of course, in that they both involve killing.

We perpetuate that by still training young boys to be 'rough and tough' and play sports like rugby, comparable to the 'do as you're told' (regardless) and 'charge' the enemy in trench warfare. If men are somewhat more inclined to physical violence than women, therefore, it is hardly surprising.

Young girls, in contrast, are brought up playing with dolls and trying to look nice.

[5] Intelligence.

The Gaussian distribution of IQ spreads more widely for men than for women (Mohr, 2012c, 2018):

There are, it should be noted, considerable sex differences,
female being relatively superior in spelling
and inferior in arithmetic [results for 15-year olds].
Many surveys of intelligence and attainments have also
demonstrated that the range or spread of ability (as distinct
from the average performance) is slightly more restricted in
girls. P.E. Vernon, *Intelligence and Attainment Tests,*
University of London Press (1960).

Today, however, this may be changing somewhat with more women attending University than men in some Western countries, an unimaginable situation 100 years ago.

The bottom line, however, is that, increasingly, the differences between men and women are becoming divisive issues when once it was *'vive la difference,'* so that the D term in Equation 10.1 makes a negative contribution to attitudes towards the opposite sex these days.

Hostility and conflict

Around the world there is now a good deal of pressure from women's groups wanting an ever better deal for women, for example paid maternity leave.

In the workplace women have taken over much of the education industry where now child day-care is a massive industry in its own right, employing many women who, in turn help other women take jobs that men once had.

Women are much more accomplished gossipers and liars than men, something they seem to learn early in life. For example, they will seldom be honest about their past, particularly their sex life, whereas they will expect to know all about a man's and will then gossip about it, and anything else he says or does. One woman the first author knew, for example, always put her age down by about 10 years when applying for a job, telling him: *"You have to lie to get jobs."*

Violence against women has also become a major issue. This issue lacks balance, however, for example women often incite violence by (sometimes hysterical) 'verbal assault'. As on the football field where insulting remarks are made to incite an opposition player to violence with the hope of the referee noticing, so too women can try and catch men out in this way to get them into trouble and gain evidence against them which might support claims for custody and child maintenance after a marriage breakup.

As for conflict, in part because of feminism, in the decadent West 50% of marriages now end in divorce.

Another cause of some hostility, there is still frequent complaint about the predominance of men in upper management.

Changing behaviours

In the decadent West behaviour throughout society seems to be degenerating. In the media, as in society itself, violence and sex are pervasive to the extent that ads for brothels appear in the local papers that children can take from the letter box when they get home from school.

Women becoming more 'butch,' however, is widespread and, of course, comes part and parcel with Feb Lib, and the first of the quotations that opens this chapter is an example of this.

Once, for example, jeans were, of course, intended for male labourers, but thanks to the ubiquitous marketing of the modern age a high proportion of women wear them day in, day out.

The incredibly ubiquitous advertising of our consumer society, together with junk food outlets prominently located throughout our cities, has helped create an obesity epidemic. In addition, increasing numbers of people are experimenting with and becoming addicted to alcohol and drugs.

With increasing levels of unemployment and homelessness in the West, and circa 2 billion of the world's people being undernourished, the authors feel that we are, indeed, experiencing *reverse evolution* both physically and mentally with IQ decreasing significantly in the West in the last 100 years (Mohr, 2012a).

Societal influences

Throughout society there are many influences contributing to the War of the Sexes, including:

[1] The Feminine Liberation movement.

This, of course, affects most women to some extent, Fem Lib views often being aired extensively in the media.

[2] The Media.

Media coverage of divorce cases and violence against women is frequent.

[3] The Sex Industry.

The pervasiveness of the sex industry throughout Western society degrades our view of women significantly.

[4] Increasing numbers of women in the workforce.

With more women in the workforce than ever before, there is far more opportunity for them to help each other gain promotions at the expense of men.

Here women's capacity for lying can come to the fore. For example, more than once we have known of a woman using a relative as a referee for her job applications, the person in question not being a 'blood relative' but a relative by marriage and thus having a different surname. Indeed, women have been known to use their married sister as a referee in this way.

Declining Western civilizations

As the world's population exponentiates Western civilization is in decay. Our societies are becoming meaner, nastier and more violent at an alarming rate. Violence is on the increase everywhere to the point that many people don't feel safe on the streets at night and, of course, there is no shortage of street crime during the day as well.

Experiments with rats show that when they are housed beyond a certain population density they begin to fight each other. Evidently, humans do the same and we are now accustomed to associating crime and violence with big cities like Chicago and New York.

Increasing numbers of us are addicted to booze, illegal so-called 'party drugs,' as well as prescription drugs like Valium for anxiety, Ritalin for ADHD, and lithium for bipolar disorder (formerly called manic depression).

With divorce rates around 50% we are living less safely in this respect at least than our Neanderthal ancestors did. Childhood is miserable enough at times but family breakups often make it much more so for far too many children.

In marriage, as well as in courtship, there is little or no meaningful communication. If you eavesdrop on a couple that has been married for a decade or two you will find the dialogue at all times entirely trivial, for example: "Do we need milk?," in modern times this being said as often as not over a mobile phone while one partner is in the supermarket.

Indeed, with the War of the Sexes heating up and women taking over in management, politics, and education, and running the countless industries that target women consumers, the future is bleak indeed for our decadent society.

Indeed, you can see the writing on the walls, that is, the graffiti that covers much of our miserable megacities, a sure sign that young men with nothing better to do are regressing back to grunting cave men once again.

This is, indeed, something of a reversal in roles. Once it was probably troglodyte women who did the cave painting, perhaps to teach children while the men were out hunting. Now, as manufacturing industry winds down inexorably in most countries except a few in Asia, more and more men are out of work whereas new, 'softer' jobs for women continue to be created, for example in childcare centres.

Assessments

Equation 10.2 is:

Attitude $A^{**} = A + B + C + D + S$

In the War of the Sexes the relevance of the terms on the right-hand side can be summarized as follows.

[1] ***Initial attitude A*** of women is much influenced by mainstream feminist arguments for equality etc., and to a lesser extent by extremist views that women are really superior.

[2] The *behaviour, B,* of men and women has changed with, for example, more and more people addicted to alcohol, drugs or gambling, an obesity epidemic, and society becoming more violent and sexually promiscuous.

In addition, feminists encourage women to be more assertive, or even 'butch,' giving rise to more competitive attitude and in turn more conflict.

[3] The *contact history, C,* between men and women has changed and now there is a good deal more conflict between men and women, the disastrous 50% divorce rates that now prevail in many Western countries being evidence of this as people with children to consider do not separate permanently unless there are substantial reasons such as intolerable levels of dissatisfaction, argument and conflict.

[4] The *differences, D,* between men and women are very considerable, as discussed in the third section of this chapter.

[5] *Societal attitudes, S,* tend to support the feminist movement, as discussed in the second section of this chapter, thus contributing considerably to the attitudes and behaviours of individual women.

Conclusion

It is the combination of these factors, all of them encouraging negative attitudes and conflict, that ensures that the War of the Sexes will continue for some time.

The destructive effects are great, circa 50% divorce rates affecting half a generation of children adversely, as well as having a broader impact on increasingly corrupt and decadent Western societies, for example decreasing the morale and efficiency of the workforce.

11. The War of the Sexes

Chapter 12

BULLYING IN SCHOOLS

*Show me a man who has enjoyed his school days
and I'll show you a bully and a bore.*
Robert Morley, attributed.

Introduction

Bullying has become a big issue in the media in Australia over the last decade or so. One rarely heard the word in the first author's school days, but bullying did occur occasionally and, indeed, he was sometimes the victim of it. He was also the youngest of three children and thus suffered a little on that account too. That said, however, most people have experienced bullying at some point in their life.

Now, however, there is considerable support in society at large to combat bullying in schools and quite a few books and pamphlets are available on the subject.

The psychology of bullying

Bullying must relate somewhat to the alpha-male behaviour seen in several animal species, notably our close relatives, gorillas. Thus exertion and display of 'power' and 'dominance' are key factors in bullying.

The threats or displays of aggression that are part and parcel of bullying are part of the pathology of the typical psychopath, other sociopathic behaviours including delinquency, dishonesty and aberrant sexual behaviour (Davies, 1971).

About 1% of the people in society are psychopaths, most of them undiagnosed, whilst a whopping 3-5% of people have antisocial disorders, the latter including autism which is diagnosed in school children with disturbing frequency in Western societies.

Bullying often occurs when there is a 'power imbalance', for example a student given extra authority such as being made a school prefect might be more likely to indulge in bullying some times, much in the same way as we associate with the traditional image of army sergeants in the movies.

Bullying makes such people feel important, something which they may feel a need to compensate for, perhaps feeling isolated in some way by their own rank or other circumstances.

Everyone at a certain level of stress will develop psychiatric symptoms such as anxiety and depression. Psychopaths, however, may have a low 'stress threshold', and this is usually true of bullies who, in other words, have a 'short temper.'

Victims of bullying

Bullies, will, of course, tend to pick easy or 'soft targets' such as children who:

> Are new to the school.

> Look or are different in some way, perhaps racially or ethnically.

> Lack social confidence and tend to be loners.

> Are from a poor background and perhaps are less well-dressed, have little pocket money etc.

> Prefer books to people, i.e. 'nerds' or 'academic'.

> Struggle with schoolwork or other group tasks.

> Are not good at sport.

> Are smaller, weaker or younger.

> Have a disability.

Environments conducive to bullying

Schools are, to a considerable extent, competitive environments and, as such, are conducive to bullying.

Team sports are intrinsically competitive and can quickly provoke bullying. For example, the first author (GAM) recalls catching a boy out for a duck in an inter-house cricket match in Grade 8. The boy came up to him in the changing rooms afterwards and asked: "How tall are you?"

GAM told him and he replied: "I didn't know they piled shit that high." He went on to become a top lawyer.

Class tests are also competitive, of course, and GAM recalls always finishing the arithmetic tests in fourth grade in half the time allowed and being let out of the classroom early as a reward. A couple of times, at the end of lunchtime a jealous classmate not good at arithmetic sat on him to try and keep him from going back to class. This bully too went on to be a lawyer (an academic one).

Classrooms, of course, ensure proximity and thus provide plenty of opportunity for sly bullying while the teacher is writing on the board. Miscreants will often sit at the back of the classroom, if allowed, and teachers often make them sit at the front so that they can keep a closer eye on them and thence keep them under control.

Types of bullying

These include (Healey, 2011):

[1] Face-to face or direct bullying which may involve verbal actions such as name-calling and insults, or physical actions such as punching or kicking.

[2] Covert or indirect bullying such as spreading lies or rumours or excluding people from groups.

[3] Cyberbullying through email and social networking sites and forums. Cyberbullying is often anonymous and most people who do it also bully offline.

Whatever the type of bullying, it often extends to harassment based on race, gender, religion, or disability.

Bullying behaviours

Some of the common behaviours of bullies include (Fanteux, 2011):

➢ Blaming the victim for something and becoming increasingly angry and frustrated about it, in turn blaming the victim for their frustration.

➢ Agitated body language with tight, adrenalin-flushed muscles.

➢ Menacing look, flushed face, rapid breathing.

➢ Hostile dialogue.

➢ Threats of hostile actions.

➢ Presentation of a plan to cause harm.

➢ Ignoring warnings.

➢ Bullies often lead a small group which backs them up and gives them a power advantage over victims.

The effects of bullying

Bullying can affect victims in such ways as:

➢ Feeling alone and helpless.

➢ Feeling depressed and rejected.

➢ Feeling confused, not knowing what to do or why they are being bullied.

➢ Feeling unable to stop the bullying.

➢ A loss of self esteem.

To reduce these effects victims should work on building self-esteem, making sure they have a few friends, and becoming a confident communicator (Field, 1999).

Dealing with bullying

One of the first rules in dealing with bullying is don't reciprocate any threats as this will, of course, only escalate the level of hostility and make open conflict more likely.

Instead, keep calm and stand your ground confidently, but don't stand too close and stand to the left if you are right-handed in case the bully tries to hit you.

If the bully moves closer tell them to stop.

To try and defuse the hostility, confidently and quietly say something like: "I agree" or "I'm sorry if you are upset."

To restore control say: "Relax" or "Calm down".

Then try and get the bully to say what irks them and express empathy for their position verbally and using concerned facial expressions, remembering all the time that it is the bully who really has the underlying problem(s) (which he is venting on you).

Collectively dealing with bullying

Schools should openly address the subject of bullying early on and give advice on dealing with bullying such as:

> - Assure any bullies that bullying is wrong and not allowed in the school.

> - Make a list of bullying events and the students involved.

> - Tell parents about it so that they can contact teachers about it.

> - Make sure they have at least a couple of friends at school to support them.

> - If they feel isolated and 'foreign' join a team or group in the school to find friends.

> - Contact 'Kids Help Line' on 1800 55 1800 or at www.kidshelp.com.au.

To deal with individual cases of bullying the parents of the bullies should be told and a meeting of a school counsellor or teacher with the bully and the victim should be arranged to talk through the problem.

Then in more serious cases the bullies, and perhaps the victims also in some cases, should be referred to independent counselling.

Assessments

The components of Equation 10.2, that is:

Attitude $A^{**} = A + B + C + D + S$

have considerable relevance to bullying in schools:

[1] The *initial attitude, A,* of bullies is that they are superior, justifying that feeling perhaps because they are bigger than most other students in the class, for example.

Their victims, on the other hand, are deemed to be inferior because they are smaller, weaker, of different race or gender, or simply new to the school and thus have few friends as yet. Almost any excuse can be found for bullying, of course, so long as the bully is bigger, or has one or two other fellow bullies to back him up.

[2] With greater confidence the bullying ***behaviour*** (***B***) is likely to grow worse over time, eventually requiring intervention in many cases.

Often, however, bullying affects the victim's performance at school and their psychology. Indeed, the results can be serious, ranging from poor school results which limit career opportunities later on, to suicide in extreme cases of depression and anxiety.

[3] Soon a negative ***contact history*** (***C***) builds up between the bully and the victim and the bully becomes increasingly confident if not opposed in any way.

[4] It is such ***differences*** (***D***) as noted in [1] that are the excuse for bullying.

[5] ***Societal attitudes (S)*** are now very strongly against bullying to the point at which victims stand a much better chance of gaining help and support.

Finally, the movie *Revenge of the Nerds* is a good example of bullying. In this a group of nerds new to an American college are bullied by a group of 'sporty' types but eventually win popular support by winning an important annual inter-fraternity competition, clinching this win with a far superior musical performance.

Conclusions

Bullying no doubt relates to alpha male behaviour in several animal species, humans with such behaviour being said to have type A personality syndrome, a set of traits including ambition, impatience, competitiveness, and hostility. Schools, therefore, prove an ideal place for children with type A personality to become bullies, for example when, despite their competitive nature, they do not do as well in class tests as better students.

Here the cause of bullying is jealousy, and there are many other possible causes of this ranging from the bullied child having more money or being better looking.

Alternatively, competitive type children who sense some weakness in another, for example them simply being smaller, may use this as an excuse for bullying, comparable to the 'chest thumping' behaviour of dominant male gorillas.

Thus competitive type A children will bully both when they are superior in some way, or inferior in some way, in other words their competitiveness can always find an outlet.

Whilst bullies may do considerable harm to their victims, however, it is they who are probably in more need of extensive psychological therapy.

12. BULLYING IN SCHOOLS

Chapter 13

BULLYING IN THE WORKPLACE

*[The boss] told a woman she "should have been drowned at birth
and called another "porky", "wog" and a "big fat bush pig".
He threatened to dissolve employees in acid, told a woman
a rapist was "waiting for you" and said all women
were "dogs" who were "only good for one thing."*
Article by Steve Butcher, *The Age*, 6th December 2012.

Introduction

Like bullying in schools, workplace bullying is also a big issue now, the foregoing quotation from a newspaper article being an extreme example of it that occurred in a small business.

Estimates of prevalence rates for workplace bullying in Australia range from 3.5% to 15% and according to Healey (2011): *About one in six people are bullied at work; in some industries the figure is higher, ranging from 25 percent, 50 percent to 97 percent.*

A survey of 5,300 employees in the UK found a prevalence rate of 10.5%, whilst a survey of the population of Michigan in the USA found a prevalence rate of a whopping 21.5%. At such a rate 1.5 million Australian employees would have been victims of bullying in 2000 with a cost to businesses of between 17 and 36 billion dollars (Healey, 2011).

Bullying behaviours

There are five main types of workplace bullying:
➢ Work-related.
➢ Personal attacks.
➢ Social isolation
➢ Verbal threats.
➢ Rumour spreading.

Bullying behaviours can vary from easily noticed, aggressive and loud blaming and threats, to 'backstabbing' that damages the victim's reputation in the organization.

Usually the victim eventually suspects he or she is being backstabbed but is unsure of where the rumours are coming from, if not paranoid about it.

Usually bullying will involve both open aggression and covert backstabbing, the full range of behaviours being:
➢ Banter and teasing.
➢ Blame and verbal abuse.
➢ Personal abuse and humiliation.
➢ Yelling, screaming and offensive language.
➢ Professional denigration.
➢ Overt threats and intimidation.
➢ Racial, religious, gender or sexual slurs.
➢ Discrimination on the basis of age, gender, religion or culture.
➢ Harassment with repeated "hurry ups" etc.
➢ Manipulation of job specifications or withholding vital information to undermine work performance.
➢ Unrealistic workload or impossible tasks.
➢ Micromanagement.
➢ Changing work rosters to inconvenience particular employees.
➢ Assigning meaningless tasks unrelated to the job.
➢ Cyberbullying.
➢ Professional and personal exclusion or isolation.
➢ Career sabotage.

> Unjustified whistleblowing.
> Blackmail.
> Physical abuse or violence.
> Criminal assault.

Types of bullies

There are several typical types of bully, including:

(a) Ordinary workmates who are competitors wanting to impress the boss and weaken the position of those they bully. Often they are not very aware of their behaviour and will be repentant when it is pointed out.

(b) A manager or trade union official, often those new in the role who may lack confidence and/or competence and feel under pressure to prove themselves.

Managers who bully will tend to create a poor role model for others and be more likely to turn a blind eye to others that bully.

(c) People with type A personalities who are ambitious, driven, assertive and hostile.

(d) The psychopathic serial bully who bullies instinctively and may have an anti-social personality disorder. 1% of the population is psychopaths, the pathology of their condition including aggression, threats, lying and cheating.

Typical targets

Victims of bullying may:
> Be new on the job.
> Look or be different in some way, perhaps racially.
> Lack social confidence and tend to be loners.
> Show vulnerability and avoid conflict.
> Be from a different social or ethnic background.
> Be an academic type or 'nerd'.
> Struggle with some tasks.
> Be smaller or weaker, or have a disability.
> Be much younger or much older than the bully.

The effects of bullying

The effects of bullying can range from anxiety disorders, stress and depression to loss of confidence and eventual loss of job or career, as shown in Table 13.1.

Table 13.1. Effects of workplace bullying.

Type of effect	Effect
Physical	Insomnia Eating or drinking to excess Heart problems Stress-related illness Suicidal thoughts
Work performance	Distraction and poor concentration Loss of motivation Difficulty with new tasks Accidents working overstressed
Emotional	Fear and panic attacks Anger and frustration Depression Anxiety disorders Post-traumatic stress disorder
Financial	Loss of promotion Loss of second job Forced retirement Loss of income Loss of career
Social	Social difficulties Social isolation
Family life	Marital arguments over money etc. Separation/divorce

In short, bullying can ruin a person's life, leaving them unemployed for a long period, if not permanently.

For example, in moving to another University the first author was backstabbed with vicious rumours by his jealous previous boss and subsequently bullied also by a newly appointed boss. Eventually he resigned and, having had two mad and bad bosses in a row (and thus not having adequate referees) he never got another job.

Workplace bullying is also costly to industry because (Phillips, 2001; Burrell, 2001; Healey, 2011):
- Productivity and profitability are reduced.
- Motivation, teamwork and efficiency are reduced.
- Absenteeism increases.
- Expensive mistakes are made.
- An unsafe work environment results.
- Good employees leave.
- Time is wasted by bullying and in dealing with it.
- Unethical and fraudulent behaviours may occur.
- Adverse publicity circulates.
- There are costly compensation claims.

Dealing with bullying

Organizations can do a great deal to help reduce workplace bullying, for example by:
- Improving management training and skills.
- Running occasional workshops on proper workplace practices.
- Having a designated counsellor to whom complaints about bullying may be addressed.
- Conducting surveys to determine the extent of bullying in the organization.
- When bullies are identified, any previous history of bullying in the current or previous jobs should be identified and investigated.
- Check the work performance of bullies.
- Refer bullies for psychological and/or psychiatric assessment.

Assessments

The components of Equation 10.2, that is:

Attitude $A^{**} = A + B + C + D + S$

have considerable relevance to workplace bullying:

[1] The ***initial attitude A*** of bullies is that they are superior, perhaps because they have a higher rank in the organizational hierarchy.

Their victims may be deemed to be inferior because they are smaller, weaker, of different race or gender, or simply new to the organization and thus have few friends in it as yet.

Highly competitive work environments can encourage bullying, the armed services being a well-known example:

Colleague: a competitor known to you by his first name, often working in your organization and vying with you for promotion and other perks (Marks et al., 2006).

[2] With greater confidence the bullying ***behaviour (B)*** is likely to grow worse over time, eventually requiring intervention in many cases.

Often, however, bullying affects the victim's workplace performance and their psychology. Indeed, the results can be serious, ranging from loss of promotion or job, to loss of career, divorce and suicide.

[3] Soon a negative ***contact history (C)*** builds up between the bully and the victim and the bully becomes increasingly confident if not opposed in any way.

[4] It is such ***differences (D)*** as noted in [1] that are the excuse for bullying. Bullies might also have type A personalities and thus be ambitious, driven and hostile.

[5] ***Societal attitudes (S)*** are now very strongly against workplace bullying to the point at which victims stand a much better chance of gaining help and support. Occasional media coverage of bullying is also helpful.

For example, an article in 'The Age' on 27/12/2012 entitled *Inquiry call on CSIRO 'bullying'* which reported that at a single site: "There may have been tens of claims of workplace bullying, intimidation and/or harassment, and other forms of misconduct that have not been fully or adequately investigated, and where a strong possibility exists that, at the very least, due process has been breached."

There have been many such articles in recent years, most of them about schools, and this repeated exposure of the issue has raised the level of public concern and helped instigate remedial actions in some schools and other organizations.

Conclusion

The following section from a book on personnel management (Stone, 2002), sums up the subject of workplace bullying well:

Bullying in the workplace is a health and safety hazard. It is also illegal. Bullying includes persecuting or ganging up on an individual, making unreasonable demands or setting impossible work targets, making restrictive and petty work rules, constant intrusive surveillance, shouting, abusive language, physical assault and open or implied threats of dismissal or demotion. One survey, for example, showed that lazy workers put pressure on colleagues not to work too hard. If ignored, verbal and physical abuse are suffered. An ACTU survey found that more than half of all employees reported experiencing shouting, ordering, belittling and other intimidating behaviour. Bullying can be anywhere in the organization but most bullies are managers. The incidence of bullying is higher in workplaces with autocratic and arbitrary management.

13. Bullying in The Workplace

Chapter 14

URBAN CRIME

*Reports from the Federal Bureau of Investigation
indicate that in 1968 one American in 50 was either murdered,
raped, robbed, beaten, or had his car stolen.*
From *The Sores of Civilization*, Hamlyn, London (1970).

Introduction

Human societies are more crime-ridden than ever before in history. Now 'white collar' crime is rife, guns are widely available, the illegal drugs industry is now one of the world's two largest, and crowded modern cities like Mexico City and Chicago encourage high crime rates.

In the USA more and more people feel forced to keep at least one gun at home to protect themselves. According to Thomas (2007):

➢ 1,135 companies in 98 countries make small arms.
➢ There are 640 million small arms at large in the world.
➢ 8 million new small arms are bought each year and 60% of these end up in the hands of criminals and civilians.
➢ 1 person is killed every minute with small arms.

Increasingly our cultures seem to celebrate bestiality and violence, whether in sports like boxing and martial arts, movies filled with scenes of sex and violence, or video games involving constant shooting and killing. Then, of course, constant media reports of violence seem to encourage 'copy cat' killings.

Mass shootings

In the USA, in particular, mass shootings have become increasingly frequent, in part because assault rifles with 50 round magazines can be purchased by ordinary citizens.

At the time of writing, there have been 186 mass killings in the USA since 2006, this including 146 mass shootings.

The FBI defines a 'mass shooting' as an incident in which four or more people are killed and nearly half of such incidents involve killing family members. Some of the major mass shootings in the USA since the Columbine High School shooting in 1999 have included:

- ➢ 14/12/2012. 27 killed, including 18 children at an elementary school in Newtown CT.
- ➢ 20/7/2012. 12 killed and 58 wounded in a movie theatre in Auroro CO.
- ➢ 8/1/2011. A woman killed 6 and wounded 13 in a supermarket in Tucson AZ.
- ➢ 5/11/2009. 13 killed and 29 wounded at Fort Hood army base in Texas by an Army psychiatrist reportedly yelling "Allahu Akbar!"
- ➢ 3/4/2009. 13 killed and 4 wounded at an immigration centre in Binghampton NY.
- ➢ 5/12/2007. 10 killed & 4 wounded in a department store in Omaha NE. The 19-year old gunman killed himself.
- ➢ 16/4/2007. 32 killed and 24 wounded at Virginia Tech by student Seung-Hui Choi.
- ➢ 21/3/2005. A teenager killed two relatives, then 9 at Red Lake Senior High School, then killing himself.
- ➢ 12/3/2005. A church member killed 9 at a church meeting in Brookfield WI, and then killed himself.
- ➢ 29/7/1999. An Atlanta man killed his wife and 2 children with a hammer, then shooting 9 people before killing himself.

➢ 20/4/1999. Two teenagers killed 13 & wounded 21 at Columbine High School in Littleton CO, then killing themselves.

Mass shootings happen elsewhere in the world, of course, an example being the mass shooting in Australia at the Port Arthur prison colony site in Tasmania where 35 people were killed and 23 wounded in April 1996.

An analysis of 56 mass shootings in the USA in the period 2009 to 2012 found that 57% of cases involved domestic violence. In 60% of mass public shootings in the last century in the USA, officials found signs of mental illness. According to USA today, Northeastern University criminologist Alan Fox said: "Mass murderers don't take you up on treatment. They tend to externalize and blame other people for their problems. They blame the spouse, the co-workers, immigrants. They feel persecuted."

An epidemic of gun-related homicides

934 people died in mass shootings in the USA during the period 2006 – 2012. This number is less than 1% of all gun-related homicides and 33 Americans are killed every day, most of them by handguns, and often by a family member or intimate partner. Many other homicides involve acquaintances, neighbours, and co-workers.

Each time a major mass shooting such as that at an elementary school in Newtown in December 2012 occurs, there is a public outcry and calls for limiting gun sales and banning the sale of powerful assault rifles.

The National Rifle Association of America remains recalcitrant, however, claiming that it is every American's right to carry whatever gun he chooses to protect himself in case of need. In addition, there are a great many gun shop owners who protest that their businesses would be harmed by stricter gun control laws. No doubt the huge arms industry also provides financial support for campaigning against stricter gun laws.

International murder rates

Murder rates vary considerably around the world, examples of the rates per year, per 100,000 people being:

- ➢ Africa 17.0.
- ➢ Americas 15.4.
- ➢ Asia 3.1.
- ➢ Europe 3.5.
- ➢ Oceania 2.9.
- ➢ World 6.9.

Examples of the full range of rates in different countries are:

- ➢ Australia 1.0.
- ➢ Colombia 31.8.
- ➢ Congo 30.8.
- ➢ Ivory Coast 56.9.
- ➢ Papua New Guinea 13.0.
- ➢ Russia 10.2.
- ➢ South Africa 31.8.
- ➢ UK 1.2.
- ➢ US 4.8.
- ➢ Venezuela 45.1.

Whilst murder rates and the gun law issue in the US command a lot of attention in the press in this country (Australia), however, murder rates in many other countries are higher, in some cases far higher, though admittedly those countries with the highest rates have epidemics of crime and civil unrest, a few being in a state of civil war involving large numbers of displaced people.

Other crime

There is plenty of other violence in society, with or without guns, for example:

➢ Random street violence and theft.
➢ Violence in and outside pubs and clubs.
➢ Violence and theft on trains and train stations.
➢ Robbery of shops, often late at night, and often with real or fake guns.
➢ Sexual assault and rape, usually with some violence.
➢ Domestic violence which contributes to a high proportion of shootings and mass killings.

Assessments

The components of Equation 10.2, that is:

Attitude $A^{**} = A + B + C + D + S$

have considerable relevance to urban crime:

[1] *Initial attitude, A.* The general public, of course, abhors crime and, indeed, lives in increasing fear of it.

Criminals on the other hand, are tough and uncompromising and, whether for reasons of profit or grievance, they feel entitled to carry out crimes.

Often, however, ordinary people who 'would not dream' of committing any sort of crime lose control under the stress of marital arguments, sudden loss of a job, or financial problems.

[2] *Behaviour, B.* Hardened criminals are tough and uncompromising and will plan their crimes, many of them being psychopathically aggressive and hostile.

Ordinary law abiding people, however, may lose control under stress and commit serious crimes that are quite 'out of character'. Lawyers often defend such crimes as being so-called 'crimes of passion' involving some degree of temporary insanity.

[3] *Contact history, C.* Many crimes, especially serial crimes or mass shootings, are committed by social outcasts, people who feel alienated or wronged by society.

Domestic violence, of course, usually involves a long history of contact during which grudges and bad feeling have developed, often culminating in a 'scene' involving heated verbal exchanges which then provoke immediate violence, or a subsequent plan for perhaps violent revenge.

[4] *Differences, D.* Hardened criminals usually see themselves as 'tough' and their victims as weak.

In crimes involving weapons, of course, the perpetrators seek to give themselves an unfair advantage in numbers and/or firepower.

As noted in Chapter 11, in the 'War of the Sexes' the physical and mental differences between men and women are many.

[5] *Societal attitudes, S.* Society is 'conditioned' to some extent to accept violence by a culture of:
- Violent sports such as boxing and martial arts.
- Bruising contact sports frequently involving on-field violence such as rugby.
- Movies rife with sex scenes and extreme violence.
- Video games filled with violence and constant shooting.

Nevertheless, society at large does not condone crime and the media constantly reinforces a negative attitude to crime, often calling for greater police numbers to keep crime in check.

Conclusion

As the figures for small arms sales given at the start of the chapter show, small arms are far too widely available in modern society and greater restrictions are needed.

In response to the Port Arthur shooting in Australia the government instituted a successful gun 'buy back' scheme that took thousands of handguns and rifles off the streets.

In response to public concern, in Melbourne the government has recruited a special force to police suburban rail stations at night. Such measures, along with higher penalties for crimes of violence, may help reduce them in number.

As noted in Chapter 11, 50% divorce rates are now common in the West and there is a need to reduce this by providing more counselling services for married couples. Often their problems are financial, however, and more needs to be done to decrease the widening gap between rich and poor in capitalist societies.

Chapter 15

TRIBAL & TERRITORIAL CONFLICT

Altogether, national hatred is something peculiar.
You will always find it strongest and most violent
where there is the lowest degree of culture.
Johann Wolfgang von Goethe, quoted by Johann Peter Eckermann,
Conversations with Goethe, Mar. 14, 1830.

Introduction

The best known studies of chimpanzees, with which we share 96% of our genes, were conducted by Jane Goodall and associates in the Gombe National Park on the edge of Lake Tanganyika in Tanzania (Goodall, 1971).

Ultimately, Goodall was quite disillusioned to find that *tribes* of chimps were led by an alpha male and would occasionally have small wars with neighbouring tribes, these resuming at intervals over periods of many years. She concluded that they were all too much like humans!

The first definition given by the 9th edition of the Concise Oxford Dictionary for tribe is: *a group of (esp. primitive) families or communities, linked by social, economic, religious, or blood ties, and usu. having a common culture and dialect and a recognized leader.*

The first use of the word *tribe* in English referred to the 12 tribes of the ancient Hebrews, 10 of which were named for the sons of Jacob, and 2 for sons of Jacob's son Joseph. After Israel was conquered by Assyria in 721BC only 2 tribes remained, the others being referred to by posterity as 'the 10 lost tribes of Israel'.

Early Greek and Roman tribes

In ancient Greece (circa 1200BC) tribes were distinct by location, dialect, and tradition, and included the Ionians, Dorians, Achaeans and Aetolians. In Attica in 508BC (the region in which Athens is now located) Cleisthenes replaced four Ionian tribes with 10 new ones, each named after a local hero. All 140 villages or demes were represented in The Council of Five Hundred or *Boule* according to their size. At first this council's main function was in dealing with two invasions of the new state, but it may have been the crude beginning of democracy.

The first Roman tribes were the Titienses, Ramnenses and Luceres. These were later replaced by 4 urban and 16 rural tribes, the number of the latter increasing to 35 by 241BC. Provincial communities and people granted Roman citizenship of the empire after 27BC were all enrolled in a particular tribe, these serving as units for the purposes of census taking, taxation, and military conscription.

The German tribes

The Germanic peoples originated at the beginning of the Bronze Age (circa 1800BC) from the mixing of Battle-Ax people from the Corded Ware Culture of middle Germany with the megalithic culture on the eastern North Sea coast.

They spread over southern Scandinavia and into Germany but during the Iron Age (which lasted until the Roman period) they were cut off from the Mediterranean by the Celts and Illyrians. Increasing population and worsening climate forced them further south and before 200BC Germanic tribes had reached the lower Danube.

Circa 110BC the Germanic Cimbri and Teutonic tribes combined to invade the Roman province of Transalpine Gaul and then defeated a Roman army sent to deal with them at the Battle of Arausio on Oct. 6th, 105BC. They were eventually defeated by the Romans in 101BC in the region of the Upper Po River.

Land-hungry German tribes continued to advance, however, but were stalled by Julius Caesar in 58BC after they had crossed the upper Rhine, and from about 70AD the Germans were pushed back. Eventually the Germans advanced again, by 150 threatening Italy itself.

The Goths reached the Black sea circa 200, plundering the Balkan Peninsula and Anatolia as far as Cyprus.

Circa 260 – 300 the Alemanni and Franks moved towards Gaul and Italy.

After 375 the Huns from central Asia also became a force competing for space in Europe but the German tribes continued to advance, crushing the Romans at Adrianople in 378, after which the Roman Empire began to shrink.

Finally, in 476 the German leader Odoacer deposed emperor Romulus Augustulus at Ravenna, ending the Western Roman Empire and becoming the first barbarian ruler of Italy.

Mongolian invasions

Born in 1162 into a clan that had a tradition of power and rule, Genghis Khan's success in tribal warfare resulted in him being made ruler of Mongolia. From 1207 to 1215 his armies probed deep into North China, taking the Chin capital Chung-tu (modern Peking). Then he moved westward, taking over Turkistan and then northern Iran.

Leaving his sons and generals to continue campaigns into Russia and Eastern Europe, Genghis Khan launched a successful campaign against the Hsi Hsia, a Tangut tribe near the northwest border of China but died during it.

India

Excavations place the Indus valley civilizations back at least 5,000 years. Sanskrit-speaking Aryan tribes invaded from the northwest circa 1500BC, merging with the inhabitants.

Asoka, the third Mauryan king of Magadha, ruled most of the Indian subcontinent in the 3rd century BC, establishing Buddhism as the main religion. Hinduism eventually revived, however, and predominated.

Arabs invaded the West and established a Muslim foothold in the 8th century, Turkish Muslims gaining control of North India by 1200.

Vasco de Gama established Portuguese trading posts circa 1500 and the Dutch also established a presence. The British gained trading concessions in 1609 and the East India Company eventually gained control of most of India.

The Americas

Families of Indians of the Americas joined to form local *bands* of 20 – 500 people, their size depending upon how many people the nearby area could support.

Tribes were a collection of bands in the same general area and there were hundreds of tribes in the Americas when Columbus arrived. Some tribes in North America joined in *federations*, it is thought to prevent inter-tribal conflict.

The Aztecs in Mexico and Incas in Peru were advanced civilizations that developed empires and systems of government. In Middle America large Mayan cities with tens of thousands of people ruled over the surrounding areas.

In the Indian Wars (1622 – 1890) Europeans invaded, conquered and settled the USA, the native Indian population being reduced from about 1 million at first contact to about 250,000 at the end of the 18th century (Chambers, 1993).

The Tasmanian aborigines

The Tasmanian aborigines had three groupings:
[1] The 'hearth group' of a husband and wife, their children, and other relatives that cooked and camped around a single fire.
[2] The 'band', a landowning group consisting of several hearth groups. Bands could allow or deny others from foraging in their territory.
[3] The 'tribe' of 250 to 700 people from bands with adjoining territories. There were nine Tasmanian tribes, each with their own language or dialect and cultures.

In 1768 Captain James Cook set out on a 3-year voyage that was to awake England's interest in Australia, and his further two voyages in the 1770s cemented that interest. With the invasion of white settlers from Britain, however, the Tasmanian aborigines were completely exterminated.

Palestine and Israel

According to Bell and Hall (1991): *It is also estimated that since World War 2 there have been 100 wars, fought in more than 60 countries or territories. During no year have there been less than four wars, and in some years as many as 18 wars have been fought.*

Perhaps the best example of territorial conflict at present is the ongoing conflict between Israel and Palestine. The Palestinians do, indeed, have great cause for grievance, Palestine having been mandated as a British protectorate which was then divided between Jordan and Israel. Subsequently Egypt, Jordan, Syria, Lebanon, Iraq and Saudi Arabia invaded but were repelled by the Jewish state which gained territory.

Separate armistices were signed with Arab nations in 1949, Jordan occupying the West Bank and Egypt occupying Gaza. Neither granted Palestinian autonomy.

Israel, with the brief help of British and French forces, invaded Egypt in 1956 after repeated terrorist attacks. A cease-fire was arranged by the UN on November 6th.

With the help of a UN Emergency Force an uneasy truce lasted until 1967 when the UN force withdrew at Egypt's demand. Egypt reoccupied the Gaza Strip and closed the Gulf of Aqaba to Israeli shipping.

On June 5th the 6-day war began and Israel took the Gaza Strip, the Sinai Peninsula to the Suez Canal, East Jerusalem, Syria's Golan Heights, and Jordan's West Bank.

Egypt and Syria attacked Israel on Oct. 6th 1973, this day being the major fast day of Yom Kippur, but were driven back by Israeli forces which crossed the Suez Canal.

Israel invaded Lebanon in 1978 after a Lebanese terrorist attack, withdrawing to be replaced by a 6,000 strong UN peace-keeping force.

In 1979, Israel and Egypt signed a formal peace treaty, ending 30 years of conflict.

In 1981 Israeli jets destroyed an Iraqi nuclear reactor near Baghdad, claiming it could have been used for nuclear weapons. In 1982 Israeli jets bombed PLO strongholds in Lebanon and invading Israeli forces encircled Beirut which was then evacuated after massive Israeli bombing of West Beirut.

During the Persian Gulf War of 1991 Iraq fired several scud missiles at Israel.

After decades of conflict peace talks with the PLO resulted in historic agreements but the conflict continues with talk by the US of a "two state solution" making no progress:

[1] Israel invaded Gaza in 2008.

[2] Hamas continued to fire rockets from Gaza into Israel, some landing close to Israel's central city of Tel Aviv in 2012, prompting Israel to call in reserve forces ready for action.

{3] Israel continues to build housing in the West Bank, despite growing international opposition.

Assessments

The components of the equation $A^{**} = A + B + C + D + S$ (Equation 10.2) have, of course, much relevance to tribal and territorial conflict:

[1] *Initial attitude, A.*

It is, perhaps, natural for people that live in a relatively small tribe to regard any outsiders as a threat should they trespass into the relatively small territory that the tribe regards as its own. In the case of primitive tribes such trespass is quite likely to be for the purpose of hunting and gathering foods that the local tribe believes it has a sole right to. Notably, by custom Tasmanian aborigine bands were able to deny outsiders right of access to their territory and, no doubt, those that broke such agreements risked sparking conflict.

[2] *Behaviour, B.*

Some cultures developed the habit of conflict and conquest and became more aggressive than others, so that acquisition of new territory as the population expanded became something of a habit, each new leader striving to live up to or exceed his predecessor's record of conquest.

Such behaviour undoubtedly relates to the alpha-male behaviour of several animal species, in the case of humans this exhibiting as type A personality.

Type A personality is a cluster of traits including ambition, impatience, competitiveness, and hostility. Only some type A's are abnormally hostile and it is this trait that is harmful to the health of all concerned, hostile people being more prone to CHD, whilst the health of the victims of their hostility is often imperilled also (Larsen & Buss, 2002).

[3] *Contact history, C.*

From our early hunter-gatherer days humans have not ventured far without carrying tools and weapons for gathering and hunting. Other tribes on seeing strangers with weapons might, of course, fear conflict.

Once a history of conflict has been established, however, conflict seems to become something of a habit or 'practice' that tribes might use to gain new territory to house and feed rapidly expanding populations.

The problem here, therefore, is that we are still not able to communicate positively and *negotiate* well enough to prevent wars.

[4] *Differences, D.*

People with markedly different languages, cultures, and religions that have taken centuries to develop are likely to regard 'outsiders' as 'foreign', of course, and throughout history this seems to have been sufficient grounds for prejudice and conflict. Religion, in particular, has always been a source of conflict, as discussed in Chapter 17.

[5] *Societal attitudes, S.*

With war having reached such a massive scale at times our attitudes against large scale war are, of course, very negative. Attitude towards conflict on a smaller scale, however, remains relatively supportive if one is to believe politicians and the media.

The primary problem is that much of mankind's lamentable history of conflict has been caused by leaders, in part by supporting the maintenance of large military forces, and then by occasioning the use of them.

The secondary problem is that governments have always been able to influence the public and persuade them to support wars with the use of subtle propaganda campaigns.

Conclusion

As with most animal species, humans are naturally suspicious and fearful of invasion of their 'space' and much human conflict has been caused by such invasions, sometimes growing populations seeking food, and sometimes ambitious leaders seeking greater power.

Chapter 16

IMPERIAL POSSESSION & CONFLICT

*It has been a characteristic of collective human activity for centuries
that one group attempts to dominate another. When the area of
domination is large enough it may be called an 'empire'.
The act of setting up an empire is called 'imperialism'.*
Cowie HR, Collins MB, Ryan DB, *Imperialism, Racism and
Re-Assessments,* Nelson, Melbourne (1994).

*No body can be healthful without exercise,
neither natural body or politic; and certainly to a kingdom
or estate, a just and honourable war is the true exercise.*
Sir Francis Bacon,
"Of the True Greatness of Kingdoms and Estates", *Essays* (1625).

Introduction

Some of man's long history of Imperial possession and conflict has already been described in Chapters 3 and 4, including the exploits of Alexander the Great, the Roman Empire, Ottoman Empire, the Spanish and Portuguese Empires, the Dutch and French Empires, the Austro-Hungarian Empire, Hitler's Third Reich, and the British Empire.

In the present chapter discussion will concentrate upon European imperialism in the 'Age of Discovery' and subsequent developments that still affect us today.

The Crusades and the Renaissance

Muslim invaders captured large areas of land at the eastern end of the Mediterranean Sea between the 8th and 15th centuries BC, including Jerusalem and the surrounding 'Holy Lands.' In 1095 the emperor of the Eastern Roman or Byzantine Empire appealed to the Pope for help to repel the Islamic threat. The result was a series of crusades over the next 200 years and these are discussed further in the following chapter (Chapter 17).

The crusades, though launched for religious reasons, generated a lucrative trade in silks, spices, and elaborate carpets. The exchange of peoples, products and ideas that this trade generated encouraged a wider view of the world than the feudal way of life that had prevailed for a thousand years. Thus a new desire for knowledge emerged, one focus of it being the civilizations of ancient Greece and Rome, bringing Europe out of the Middle Ages and into the Renaissance (14th century to circa 1650).

Islamic control over the eastern Mediterranean greatly inhibited overland trade with Asia. Portugal and Spain and had gained little from this trade and in the period 1480-1530 their monarchs sponsored numerous expeditions seeking sea routes to India and China for the purposes of trade (Cowie et al., 1994).

The results changed history:
- In 1487 Bartholomew Diaz found and named the Cape of Good Hope at the 'bottom' of Africa.
- In 1492 Colombus sailed Westward across the Atlantic to discover the Americas for Spain.
- In 1498 Vasco da Gama sailed to India.
- In 1521 Magellan claimed the Philippines for Spain, naming it after his king, and then completed a circumnavigation of the globe in 1522.

In the 'Age of Discovery' that followed Europe rapidly discovered and colonized huge areas of the world.

Motives for European Imperialism

Motives for acquiring new colonies included importing silks, spices and Chinese porcelain to sell for profit, and obtaining new sources of raw materials and precious metals. Soon, however, overseas colonies became large markets for goods made in the 'home' nations.

European monarchs also 'claimed' to be ruled by 'divine right' and that their principal motives for colonization where to bring 'faith' to the 'heathen' peoples of the world:

> *Look at him well. This is a heathen; a being condemned*
> *to eternal flame unless you help him*
> *Don't think we are merely going to destroy his people*
> *and lift their wealth. We are going to take from them*
> *what they don't value and give them instead*
> *the priceless mercy of heaven.*
> P. Shaffer, *The Royal Hunt of the Sun,* p. 5,
> Hamish Hamilton, London (1964).

Imperialist expansion was also a demonstration of relative strength and thus status of rival nations and the kings of Spain and Portugal believed that their empires increased their prestige (Cowie et al, 1994).

Colonies also had many other important uses:

[1] As settlements for people from the crowded inner areas of major European cities.

[2] As plantation colonies for which purpose sometimes both the crop and the labour were imported from another area, an example being the sugar and tobacco plantations in the West Indies for which slaves were imported from Africa.

[3] As trading posts.

[4] As military bases from which a large surrounding area could be kept under control.

The British raj in India

After the arrival of Vasco da Gama in India in 1498, the Portuguese, and then the Dutch, French and British established trading bases there. After many years of rivalry between these powers the British established military and commercial supremacy and dominated India for almost 200 years (1757 – 1947).

The British East India Company, founded in 1600 and revived in 1702, gradually grew but was in competition with the Portuguese, French and Dutch.

British domination in India can be dated from 1757, when the British army seized the French settlements in Bengal and defeated the opposing army of the Nawab Suraj-ud-Daulah in the Battle of Plassey. By 1772 Bengal was under British control.

The British East India Company gradually expanded its influence, forcing the British Government to appoint a governor-general to take partial control over it.

Missionaries entered the region with government support, schools were opened, English was encouraged as the official language, and improved communications and irrigation were developed.

In 1857 Muslim and Hindu soldiers in the East India Company mutinied against the aloof and rigid discipline of English officers who ignored caste rules. This forced the British Government to take full control in 1858, but relations between the two peoples were irreparably damaged.

In 1885 the Indian National Congress was formed as a forum in which people could vent their grievances and suggest reforms. Subsequently, a more assertive branch of this movement was formed which demanded that Britain should "quit India" (Cowie, at al., 1994).

At the time of Queen Victoria's Diamond Jubilee celebrations in 1897 the British Empire was the world's largest, covering approximately a quarter of the globe, and a quarter of its people (Cowie et al., 1994).

India was an 'empire within an empire', being said to be over twice the size of the Roman Empire at its peak and having a population of 300 million.

In 1906 Indian Muslims formed the All India Muslim League, turning the religious division in India into a political one.

In 1909 educated Indians were allowed to elect representatives to advisory provincial councils, and Indian representatives were allowed to sit on executive councils in both the provinces and the capital. These reforms were widely interpreted as "window dressing" (Cowie et al, 1994).

During WW1 the Indian army grew to 1.2 million, more than half of that number serving overseas. Many British troops and officials left India during WW1, however, resulting in increased Indian participation in the civil service and strengthening claims for self-government.

In April 1919 a British general ordered his troops to fire at unarmed anti-British demonstrators in Amritsar in the Punjab province, killing 379 and wounding 1200.

In December 1919 the British Parliament passed the Government of India Act which introduced a system of government called a 'dyarchy' which gave control of such departments as education, health, agriculture and public works to Indian cabinet ministers. The central government, however, retained control of the key areas of law and order and finance.

Between 1919 and 1945 there were many conflicts and negotiations. In 1931 Gandhi represented the Indian Congress Party at a conference in London.

In 1935 the British Parliament passed the Government of India Act which gave self-government in the provinces but not full dominion status at federal level, defence and external affairs remaining under the control of the British-appointed viceroy.

In 1941 a small volunteer force called the Indian National Army was formed to help the Japanese drive the British out of India.

In 1942 Britain promised India self-government in return for co-operation in the war effort. The Indian Congress Party, however, claimed that the presence of British forces made Japanese invasion more likely and repeated 'quit India' demands. Anti-British riots broke out and 1000 Indians were killed, 1600 injured, and 14,000 people were imprisoned, including Gandhi and other Indian leaders.

Finally, in 1947 India was granted independence with Pakistan partitioned off as a separate and independent Islamic state. This caused a mass exodus of Hindus leaving Pakistan, and Muslims leaving India, and it is believed that 500,000 people died in the resulting riots and conflicts (Cowie et al., 1994).

Benefits of European Imperialism

Some Asian societies were unified by new European-generated activities, a common currency, a common language of commerce (for example English in India or French in Indo-China), and a coordinated railway system.

Some Asian countries, particularly Japan, saw a need to improve their economies using Western production and marketing methods. Japan grew in strength and, in part thanks to an alliance with England, had major naval victories over Tsarist Russia in 1904-5, thus gaining much additional territory.

Most colonized peoples resented European intrusion, and could not accept European customs and religious beliefs. Thus it was inevitable that they would eventually seek their own national identity and independence.

Many of the former Asian colonies of European powers that eventually obtained their independence have been able to function as separate nations because of their adoption of European technology and the European style of centralized administration that their nationalist leaders used to criticize.

India gained much from British rule, including unification of the country, a British form of government, and an efficient civil service. One of the world's largest railway networks had been built, along with many dams and irrigation works, transforming agriculture from a subsistence level to a commercial scale.

Having been largely tribal, few of the African civilizations were coordinated enough to resist Western colonization. After World War 2, however, the African colonies gradually gained independence peacefully but since then there have been many national and international conflicts in Africa, much of which is still considered to be part of the impoverished 'Third World'.

In the twentieth century the expansion of the USSR as a result of World War 2 was an imperialist act of major proportions and this and the decades of 'Cold War' that followed are discussed in Chapter 20.

Assessments

The components of the equation $A^{**} = A + B + C + D + S$ (Equation 10.2) have, of course, much relevance to imperial possession and territorial conflict:

[1] *Initial attitude, A.*

Initially, at least, many of the peoples of colonized countries accepted their fate quietly, perhaps hoping for greater prosperity.

The greed and vanity of the imperialists, however, was excessive to the point of insanity (Panniker, 1959):

[An] ... aspect of British authority in India at this period was the conviction held by every European in India of enduring racial superiority. Seton Kerr, a Foreign Secretary of the Government, explained it was "the cherished conviction of every Englishman in India ... that he belongs to a race whom God has destined to govern and subdue".

[2] *Behaviour, B.*

As noted earlier in this chapter, the sheer arrogance and assertiveness of British rule was one reason for discontent in India, another, no doubt, the perception that the British were simply taking advantage of the country to increase their own power and wealth. The will of Indians to retain their own identity, culture and religion was also a motivating force, a tragic example of the latter being the great loss of life during the mass migrations after the partition of Pakistan.

[3] *Contact history, C.*

As in the case of British rule of India, unrest develops periodically in occupied territories, usually culminating in considerable loss of life. Over time levels of resentment and hostility tend to grow, eventually forcing the eviction of the colonial power.

[4] *Differences, D.*

People with markedly different languages, cultures, and religions that have taken centuries to develop are likely to regard 'outsiders' as 'foreign', of course, and throughout history this seems to have been sufficient grounds for prejudice and conflict. Religion, in particular, has always been a source of conflict, as discussed in Chapter 17.

[5] *Societal attitudes, S.*

The attitude of the peoples of colonizing nations is usually supportive so long as their colonies are turning a profit without undue resistance from the exploited peoples.

When there is any significant degree of revolt against the ruling power, however, especially when this results in significant casualties, public support at 'home' wanes and pressure is put on the colonizing government to consider freeing the occupied territory.

Conclusions

With the dawn of the 20th century several countries began to strive for independence, encouraged perhaps by the final demise of the Spanish Empire in the Spanish-American War of 1898.

After India gained independence in 1947 a series of colonies in Africa gained independence in the 1950s and 1960s.

Thus, one by one the world's colonies have disappeared and only a few remain, and those largely small and in name only.

Now, indeed, the world's populations have intermingled to a significant extent, for example many native people from countries once colonized by Europe escaping from bad governments and conflict to live in Europe.

Hopefully, therefore, the multicultural societies that result will be stable ones and freer from internal and external conflict than in the past.

Chapter 17

RELIGIOUS CONFLICT

In all ages, hypocrites, called priests,
have put crowns upon the heads of thieves, called kings.
Robert G. Ingersoll, *Prose-Poems and Selections* (1884).

Old religious factions are volcanoes burnt out.
Edmund Burke, Irish-born Whig politician and writer.
Speech on the Petition of the Unitarians, 11 May 1792.

The Jews

Nomadic *Hebrew* tribes lived in the eastern Mediterranean area before 1300BC and circa 1020BC they conquered Canaan or ancient Palestine. They united under King Saul as a nation which included present-day Israel and parts of Jordan and Syria, but the nation was fraught with conflicts among its states.

After King Solomon's death in 922BC the nation was divided into the kingdoms of *Israel* (in the north, Samaria being founded in 870BC as its capital), and Judah (in the south and including Jerusalem). The kingdom of Israel was destroyed by the Assyrians in 734BC. In 721BC they annexed Judah but it retained nominal independence for the next 135 years.

The word Jew comes from the Hebrew *yehudhi,* meaning a member of the ancient Hebrew tribe of Judah, the ancient territory that became the Roman province of Judaea in AD6. The English word Jew is derived directly from the Latin *Judaeus,* meaning an inhabitant of Judea.

In 597BC Nebuchadnezzar II captured Jerusalem and Jewish nobles, warriors and artisans were deported to Babylon. Troubled by revolts in Babylonia (594BC) and Judah (588-587BC) Nebuchadnezzar destroyed Jerusalem and many more Israelites were deported to Babylonia in 586BC, many others fleeing to Egypt. Thus many Jews become part of the Diaspora, those Jews dispersed among nations outside Palestine

Persia conquered Babylonia in 539BC and, though the majority of the Jews living in Babylonia remained, many did return from exile to Palestine.

It was not until 168BC, however, that an independent Jewish kingdom was revived. Rome took control of this in the next century, suppressing Jewish revolts in AD70 and AD135.

In 1948 the modern state of Israel was established and the conflict-ridden history of this is outlined in Chapter 15.

Zoroastrianism

Zoroastrianism originated in Iran in the 6th century BC and was based on the teachings of Zoraster which accepted one supreme god, Ahura Mazda. This religion included an initiation ceremony, fire worship, rituals of purification to ward off evil spirits, and sacrifice of the sacred liquor haoma accompanied by recitation of large parts of the primary scripture, the Avesta.

The city of Rhagae (near Tehran) dates from the 3rd millennium BC and from the 3rd to 7th centuries AD it was a centre of Zoroastrianism. It was captured by the Muslims in 641 and followers of Zoroastrianism were persecuted in the 8th to 10th centuries, some migrating from Iran to India.

Islam

The Shiites were supporters of the 4th caliph Ali and when he was assassinated in 661 they claimed that only the descendants of Ali and his wife, Fatima, Muhammad's daughter, were entitled to rule the Muslim community.

During the early centuries of Islam, the Shiites, politically defeated and persecuted, became an underground movement. Shiites pay the tax called zakat (originally levied by Muhammad to help the poor and later levied by Muslim states) to their religious leaders rather than to state authorities. As a result, many Shiite leaders in Iran and Iraq have immense wealth and property.

During the 10th and 11th centuries, Shia Islam had a large following throughout the Middle East, but the spread of the popular mystical movement known as Sufism seems to have greatly diminished its strength.

At present Shiites are in the majority in Iran, and large numbers are found in Iraq, Syria, Lebanon, India, Pakistan, and parts of Central Asia, their total number exceeding 165 million.

The Sunnites constitute the vast majority of the world Islamic community. The doctrines and theology of the Sunnites were developed toward the end of the 9th century, and their theology was developed as a complete system during the 10th century.

Despite appeals from some Shiite leaders for rapprochement and solidarity with Sunni Islam, there has been considerable conflict between the two factions of Islam in recent decades, particularly in Iraq where it is ongoing on an almost daily basis.

In recent decades there has also been a spate of terrorist attacks against the West committed by Muslim extremist groups and this is discussed in Chapter 22.

Regional Italian conflicts

Alboin became chief of the Lombards in 565, when the tribe lived in the region between the Danube River and the head of the Adriatic Sea. Three years later, with the assistance of the Avars, Alboin defeated the Germanic people known as the Gepidae. Then Alboin led the Lombards and 20,000 Saxons across the Alps into northern Italy and established the kingdom of Lombardy in the valley of the Po River, with Pavia as its capital.

When Albroin died in 572 separate bands united under regional leaders called 'duces'. The Lombards, like the Goths, followed the heretical creed Arianism which held that Christ was fully human and not divine, and were thus always in conflict with the native Italians.

The Lombard king Agiluf (r. 590-615) converted to orthodox Christianity which reduced conflict. Then the Lombards, seeking to increase their power, began to threaten Rome. In 754 Pope Stephen II sought help from the Franks and in 774 Charlemagne defeated the Lombards and deposed their last king. In 800 he was crowned emperor of the West by Pope Leo III.

When the Saracens took Sicily and threatened Rome in the 9th century Charlemagne's great-grandson, King Louis II, held them back. After Louis died Muslims overran southern Italy, forcing the popes to pay tribute.

The Crusades

The First Crusade was proclaimed by Pope Urban II in 1095 to assist the Byzantine emperor deal with territorial threats by the Turks. It defeated the Turks at Dorylaeum in 1097, established a foothold in northern Syria at Antioch in 1098, and liberated Jerusalem from Muslim control in 1099 (Chambers, 1993).

The Second Crusade was proclaimed by Pope Eugenius III in 1147 in response to the capture of Edessa in 1144 by the Turks but was a failure.

The Third Crusade was proclaimed by Pope Gregory VIII in 1189 after Saladin had captured Jerusalem in 1187. It was led by Frederick I of the Holy Roman Empire, Phillip II of France, and Richard I, 'the Lionheart'. It failed to regain Jerusalem but Richard negotiated a compromise allowing pilgrimage to the Holy Places.

The Fourth Crusade was proclaimed by Innocent IV in 1202 but was directed by Venetian interests to take Dalmatia and then Constantinople, and its original objectives were ignored.

Later Crusades were directed mostly at Egypt and North Africa. The 5th captured Damietta in 1219, and the 7th captured it again in 1249, but both crusades stalled in the Nile Delta.

The 8th Crusade (1270-2) succeeded only in establishing treaties with the Mamluks in Egypt, and with Tunis. The 6th Crusade gained control of Jerusalem from 1229 until 1244, when the Latin forces were defeated by a joint Egyptian and Khwarizmian army, Latin forces finally being driven out of the Holy Land in 1291 (Chambers, 1993).

The Spanish Inquisition

The Spanish Inquisition was ordered by papal bull in 1478 to force Jewish and Muslim minorities to accept the Catholic faith. Between 1500 and 1526 fourteen permanent tribunals were established, two more being established in 1574 and 1640.

In the first 10 years 2,000 people were burnt and 15,000 others punished.

A further papal bull in 1547 saw the inquisition extended to Portugal, and then Brazil.

The Spanish Inquisition was established in Peru in 1570 and in Mexico in 1571. It was finally abolished in 1834.

The Reformation

The Protestant Reformation of Europe in the 16th century swept Europe, the seeds of discontent that led to it having been sown much earlier. The 14th-century English reformer John Wycliffe (1328 – 1384) attacked the papacy itself, objecting to the sale of indulgences and questioning the moral and intellectual standards of ordained priests.

His teachings found an advocate in the religious reformer John Huss in Bohemia. The execution of Huss as a heretic in 1415 sparked the Hussite Wars, a violent expression of Bohemian nationalism, a precursor to religious civil war in Germany in Luther's time.

In France in 1516 a concordat between the king and the pope placed the French church substantially under royal authority. Earlier concordats with other national monarchies also prepared the way for the rise of autonomous national churches.

The Protestant revolution was initiated in Germany when Luther published 95 theses challenging the practice of indulgences in 1517. After publicly burning a papal decree ordering him to recant Luther went into hiding for a year but continued circulating pamphlets and translated the New Testament into German.

When Luther re-emerged he became a revolutionary leader able to exploit the religious and economic divide that had developed in Germany. The Peasant's War, inspired by Luther's teachings, began in 1524. Luther disapproved of the violence and the peasants were defeated in 1525.

A number of attempts at reconciling the Catholic and opposing views were made. When the Lutherans protested against the Catholics revoking an agreement the term 'Protestant' came into usage.

In 1530 the German religious reformer Melanchthon drew up a conciliatory statement of the Lutheran tenets, known as the Augsburg Confession, which was submitted to Emperor Charles V and to the Roman Catholic faction.

Although the Augsburg Confession failed to reconcile the differences between Roman Catholics and Lutherans, it remained the basis of the new Lutheran church and creed.

In 1546 the German emperor, in alliance with the pope and the Duke of Saxony, made war against the Schmalkaldic League, an association of Protestant princes. The Roman Catholic forces were successful at first but eventually the emperor had to end the religious civil war with the Peace of Augsburg in 1555.

Its terms allowed the rulers of the 300 German states to choose between Roman Catholicism and Lutheranism and enforce the chosen faith upon the ruler's subjects.

Lutheranism, by then the religion of about half the population of Germany, had spread to Scandinavia and became the state religion of Sweden in 1529, whilst in 1536 Denmark abolished Roman Catholic authority throughout its territories, then including Norway and Iceland.

In Switzerland Huldrich Zwingli became known in 1518 for denouncing the sale of indulgences. Like Luther, he considered the Bible the sole source of moral authority and strove to eliminate everything in the Roman Catholic system not in accordance with the Scriptures. In Zurich from 1523 to 1525 Zwingli lead people in burning religious relics.

As in Germany, the government was unable to prevent civil war and two short-lived conflicts broke out between Protestant and Roman Catholic regions in 1529 and 1531, Zwingli being killed in the second of these. Peace was restored when each region was allowed to choose its own religion, Roman Catholicism prevailing in the mountain regions and Protestantism in the valleys and cities, much the same situation persevering to this day.

In the generation after Luther and Zwingli French-born Calvin was even stricter in his beliefs and under his regime in Switzerland nonconformists were persecuted and even executed. His established a University in Geneva and his influence extended to France, the Spanish Netherlands, and Scotland.

The Reformation in France was led by Lefèvre d'Étaples who in 1523 translated the New Testament into French but he was soon regarded by the authorities as a radical and he and his followers were persecuted, many fleeing to Switzerland. By 1567 more than 120 pastors trained in Geneva by Calvin had returned to France to establish Protestant churches whose members were known as Huguenots.

The division of France into Protestant and Roman Catholic factions led to a series local conflicts and civil wars which were ended by the Edict of Nantes (1598). As over 90% of the French population remained Catholic, however, Protestant influence in France remained limited.

Most of the Dutch embraced Calvinism, which served as a potent bond in their nationalistic struggle against their Spanish Roman Catholic overlords. They revolted in 1568 and warfare continued until 1648, when Spain relinquished its claim to the country and the former Spanish Netherlands then became an independent Protestant nation.

In 1560 John Knox persuaded the Scottish Parliament to adopt a confession of faith and book of discipline modelled on those in use at Geneva. The Parliament subsequently created the Scottish Presbyterian church. The Roman Catholic Mary, Queen of Scots, attempted to overthrow the new Protestant church, but after a 7-year struggle, she was forced to leave the country.

In England Henry VIII was in dispute with the pope over his refusal to annul his first marriage to the childless Catherine. He sought opinions on the dispute from major European universities, eight of which supported his views.

Henry married Anne Boleyn in 1533 and two months later had the Archbishop of Canterbury declare his marriage to Catherine void. He was then excommunicated by the pope but retaliated by having Parliament pass an act appointing he and his successors head of the Church of England. Between 1536 and 1539 the monasteries were suppressed and their property seized.

Subsequently many Lutherans were burned as heretics and Roman Catholics who refused to recognize the king's leadership of the church were executed. Eventually, however, the Anglican Church adopted Protestant views.

Later Mary I attempted to restore Roman Catholicism as the state religion, and during her reign many Protestants were burned at the stake. A settlement was reached under Queen Elizabeth I in 1563 and Protestantism was restored, and Roman Catholics were often persecuted.

Europe's 30-year war (1618-1648)

The religious hatreds that flared into the Thirty Years' War had smouldered for more than half a century, in part because of the weaknesses of the 1555 Peace of Augsburg agreement between the Holy Roman emperor and the Lutheran princes of Germany. The result was a struggle between the Hapsburg-controlled Holy Roman Empire and the Protestant municipalities which spread to involve most of Western Europe. The war, one of the most destructive conflicts in European history, had four main phases:

1618-25: The Palatine-Bohemian conflict in which Protestant forces initially had the upper hand. Then, in part because of dissention amongst the Protestant forces, the pro-Catholic forces were ultimately victorious.

1625-29: The king of Denmark and Norway came to the aid of the German Protestants, in part wishing to end Hapsburg control of the Danish duchy of Holstein, Germany. Again the Protestants were defeated and Denmark had to give up small landholdings in Germany.

1630-35: Having earlier been asked for support by the North-German Protestants, the Swedish king, encouraged by a promise of French support, landed a well-trained army on the coast of Pomerania in 1630. While he was waiting for support from Brandenburg, Pomerania and Saxony to materialize, however, pro-Catholic forces captured and sacked the city of Magdeburg in 1631, after which Protestant inhabitants were massacred.

The Swedes then defeated the Catholic forces in three successive battles and moved into southern Germany for the winter. In 1632 they captured Munich. Further battles followed but ultimately the Protestant coalition abandoned its struggle and the Peace of Prague ended the third phase of the 30-year war.

1635-48: In 1635 France declared war against Spain, the chief Habsburg dominion aside from Austria, and allied with Sweden and German Protestant leaders, defeated a combined force of Saxons and Austrians at Wittstock, 93km northwest of Berlin, in 1636. The Habsburg position in Germany was further weakened by a defeat inflicted at Rheinfelden on the Swiss-German border in 1638.

After these setbacks the imperial armies were forced to surrender their European strongholds one after another. Between 1642 and 1645 the Swedes had numerous triumphs, overrunning Denmark, which had become allied with the empire, and ravaging large sections of western Germany and Austria.

In the west the French routed a Spanish army at Rocroi, France, in 1643. They were then defeated at Tuttlingen, Germany, but thereafter the French gained the upper hand, routing a Bavarian army at Freiburg in 1644, and an Austro-Bavarian army near Nördlingen in 1645. After central Bavaria was invaded, however, Bavaria agreed to a truce with Sweden and France in 1647.

Despite this, fighting continued in Germany, Luxembourg, the Low Countries, Italy, and Spain throughout the remainder of 1647. After further defeats, the Holy Roman Emperor signed the Peace of Westphalia agreement on Oct. 14, 1648. This established Switzerland and the Dutch Republic (the Netherlands) as independent states, gravely weakened the Holy Roman Empire and the Habsburgs, ensured the emergence of France as the chief power on the Continent, and disastrously retarded the political unification of Germany, the population of which had fallen by 20%.

Assessments

The components of the equation $A^{**} = A + B + C + D + S$ (Equation 10.2) have, of course, much relevance to religious conflict:

[1] *Initial attitude, A.*

It is clear that the greed, vanity and incompetence of religious leaders is often as great as that of political leaders. Thus they too have also sought wider influence and thus greater power, often resulting in conflict

All too often, however, the brainwashed masses believe in their propaganda and lies and follow their misguided policies blindly and enjoin in conflicts that arise from them.

[2] *Behaviour, B.*

Large, advanced societies, of course, require control and thence leaders, and from man's tribal days religious leaders have had great influence.

Throughout history many of them, like political leaders, have also indulged in ambitious and driven type A personality behaviours in seeking wider influence and thus greater power, all too often resulting in conflict, sometimes on a grand scale. Such people are undoubtedly psychopathic, the pathology of their condition including aggression, lying and cheating.

[3] *Contact history, C.*

Much of the discontent and conflict over religion throughout history has been of the 'revolutionary' kind, that is, people have come to resent abuses of power, hoarding of money and assets, and discrimination by religious authorities. Over time levels of resentment and hostility tend to grow, sometimes resulting in attempts to overthrow a particular religion or sect and adopt another.

Being preached from on high, religions have a tendency to spread, of course, so the newly adopted religion may then spread to other regions, and then countries, and the spread of Catholicism and later Protestantism are good examples of this.

[4] *Differences, D.*

Religion has always been seen as a major difference between people, even when they only belong to different sects of the same religion. This was particularly true in the past when religious rites and prayer simply helped pass time, but is less true in modern societies where radio, TV, fast travel, phones, the Internet etcetera leave much less time for religion, if any, for most people in the West.

[5] *Societal attitudes, S.*

Throughout history any given society has, generally, had one religion and people have been 'brainwashed' by religious cant to believe it is 'right'. Thus most religions involve zealotry that leads to other religions being regarded as wrong, if not evil, such prejudice being used by religious leaders and monarchs as an excuse for all too many wars throughout history.

Then, when other religions are seen to be a repeated source of conflict, however, the views of outsiders towards that religion will be negative.

Conclusion

Religions insist their creed is 'right' and to break its rules is evil. Thus 'non-believers' can be regarded as evil, encouraging religious prejudice and conflict. Religious leaders too can be ambitious type A personality people and thus throughout history have often encouraged conflict (Mohr & Fear, 2015; Mohr et al. 2018c).

Chapter 18

ETHNIC CONFLICT

There is no contradiction between saying (a) that contact tends to reduce the cultural differences among ethnic groups and (b) that contact also tends to stimulate efforts to preserve or increase these differences.
H. D. Forbes *Ethnic Conflict, Commerce, Culture, and the Contact Hypothesis* (1997).

Introduction

Ethnic discrimination, exploitation, and conflict have occurred throughout history. As noted in earlier chapters, there were centuries of exploitation of the peoples in the many Western colonies throughout much of the world, and ethnic conflict inevitably occurred frequently as a result.

As for more recent times, one study identified 58 ethnic civil wars between 1945 and 1999, these being 51% of the total number of civil wars (Caselli & Coleman, 2012).

Encyclopaedia Britannica Ready Reference 2003 defines *ethnic group* as: *Social group or category of the population that in a larger society is set apart and bound together by common ties of race, language, nationality, or culture.*

Macquarie dictionary's (1991) entry for *ethnocentrism* is: *the belief in the inherent superiority of one's own group and culture accompanied by a feeling of contempt for other groups and cultures.*

The third edition of the Shorter Oxford Dictionary defines *ethnomaniac* as: *one who is crazy about racial autonomy.*

The seventh edition of the Concise Oxford Dictionary defines *ethnic cleansing* as: *the mass expulsion or extermination of people from opposing ethnic or religious groups within a certain area.*

In the present chapter, therefore, discussion of ethnic conflict includes 'racial conflict'.

The Boer War

Throughout the 19th century ill feeling mounted between the Boers, Dutch-descended Afrikaners, and British settlers, resulting in the Afrikaner migration called the Great Trek (1835-1843) and the establishment of the Afrikaner republics Orange Free State and Transvaal (which became 'The South African Republic').

The discovery of gold in southern Transvaal in 1884 lured thousands of British prospectors to the area. The Afrikaners resented the newcomers or Uitlanders (foreigners) and taxed them heavily and denied them voting rights. The resentment on both sides grew, ultimately leading to a failed British-supported revolt by the Uitlanders against the Afrikaner government in 1885.

When the British refused to remove troops from border regions in 1889 the Orange Free State declared war and the Boers invaded Natal and Cape Colony, winning three battles in December. The British recovered and won a major victory in The Battle of Spion Kop and annexed the Orange Free State and then Transvaal in September 1990.

Refusing to surrender, the Boers continued a guerrilla campaign in the conquered territories. The British responded by establishing concentration camps, burning farms, and executing Boer irregulars.

In 1902 The Peace of Vereeniging promised the Boers self-government if they became British subjects.

In 1906 the British granted responsible government to the Transvaal and Orange Free State, and in 1910 the Union of South Africa was formed to unite them with Cape Colony and Natal (Natkeil, 1982).

Anti-Semitism

Scattered communities of Jews were always a minority that was easily identifiable. During the Middle Ages they had to exist outside the feudal system based on land and many engaged in trade and commerce.

In the early days of capitalism the Church forbade profit and money-lending with interest and most Christians left this activity to Jews. The growing wealth of Jews, however, led to resentment and anti-Jewish sentiment in Europe and in the 19th century thousands fled to the USA to escape it.

In his down-and-out days in Vienna Adolph Hitler wrote:

Was there any shady undertaking, any form of foulness, especially in cultural life, in which at least one Jew did not participate? On putting the probing knife carefully to that kind of abscess, one immediately discovered, like a maggot in a putrescent body, a little Jew who was often blinded by the sudden light. Adolf Hitler, *Mein Kampf,* q. in *Hitler: A Study in Tyranny,* A. Bullock, Penguin, Harmondsworth (1962).

It is believed that the brutal ethnic cleansing of Hitler's 'Final Solution' during World War II killed circa 6 million Jews. Notably, however, IBM's German subsidiary Demohag collected the detailed data on Germany's Jewish population whilst Du Pont made the Zyklon B gas used to kill them (Aarons & Loftus, 1999; Black, 2001)

The Ustashi

There can have been no more barbarous group that the Catholic, right-wing Croatian Ustashi. Formed in the 1930s, with the help of the Macedonian Internal Revolutionary Organization they assassinated King Alexander I of Yugoslavia in Marseille in 1934.

After the German invasion during WW2 a nominally independent Croatian State existed and the fascist Ustashi government set up concentration camps in which thousands of Jews, Gypsies and Orthodox Serbs were murdered in conditions of the utmost barbarity.

Towards the end of WW2 the invading Soviet Army saw an end to Croatian independence but the legacy of hatred between the Croats and Serbs lived on.

Death camps were again set up during the bitter conflict in the former Yugoslavia during the early 1990s.

The break-up of Yugoslavia

After the break-up of the Soviet Union in 1991 there was political and ethnic conflict in some former member states, particularly Yugoslavia where Slobodan Milosevic was one of the key figures. He had become president of Serbia in 1989. In 1990 he was re-elected, his Socialist Party of Serbia winning 194 of the 250 seats.

There was civil war in Croatia in 1991, and in Bosnia and Herzegovina in 1992, both of which have large Serb minorities. With support from the Yugoslav army, Serbian forces seized large parts of Croatia and Bosnia and Herzegovina. In April 1992 Serbia and Montenegro proclaimed themselves the successor state to Yugoslavia, taking the name Federal Republic of Yugoslavia (FRY).

Milosevic was widely blamed for providing financial and military backing to nationalist Serbs fighting in Croatia and Bosnia and received international criticism for the brutal atrocities that were committed by Serbs in those conflicts.

In February 1998 Milosevic ordered Yugoslav military forces into Kosovo to join Serbian police in suppressing growing unrest among the region's Albanian population. The Serbian forces killed more than 150 ethnic Albanians, including women and children, over a three-month period.

Conflict in the former Yugoslavia in the 1990s was widespread and tens of thousands of people were killed and hundreds of thousands displaced. Some of the conflict was religious and directed at the substantial Bosnian Muslim community.

Today the term Yugoslavia is still used to describe today's independent components of Bosnia & Herzegovina, Croatia, Macedonia, Serbia & Montenegro, and Slovenia.

Azerbaijan

Once part of the Roman and then Ottoman Empires, Azerbaijan joined the USSR in 1922. In 1992 fighting between mostly Muslim Azerbaijan and mostly Christian Armenia broke out over claims to Nagorno-Karabakh, an enclave in Azerbaijan mostly populated by Armenians. In 1994 a ceasefire was negotiated, leaving Armenian forces in control of the enclave.

Georgia

Georgia, having been annexed by Russia in 1801, became part of the USSR in 1922. It became an independent state in 1991. During 1991 rebellion forced the president to flee and he was replaced by a former USSR foreign minister.

In Abkhazia ethnic Abkhazis, reportedly aided by Russia, launched a bloody military campaign which by late 1993 had gained control over much of the region. In May 1994 a cease-fire agreement was reached and was supported by Russian peacekeepers.

Moldova

Moldova left the USSR and became an independent state in late 1991. In March 1992 fighting erupted in the Dnestr region between Moldovan forces and Slavic separatists, ethnic Russians and ethnic Ukrainians, who feared Moldova would merge with neighbouring Romania.

A peace accord with the separatists was signed in Moscow on May 8, 1997.

The American Negroes

Racial discrimination against Negroes in the USA was originally severe, of course, as they were imported as slaves. Slavery was abolished more than a century ago in the USA but Negroes continued to be discriminated against and live in relative poverty compared to whites.

In 1962, before the Civil Rights movement had had much impact the average black was in an occupation that ranked 24 points below the national average on the 96 point Duncan Scale (Jencks et al., 1975).

Gradually campaigns for a better 'deal' for Negroes made progress, but not without considerable conflict and violence, particularly in the 1960s.

Nevertheless, in the 1970s studies found that the average white child scored about 15 points better on standard tests than the average black child. Much of this difference can be attributed to environment, an American study of 19 pairs of identical twins reared apart finding that 4 of the pairs had IQ scores that differed by 15 points or more (Jencks et al., 1975).

In 1970, white men who worked full-time earned an average of $200/week, whereas black men averaged only $130/week, black women averaging only $90/week.

Since then, of course, the situation for blacks has improved considerably and, of course, the USA now has a black President for the first time.

Cyprus

The British colony of Cyprus was granted independence in 1959 after the murder of many British servicemen and colonial officials by the Greek terrorist organization EOKA which supported the Enosis movement for union with Greece. Thirty percent of key positions were reserved for Turks who were 18% of the population.

In 1974 a coup organized by Enosis and EOKA installed a local Greek Cypriot as president. In response Turkey invaded and took control of the northern third of the island before a ceasefire was declared. This zone was declared a separate Turkish Cypriot federated state in 1975 and 200,000 Greeks were expelled and replaced by thousands of Turks from the mainland.

South Africa's apartheid regime

The British colonies of Cape Colony, Transvaal, Natal and Orange River were unified to form the Union of South Africa in 1910. The priority of South African politics was maintaining white supremacy over the black majority.

In 1948 South Africa formally instituted its apartheid policy that enforced racial segregation. There was much protest against this, most famously in 1960 at Sharpeville, a suburb of Vereeniging, when 20,000 Africans gathered to demonstrate near a police station.

After the protesters began stoning police and their armoured cars, the police opened fire with submachine guns and 69 Africans were killed and 186 wounded, 48 women and children being among the victims. A state of emergency was declared in South Africa, and nearly 2,000 persons were detained. Reports of this incident helped focus international criticism on the apartheid policy which ended in 1989 (Encyclopaedia Britannica CD 1999).

The Rwandan genocide

The culmination of longstanding ethnic competition and tension between the Tutsi and Hutu peoples, over 500,000 people were killed in about 100 days in 1994. Estimates of the death toll have ranged as high as one million or 20% of the country's population. Organized Hutu militias, supported by many Hutu civilians, carried out the killings.

In response the rebel Tutsi Rwandan Patriotic Front defeated the army and seized control of the country.

The Australian Aborigines

The colonizing of Australia exacted a great toll on the aborigines, for example the Myall Creek massacre, The Black War in Tasmania, and the long battle between blacks and whites in the Hawkesbury region of New South Wales (Bell & Hall, 1991).

Numerous North American studies found that status attainment for blacks was not the same as for whites and that even when blacks were as well educated they were unable to achieve the same occupational and economic rewards. The same situation applies in Australia and may also result from discrimination (Broom et al., 1980).

In part because the aborigines are only a small minority, ethnic conflict between blacks and whites in Australia has only been on a small scale. Riots by aborigines in poor western suburbs of Sydney a few years ago were, however, of significant proportions.

Assessments

The components of the equation $A^{**} = A + B + C + D + S$ (Equation 10.2) have much relevance to ethnic conflict:

[1] *Initial attitude, A.*

The attitudes of ethnic groups typically relate to their history of living in a particular region. When that region is overtaken by others, of course, this is certain to cause great resentment, ultimately leading to rebellion. Sooner or later, successive conflicts wear down the foreign rulers and the region regains its independence, a story repeated dozens of times in the last two centuries.

Imperialist powers, as noted in previous chapters, often see themselves as superior and having some 'natural' or religious right to rule over suppressed peoples in the territories they occupy. Often, however, economic motives are the real incentive for imperialism.

[2] *Behaviour, B.*

Majority or more powerful ethnic groups who gain control of a region usually discriminate against and exploit weaker groups, in part for reasons of ethnic bias, but in part because of man's usual and 'animalistic' greed as seen in the rampant capitalism in much of the decadent West and comparable to the greed and ferocity with which some animal species feed and fight off other animals while doing so. In the human situation, of course, police forces and armies are used to quell dissidence, throughout history often with a great toll on human life.

[3] *Contact history, C.*

Ethnic conflict has usually been for control of a region that an ethnic group believes it has historical entitlement to. Inevitably, it may often have a racial basis also.

Religion too has often been a divisive factor leading to ethnic conflict, examples being Hitler's 'final solution' for the 'Jewish problem', the conflicts in the former Yugoslavia, and the conflicts in Azerbaijan.

Economic and political factors are often also factors leading to ethnic conflict, European resentment of Jews often being because of their apparent wealth, and Negro resentment in the USA being because of their relative poverty.

[4] *Differences, D.*
The beliefs, attitudes and customs of any human group emerge in response to the unique set of circumstances and experiences of that group. When these beliefs are commonly held, it can be said that they have passed into the culture of the group.

Social learning soon passes on this culture to new individuals born into the group. Prejudice such as 'they all look the same to me' are thus likely to be learned behaviour. Prejudiced individuals are then likely to avoid the disliked group as far as possible.

Caselli & Coleman (2012) define the term *ethnic distance*, that is, the degree of difficulty of passing from a losing/exploited group into the winning/dominant group, concluding that peaceful outcomes are more likely when ethnic distance is smaller.

[5] *Societal attitudes, S.*
Ethnic groups can easily be made scapegoats for hard times such as economic downturns. In times of high unemployment, for example, newly-arrived immigrants are often blamed. In Germany the 'Jewish-problem' was often blamed for the sufferings of the Great Depression (Bell & Hall, 1991).

Caselli & Coleman (2012) note that the ethnicity's salience varies over time and that ethnicity is a "social construct" because it results from social "discourses" that condition individuals to identify with a particular group.

Conclusions

Ethnic conflict involves disputes between human groupings which differ in race, nationality, language and culture. It is usually the result of different ethnic groups living in the same region of a country, perhaps as a result of migration of one of the groups to that region relatively recently in history. Then competition for 'space' and resources, prejudice over their differences, and jealousy over greater power and/or wealth of one group, are amongst the factors that may lead to conflict.

As in other areas of human conflict, conflict on any scale requires leaders and often these are people of importance in the ethnic community such as politicians or religious leaders. These leaders take up the 'cause' of the ethnic group and whip up prejudice and anger and eventually conflict.

18. Ethnic Conflict

Chapter 19

CONFLICTING SOCIETAL GROUPS

*Just as the human body can crave more and more of a drug
that is actually poisoning it, so a society can crave lethal weapons,
cadavers, or human organs which if freely traded,
would inflict social damage.*
Warren Dennis, *Beyond Leadership: Balancing Economics, Ethics
and Ecology* (co-authors Jagdish Parikh & Ronnie Lessem, 1994).

Introduction

Societies may consist of many factions or subgroups and
some these, of course, are prone to conflict.

The 'War of the Sexes' was discussed in Chapter 11, and
this involves the largest possible subgroup of society, about
one half, but conflict is generally via the political stance of
the feminine liberation movement.

Religious and ethnic conflicts were dealt with in Chapters
17 and 18, and throughout history these have often been
wars of considerable scale. In the present chapter the
fractions of society considered are generally smaller, as are
the scale of conflicts between them.

The class system

Most societies have had some sort of hierarchical class
system, Rome being divided between the 'populus', members
of the original Roman families, and the 'plebs' or common
people who eventually gained greater status. Later, a new
aristocracy of 'nobiles' was established, the term plebs then
coming to refer to the rest of the people.

In modern times England is the best known example of a class system which involves an upper class, a middle class, and a lower class. The upper class are those with hereditary titles and/or wealth, the middle class are the 'white collar' workers in clerical and professional occupations, and the working class are the 'blue collar' workers who work 'manually' in factories or on farms.

To these a fourth 'lower class' or 'underclass' may be added, this being a substratum of permanently jobless or underemployed people.

In the USA, for example, more than 30% of all wealth is in the hands of the top 1% of property owners.

Karl Marx held that it was only the workers who did productive work and those who ran the businesses they worked in accumulated the 'surplus value' of their work via company profits:

In proportion as capital accumulates, the lot of the labourer be his payment high or low, must grow worse.

Marx held that most of recorded history has been one of endemic class struggle and that revolution would occur in the most developed capitalist countries and that production would be controlled by the workers themselves.

Marx's writings had a great influence on the Russian Revolution of 1917 and on others since, for example that in Cuba in 1959, these events being discussed in Chapter 23.

There have, of course, been countless worker conflicts throughout history.

In 1764 James Hargreaves made his first spinning jenny which could spin several threads at once. In 1768 a mob of angry cotton labourers gutted Hargreaves' house and destroyed his machinery. He moved to Nottingham and, with a partner, took out a patent for his machine in 1770 (Odle, 1966).

In 1769 Richard Arkwright took out a patent for a horse-powered spinning-frame. In 1775 he patented a carding machine and made other machines for drawing and roving cotton, reducing it to thinner strands for feeding to the spinning-machine. In 1789 a mob smashed up his mill.

In 1790 he applied steam power to his spinning frames. In that same year a mob marched on his Derbyshire mills but Arkwright had armed his workers and the mob was dispersed (Odle, 1966).

Since those days, of course, Unions have been formed to represent the workers and these are discussed later in this chapter.

The caste system

Caste is a hereditary social group in which people share the same culture or occupation, belong to the same religious sect, or have the same level of wealth.

There are some 3,000 castes in India, each with its own customs and rituals, for example marriage or even dining with a member of another caste is not permitted.

The original caste system dates to before 1500BC and consisted of four categories or *varnas* (colours), these being:

1. White: the Brahmans who were originally priests.

2. Red: the Kshatriyas or rulers, nobles and warriors.

3. Yellow: the Vaisyas or business people and bankers.

4. Black: the Sundras or artisans and labourers.

A fifth class, the panchamas (fifths) or 'outcastes', who are today called the 'untouchables'.

India's 1950 constitution outlawed untouchability and conferred equal status on all people but remnants of the caste system remain today and still influence social behaviour considerably, arrangement of marriages, for example, still being common practice.

The caste system has, of course, been the cause of much resentment and occasional conflict throughout history.

The union movement

Since their inception workers unions have instigated many forms of industrial conflict as a means of drawing attention to their grievances. The total range of behaviour includes strikes and lockouts, peaceful bargaining, work to rules, boycotts, work bans and limitations, political actions, sit-ins, absenteeism, alcoholism, low morale and productivity, material wastage, slackness and inefficiency, go slows and labour turnover (Plowman et al., 1980).

Added to these are acts of sabotage:

. . . materials are hidden in factories, conveyor belts jammed with sticks, cogs stopped with wire and ropes, lorries 'accidentally' backed into ditches. Electricians labour to put in weak fuses, textile workers 'knife' through carpets and farmworkers cooperate to choke agricultural machinery with tree branches (Taylor & Walton, 1971).

Union action in Australia is in the middle range as regards frequency. In 1975-77 the number of working days lost through strikes per thousand people was 509 (Dabscheck & Niland, 1981).

This compares well with Canada (900), Finland (600) and Italy (1200), but less well with West Germany (8), the Netherlands (19), the UK (264) and the US (400).

Strikes in Australia are usually short, more than half between 1964 and 1979 not lasting more than a day, whereas strikes in the US tend to be longer, and thus days lost per worker each year were from 5 to 10 times greater in that period.

Union action in most countries involves, at worst, police intervention, and perhaps one of two minor acts of violence and a few people arrested. In some countries, however, prolonged national strikes have sometimes resulted in the army being called in and many people being killed.

In some countries such as Australia and England there are political parties with strong affiliations with the unions, this increasing their influence considerably.

The environmental movement

Encouraged by concerns such as pollution, resource depletion, environmental degradation, and climate change, environmental movements around the world have grown in strength greatly in recent decades. In most Western countries there is now a Green Party contesting national and state elections and their share of the vote has increased from a few percent to 10 or 20 percent in some countries.

The environmental movement has been involved in occasional conflict, for example the sinking of the Greenpeace ship Rainbow Warrior at a New Zealand port in 1985. The ship had been protesting French nuclear testing in the Pacific Ocean and investigations found that French agents had planted explosives in the ship, causing a scandal leading to the resignation of the French Minister of Defence, and the dismissal of the director of the French Secret Service.

More recently there have been mass protests against proposed logging areas and dams in Tasmania which have involved police attendance to keep control, and continuing harassment of Japanese whaling vessels in southern waters by environmental activists.

The gay rights movement

The 'gay' movement has grown in strength in several countries in recent decades to the point at which homosexuality, once looked down upon, if not deplored, has become accepted.

Annual 'gay pride' marches now pass without incident whereas once they might have involved minor scuffles between the marchers and disapproving onlookers, requiring police intervention.

Currently the movement continues to demand that gay marriage be made legal in several countries, an issue that could yet result in large scale demonstrations and conflict.

Cult groups

There are many 'cult groups' around the world, some of which have caused conflict.

In 1995 the religious cult Aum Shinrikyo released sarin nerve gas in the Tokyo subway, killing 12 people and injuring 5,500 (Lifton, 1999).

In the US there are several sectarian and religious militia groups such as the Klu Klux Klan, Aryan Nation, Posse Comitatus, The Order, The Texas Militia and many others (Dees, 1996; Jones & Israel, 1998; Snow, 1999).

The 1995 Oklahoma City bombing, in which 168 people were killed, was the most spectacular act of terrorism on US soil before the September 11 attacks. It was in revenge for the mass deaths in 1993 of most of the members of the Branch Davidian movement at Waco after a 51-day siege by federal agents.

The FBI charged Timothy McVeigh and Terry Nichols with the bombing but only McVeigh was convicted.

McVeigh's chief defence counsellor, however, found that McVeigh and Nichols had had contacts with Aryan Nation, other people with neo-Nazi sympathies and, most interesting of all, Nicholls had been to the Philippines several times where he had been in contact with Ramzi Yousef who in turn had had contact with al-Qa'ida and Osama Bin Laden (Jones & Israel, 1998).

Such groups, if their rhetoric is to be believed, may pose a serious threat to the US in future:

We must in one voice, cry out that we will not tolerate their stinking, murdering, lying, corrupt government.
Louis Beam, speech at the 'Rocky Mountain Rendezvous' (1992), a meeting of several far-right groups.

I suspect Americans will begin engaging in terrorism on a scale the world has never known.
William Pearce, author of *The Turner Diaries* (1978) and leader of the National Alliance, a US neo-Nazi group.

Urban gangs

In several Western countries there are small urban gangs such as 'bikies' and 'skinheads.'

Bikies were perhaps immortalized in the 1954 Marlon Brando movie *The Wild One* which was based on a true incident in which a motorcycle gang terrorized a small town. Such gangs can still be seen clothed in black leather and riding Harley-Davidson motorcycles. Occasionally, there is conflict between rival gangs or with the police.

Skinheads are a youth subculture that appeared first in England in the late 1960s as a working-class reaction to the 'hippies'. They had close-cropped hair and wore work-shirts, short jeans supported by suspenders, and heavy red boots often used to kick people. They were often involved in football hooliganism and attacks against Asians and other easily distinguishable immigrants.

A recent TV documentary program interviewed an aging English skinhead who said that they wanted to separate themselves from other peoples according to race, creed and religion, noting that this had never been achieved before in history without conflict. He added: "Anyone not part of our belief system was an enemy," confessing that he had been involved in bombing and killing non-Europeans.

Criminal gangs

In the last hundred years large criminal gangs have emerged in the largest cities of several countries.

The largest and best organized were the Mafia which originated in Sicily but spread, autonomous groups forming throughout Italy and in the major cities of the USA.

In the 1920s Al Capone, an Italian-American, took over a Chicago organization dealing in illegal liquor, gambling, and prostitution. He eliminated his competitors in a series of gang wars, including the Saint Valentine's Day massacre of 1929, and took control of Chicago's underworld.

Capone was convicted of income tax evasion in 1931 and sentenced to 11 years in prison but was released on parole in 1939 because of ill-health owing to syphilis.

In the major cities of many countries gang warfare has often occurred but usually been limited to murder of one or two people, often followed by a revenge killing, often resulting in a series of killings over a period of several months or a few years.

Assessments and conclusions

The components of the equation $A^{**} = A + B + C + D + S$ (Equation 10.2) have, of course, much relevance to conflicting groups in society:

[1] Initial attitude, A.

In the case of class conflict the attitudes of the upper classes are those of innate superiority, those of the lower classes being resentment of the wealth of the upper classes.

Lack of money, of course, is also the major concern of the unions who tend to represent the lower classes.

The Greens have a 'cause' which they strongly believe in, with increasingly good reason as our exponentiating population exhausts the planet's resources and pollutes it.

Gay rights movements also have a cause towards which attitudes of heterosexual people have until relatively recently usually been negative.

Smaller cult groups tend to have extremist attitudes, militia groups in particular being a potential threat in the future, particularly in the US.

Criminal organizations, of course, have little respect or concern for the law, being preoccupied with making 'easy money', these days this usually being done by selling drugs, the illegal drugs industry now being, along with the arms industry, one of the world's two largest industries.

[2] Behaviour, *B.*

The way in which richest few exploit the workers has become excessive in the extreme, gigantic executive salary packages being as much as thousands of times those of the people who actually produce something tangible, saleable products and services. It is likely that, as economic conditions deteriorate further in some countries, there will be increasing conflict and perhaps revolution.

In this context unions, along with fair-work arbitration systems, usually play a peacemaking role.

The Green and gay movements are normally orderly and peaceful.

As two examples given earlier show, the rhetoric of some cult groups is sometimes extreme, the Oklahoma City Bombing being an example of how much damage can be inflicted by just two sympathizers of such movements.

The behaviour of organized crime is particularly antisocial these days as it results in massive numbers of people becoming addicted to drugs which often ruin their lives.

[3] Contact history, *C.*

There is generally little contact between the highest and lowest classes of society, this perhaps being one motivation for having such classes.

The same generally applies to the other groups discussed in this chapter because, of course, people form such groups to share common views so they can communicate with others of like mind.

Throughout history, what inter-group contact there has been has usually been negative, polarizing groups even further. Fortunately conflict between most of the groups discussed in this chapter has, however, usually been on a limited scale.

[4] Differences, *D.*

Economic inequalities, sometimes of massive proportions, have often led to class conflict.

Money too is a major concern of unions, job security also being a major concern during all too frequent economic downturns.

The Green and gay movements have one key difference only from the rest of society, that is, their level of concern about the issues they represent.

Cult and urban groups, on the other hand, do their utmost to differentiate themselves from the rest of society.

Criminal organizations differ from society in that they routinely break the law. This, of course, is done covertly and with as little contact with the rest of society as possible, often go-betweens being used to sell drugs, for example.

[5] Societal attitudes, *S.*

Societies have always seemed to accept that people live at often massively different levels of income and status. Indeed this unjust inequality, according to Marxists, is the root of all evil. In the West media condemnation of gigantic executive salaries, if any, is very hushed, perhaps because the journalists themselves belong to an organization run by an extremely rich media mogul whom they cannot criticize without fear of jeopardizing their careers.

Society is generally supportive of the Green movement, but somewhat mutedly, whilst it tolerates the gay movement, at least. With exposure over successive decades, of course, society becomes accustomed to and more tolerant, if not supportive, of such movements.

Society dislikes cults, urban gangs, and criminals, of course, and hopes that authorities will keep them under control.

Chapter 20

POLITICAL CONFLICT

It is politics that begets war.
Politics represents the intelligence, war its instrument,
not the other way around. The only possible course in war
is to subordinate the military viewpoint to the political.
Karl Marie von Clausewitz, *On War* (1883).

Corruption, the most infallible symptom of constitutional liberty.
Edward Gibbon,
The History of the Decline and Fall of the Roman Empire (1776-88).

Introduction

The first of four definitions that WordWeb 6 gives for politics is: *Social relations involving intrigue to gain authority or power.*

It's first of two definitions for intrigue is: *A crafty and involved plot to achieve your (usually sinister) ends.*

All too often the people do, indeed, find that their political rulers are 'crafty' and corrupt and seek to overthrow them, resulting in political conflict.

Just as often, ambitious people competing for power are the cause of political conflict, often resulting in civil wars.

There have been countless examples of political conflict throughout history and a few of these are briefly described in the following chapter.

The Revolt of Ciompi

This was a popular rebellion in Florence in 1378 which was still recovering from the losses of the Black Death, a bubonic plague that killed almost half the population of Western Europe. The rebellion was led by workers who were not allowed guild membership and were thus disenfranchised. The merchant oligarchy was briefly overthrown and replaced by a popular government but a counter-coup returned it to power.

The English Civil Wars

These were England's greatest internal conflict and were between supporters of Charles I (the Cavaliers) and supporters of parliament (the Roundheads) who were in opposition to growing royal power. The king left London and raised his standard two months later in Nottingham. After an inconclusive initial battle at Edgehill in October 1642 royalist forces abandoned an advance on London when confronted by a parliamentary force at Turnham Green, the king withdrawing to Oxford to make his military headquarters there.

The Royalists won control of most of Yorkshire at Adwalton Moor on June 30th 1643, and they were victorious at Lansdown and Broadway Down (July), while Charles's nephew Prince Rupert captured Bristol. Parliament was victorious at Winceby (Oct. 11th 1643) and took Lincoln.

After the inconclusive first Battle of Newbury (September 1643), both sides sought allies. Parliament negotiated Scottish military aid and the king made peace with the Irish (who had been in rebellion since 1641), thereby freeing troops for deployment in Britain.

Despite the Parliamentary victory at Marston Moor (July 2), the Royalist operations of 1644 were generally more successful but a second Battle of Newbury (September 20) was again inconclusive.

In 1645 parliament's New Model Army had an overwhelming victory at Naseby (June 14) and the last Royalist army was beaten at Langport (July 10).

In Scotland the marquess of Montrose was defeated at Philiphaugh (September 13) and the Scots swept through the North of England while Parliamentary forces swept through the Southwest.

In 1646 the Royalist troops disbanded and Oxford surrendered. In May 1646 Charles surrendered to the Scots who in June 1647 handed him over to Parliament.

Charles escaped and, having made a deal with a Scottish group to establish Presbyterianism in England, there were a series of royalist rebellions and a Scottish invasion in July 1648. All were defeated and Charles was finally tried and executed in January 1649.

Fighting next broke out in Ireland where Oliver Cromwell suppressed a major uprising of Roman Catholics and Royalists (1649-50). A Scottish rebellion under Montrose was also crushed in April 1650.

Charles II then made terms with the Presbyterian Covenanters but Cromwell defeated them at Dunbar (Sept. 3, 1650) but then allowed Charles, recently crowned in Scotland, to march deep into England. The utter rout of the Royalists at Worcester (Sept. 3, 1651), and Charles II's subsequent flight abroad, effectively ended the civil wars.

As many as 100,000 men, or 10% of the male population, were killed in these wars.

The American Civil War

The 1860 election of Abraham Lincoln, who opposed the extension of slavery to new territories, precipitated the conflict. South Carolina succeeded from the Union and 10 other states soon followed, the 11 states forming the Confederacy early in 1861.

War broke out on 12th April 1861 when Southern forces took Fort Sumter in South Carolina. Most of the battles were in the South and the Confederacy won early victories.

The North won at Antietam in 1862, soon after which Lincoln signed the Emancipation Proclamation freeing all slaves in the Confederacy. This reduced available manpower in the South so that the North, with much greater manpower and industrial resources, began to prevail with major victories at Vicksburg and Gettysburg in 1863.

Union forces had overrun Atlanta and Georgia by 1864 and the war ended on 9th April 1945, having cost a great many lives.

Angola

In the 1950s and 1960s three organizations fought for independence from Portugal. These were the MPLA (The Popular Movement) which was Marxist, the FNLA (The National Front) which defended the interests of the northern tribes, and the UNITA (The National Union for Total Independence of Angola).

The cities mainly supported MPLA but FNLA and UNITA received support through Zaire. In 1975 South African forces moved into southern Angola, strengthening the UNITA movement.

The MPLA secured control of the capital Luanda in July 1975 and, with the help of military supplies from eastern Europe, gained control of 12 of the 16 Angolan districts.

FNLA and UNITA, helped by South African forces fought back with some success but, with the help of troops sent from Cuba, the MPLA regained control and proclaimed Angola independent in February 1976.

Namibia

Explored by the Portuguese in the late 15th century, Namibia was annexed by Germany in 1885 as German Southwest Africa. It was captured in World War I by South Africa which received it as a UN mandate in 1918 which it refused to give up after World War II.

Founded in 1960, the South-West Africa People's Organization (SWAPO) tried to achieve independence from South Africa diplomatically and in 1966 the UN passed a resolution ending South Africa's mandate but South Africa challenged the decision.

SWAPO turned to armed struggle with the support of the Angolan ruling party and the Soviet Union, using Angola as a base for launching guerrilla attacks. From 1978 South Africa made retaliatory strikes in Angola.

The same year the UN recognized SWAPO as the Namibian people's sole representative. In 1988 the UN passed a resolution that South Africa should withdraw its troops from Namibia and that free elections should be held.

South Africa accepted this resolution and Namibia finally achieved independence in 1990.

Mozambique

Mozambique became an overseas province of Portugal in 1951 and an independence movement became active in the 1960s. After years of war the country was granted independence in 1975. Run by the Marxist Front for the Liberation of Mozambique (Frelimo) the country was wracked by civil war in the 1970s and 1980s.

In 1990 a new constitution introduced a multiparty government and a market economy. A peace treaty was signed with rebel groups in 1992.

The Congo

In 1960 the Belgian Congo gained its independence but an army mutiny led to disorder during which a tribal leader, aided by Belgian residents and Anglo-Belgian companies, declared the mineral-rich province of Katanga to be an independent state. In 1961 and 1962 mercenary forces defended Katanga from UN forces but in 1963 the secession of Katanga ended peacefully.

In 1964 communist-supported rebels gained strength in the East and established the Stanleyville 'People's Republic' which was suppressed with Western help.

Political unrest continued until 1965 when a coup installed General Mobutu as president. He survived an attempt by mercenaries to oust him and in 1971 the country was renamed Zaire. Mobutu held power for over three decades, amassing vast wealth while his country collapsed. When he was overthrown in 1997 the country was renamed The Democratic Republic of the Congo.

Argentina

The Spaniards arrived in 1515-16 and by the late 19th century nearly all the native Indians had been killed. There was large-scale Italian, German, and Spanish immigration in the decades after 1880. Social reforms were enacted in the 1920s but military juntas ruled from 1930 to 1946 when General Juan Peron was elected president.

Peron allowed labour reforms but suppressed free speech and ran the country into debt. He was exiled after a 1955 coup which was followed by a series of military and civilian governments. Peron returned in 1973 and was elected president but died soon afterwards and was succeeded by his wife Eva Duarte. She was ousted by a military junta which was then under siege from leftist guerrillas. The junta killed 5,000 people and jailed and tortured many others.

On April 2nd 1982 Argentine troops seized the British-held Falkland Islands. The British navy and air force blockaded the area, British forces invading and forcing the Argentinean troops to surrender on June 14.

The 1983 Argentinean elections restored democratic government but by 1989 Argentina had severe economic problems and hyperinflation sparked rioting and looting in several cities. In the 1990s harsh economic measures were taken to stabilize the economy and reduce foreign debt.

The Korean War

Korea was a united kingdom under the Silla Dynasty circa AD 668 and was sometimes associated with the Chinese empire. Korea achieved complete independence after the Sino-Japanese war of 1894-95 but was annexed by Japan in 1910 as the province of Chosun.

After Japan's defeat in World War, 2 Korea was partitioned at the 38th parallel at the Potsdam conference in July 1945, Russian troops moving in on August 10th, and American troops on September 8th. After a series of border clashes, the communist North invaded the South in 1950.

The UN intervened and forced the invaders back to the Chinese frontier but China then entered the war and, together with the North Koreans, occupied Seoul. The UN forces counter-attacked, retaking all territory south of the 38th parallel, and an armistice was signed in 1953.

The Vietnam War

A precedent was the Indo-China War (1946-54) between France and the Viet Minh which ended with the French defeated, leaving the North and South with separate governments. When planned elections for a single government failed to take place conflict was renewed.

Fearing the spread of communism, from 1961 the USA increased its aid to the South and sent "military advisors". In 1964 the North Vietnamese attacked US ships and the US responded with continued bombing of North Vietnam.

In 1965 the US began increasing its troop commitment and by 1968 more than 500,000 US soldiers were fighting in Vietnam. Conflict against the elusive communist guerrilla forces dragged on without an end in sight and opposition to the war in the USA grew.

Peace negotiations were begun in Paris in 1968 and in 1973 a ceasefire agreement was signed. Despite this, the North Vietnamese advance continued until Saigon was captured two years later, ending the war.

The Cold War

The term Cold War was first used by Bernard Baruch during a congressional debate in 1947. It was the open but restricted rivalry that developed after the Soviet Union seized control of Eastern Europe towards the end of World War II, the US and Britain then fearing further expansion of Soviet power in Western Europe and elsewhere.

The Cold War was waged principally on political, economic, and propaganda fronts. It was at its peak in 1948-53 with the Berlin blockage and airlift, the formation of NATO, the victory of the communists in the Chinese civil war, and the Korean War (Encyclopaedia Britannica 99).

The 4m high and 45km long Berlin Wall came to symbolize the Cold War. In the years 1949 to 1961, circa 2.5 million East Germans fled to West Germany. Construction on the wall began on the night of August 12-13, 1961, and it developed into a system of concrete walls, barbed wire, watchtowers, gun emplacements, and mines.

The Cuban missile crisis of 1962 was a highlight when the US blockaded Cuba to prevent completion of construction of Soviet nuclear missile bases in Cuba. The result was an intense round of threats, counter-threats, and negotiations for several days, at the end of which the USSR finally agreed to dismantle the bases.

There was a period of détente from 1967 to 1979 during which there was increased trade and cooperation and the SALT treaties were signed. Relations cooled again when the USSR invaded Afghanistan.

In the summer of 1989 Hungary began to allow East Germans passage to Austria and West Germany. By autumn the East German regime was on the verge of collapse and on November the 9th people began demolishing sections of the Berlin Wall without government interference, and the government soon participated in the demolition. In 1990 East and West Germany were reunited, heralding the dismantling of the Soviet Union and the end of the Cold War.

Assessments and conclusions

The components of the equation $A^{**} = A + B + C + D + S$ (Equation 10.2) have much relevance to political conflict:

[1] *Initial attitude, A.*

Political conflict is, of course, about power and, as all history proves, power corrupts. Given power, it seems that many people become addicted to it. The same seems to apply to money, of course, and many a crooked politician has amassed great wealth. Such politicians, of course, are those that hang onto power until the populace is obliged to forcefully remove them from office.

Politicians made leaders being, of course, good liars but having a good 'front', people's attitude to them is usually tolerant at first. As their incompetence and/or corruption becomes more evident, however, the attitudes of the people change for the worse, often resulting in some form of conflict, be that political or physical.

[2] *Behaviour, B.*

Politicking, of course, involves a 'plot' to achieve the ambitions of groups and the individuals within them. Often throughout history, of course, both fair means and foul have been used, no better example of foul means being the 'night of the long knives' when Hitler had several hundred suspected political opponents killed.

Such behaviour, of course, is more than an exhibition of ambitious type A personality. It is more than the aggression of a psychopath, it is psychotic behaviour.

It is such ambitious, impatient, competitive, domineering and hostile behaviour that characterizes the politicians who instigate hostility directly, or indirectly, because others react to their excessive greed and corruption and rebel against it.

Such rebellion may exhibit first as strikes, protest marches, demonstrations outside government buildings, and sometimes riots. When these measures are seen by leaders to be a threat armed conflict may ensue.

[3] *Contact history, C.*

Politicians and leaders speak from 'on high' and thus communication with the people is almost entirely a one-way affair via official media channels, and then usually only via members of their political organization or government.

The only peaceful way of the people venting their grievances is such means as letters to the newspapers and there is little chance of much notice being taken of these.

The only peaceful means of changing a government is by voting for an alternative one and, all too often in history, that has not been possible, often resulting in growing frustration and eventual conflict.

[4] *Differences, D.*

The Westminster system of government is originally based on the notion of two relatively 'equal' parties so that voting will tend to be fairly evenly divided between them. Elections are often close run affairs, therefore, except when one of the parties has been in power for a few years and people have become dissatisfied with its performance, or just bored with it.

This similarity of parties emerges because if one were too radical or too conservative few people would vote for it. This, indeed, is the major flaw of the Westminster system.

[5] *Societal attitudes, S.*

The media tends to support the status quo as a rule, except when opinion polls point strongly to one party or coalition. All too often in history, however, autocratic regimes have restricted free speech, relying on dogma and propaganda to keep the people satisfied.

In recent decades increasingly expensive election campaigns have been fought in some Western countries, particularly the USA, and sometimes governments have been seen to be guilty of misappropriating public funds for publicity purposes that might enhance their election prospects.

Chapter 21

THE WORLD WARS

War is nothing but a continuation of politics
with the admixture of other means.
Karl Marie von Clausewitz, *On War* (1883).

War is one of the constants of history,
and has not diminished with civilization or democracy.
Will Durant, *The Lessons of History*
(co-written with Ariel Durant, 1968).

Introduction

Until 1914, in man's long and seemingly endless history of warfare, wars were usually 'one step at a time' affairs in which a group or nation fought only one other group. When empires were being built, of course, there would be a prolonged sequence of successive conflicts as each new territory was added to the empire.

Sometimes, of course, two parties would enjoin to tackle another, but generally that was as complex as wars needed to be.

World War 1 changed all that and two groups of nations spanning most of the globe became involved in what was later called 'The Great War.'

Then came World War 2 which exceeded it in ferocity and resulted in massive loss of human life. It ended with the use of nuclear bombing of two Japanese cities and we can only hope, therefore, that there will never be a third world war involving large scale usage of nuclear weapons.

World War 1

The 'Great War' was sparked by the assassination of Archduke Ferdinand and his wife by a Serbian nationalist at Sarajevo in Bosnia on 28th June 1914. Encouraged by Germany, Austria declared war on Serbia on the 28th of July. Russia mobilized in support of Serbia (28-30 July) and Germany declared war on Russia on August 1st.

Germany invaded Belgium on the 4th of August, bringing Britain into the war to support the French. Under the terms of an agreement with Britain (1902, 1911) Japan joined the Allies, Italy following in May 1915.

Turkey allied with Germany in November 1914, Bulgaria also doing so in October 1915.

The French army prevented the Germans from invading France via Belgium and then, with the help of the British, prevented them from reaching the Channel ports.

The Central Powers occupied Russian Poland and most of Lithuania. They then overcame strong resistance to take control of Serbia, Albania and Romania.

In April 1915 the Allies began the Gallipoli Campaign aimed at re-supplying Russia and defeating Turkey but it ended in failure. They also fought Turkey in Mesopotamia and a campaign in Macedonia lasted three years.

In 1916 the Germans attacked France but they were held back by the Battle of Verdun (Feb. – July) which was one of the bloodiest of the war. The Allies began the first battle of the Somme (July – Nov.), causing the Germans to abandon the Verdun offensive on July 16th.

In January 1917 the Germans began unrestricted submarine warfare to stop shipments of arms to Britain from the USA. That same month Germany's Foreign Secretary, Arthur Zimmerman, sent a telegram to the German minister in Mexico containing the terms of an alliance between Mexico and Germany by which Mexico was to attack the USA with German assistance in return for the US states of New Mexico, Texas and Arizona.

The 'Zimmerman telegram' and US shipping losses motivated the USA to declare war on Germany on 6th April.

The British began the Battle of Cambrai (Nov. 20 – Dec. 3) with 400 tanks, an unprecedented number, but the battle ended in stalemate.

In March 1917 the Russian Revolution began and on December 15th Russia signed an armistice with Germany.

In the spring of 1918 the Germans launched a major attack in the west which was ultimately repelled after several months of success, thanks to rapidly increasing numbers of US troops taking part. The German army was in full retreat by September.

After military losses in Palestine and Mesopotamia, Turkey agreed to an armistice on 31st October 1918.

Italian victories and advancing French and British forces ended the resistance of Bulgaria and Austria-Hungary.

When an armistice with Germany was signed in November the Allies had recaptured western Belgium and nearly all of France.

At its end The Great War had cost the lives of 8.5 million troops whilst 10 million civilians were killed or wounded. Troop casualty rates (killed and wounded) were very high, circa 75% for Russia and France, 90% for Austria and Hungary, and 65% for Germany.

World War 2

In the late 1930s Germany sought approval from Britain for its expansionist ideas. This was not forthcoming and Germany invaded Bohemia-Moravia in March 1939.

Britain, France and Russia responded by forming a pact promising mutual assistance against Germany.

To open Germany's path to Poland the German and Soviet foreign ministers signed the Hitler-Stalin pact on 23rd August 1939. This renounced the use of force against each other, promised extensive economic cooperation, and effectively partitioned Eastern Europe between them.

Germany invaded Poland on 1ˢᵗ September, overrunning it in four weeks, prompting Britain and France to declare war on 3ʳᵈ September.

Six months of relative peace followed until Germany occupied Norway and Denmark in April 1940. Belgium and Holland were invaded on 10ᵗʰ May and invasion of France immediately followed. Holland surrendered in 4 days, Belgium in 3 weeks, and France in 7 weeks.

Having declared alliance with Germany in 1936, Italy declared war on Britain and France in June 1940.

In the Battle of Britain Germany failed to achieve supremacy over England in the air. Germany then began U-boat attacks against British supply routes.

In April 1941 Germany invaded Yugoslavia, then moving on to invade Greece.

British efforts were concentrated against Italy in the Mediterranean and North Africa.

Rommel was sent to reinforce the Italians in Africa and a fierce campaign continued for three years until the Allies were finally victorious in mid-1943.

Allied forces then invaded Sicily and Italy, forcing Italy to make peace on 3ʳᵈ September 1943.

In June 1941 Germany broke the Hitler-Stalin pact and invaded Russia on a 2,000 mile front, German armies advancing rapidly on three fronts to the outskirts of Leningrad in the north, towards Moscow in the centre, and to the Volga River in the south.

Increasing Soviet resistance and heavy winter snows halted the German advance and from November 1942 they were in retreat, suffering defeats at Stalingrad (winter 1942-43) and Kursk (May 1943).

Leningrad remained under siege for almost 2.5 years (until Jan. 1944), about half its population dying from starvation and disease, but the Germans were finally driven out of the USSR in August 1944.

In June 1944 the Allies launched a second front against Germany by invading Normandy and then liberating Paris on the 25th of August. The Allies advanced into Germany in February 1945, linking with the Russians at the River Elbe on the 28th of April. Germany finally surrendered on the 7th of May 1945.

On the 7th of December 1941 Japan attacked Pearl Harbour and other US and British bases, the USA declaring war the next day. Germany and Italy declared war on the USA on the 11th December. After four months Japan controlled South-East Asia and Burma.

In June 1942 Allied naval victories in the Pacific stopped the Japanese advance. Bitter fighting continued until 1945 when the USA dropped atomic bombs on Hiroshima (6th August) and Nagasaki (9th August), forcing Japan to surrender on the 14th of August.

The human cost of the war was enormous. The Allied military and civilian losses were 44 million and those of the Axis, 11 million. Military deaths on both sides were 19 million in Europe and 6 million in the war against Japan.

The highest numbers of deaths, military and civilian, were: USSR 13M/7M; China 3M/10M; Germany 3.5M/3.8M; Poland 120k/5.3M; Japan 1.7M/380k; Yugoslavia 300k/1.3M; Romania 200k/465k; France 250k/360k; British Empire & Commonwealth 452k/60k; Italy 330k/80k; Hungary 120k/280k; and Czechoslovakia 10k/ 330k. The US had 292k battle deaths and 115k deaths from other causes but had no significant civilian losses.

The foregoing numbers may not include all of the estimated 6 million Jews murdered in German extermination and labour camps.

Spies and military intelligence

Nations have had military spies and information or intelligence gatherers since Roman times, if not before. The 'spook' business is not as glamorous as in the movies and can be sordid and messy (Doyle, 2000).

Referred to earlier, in WW1 the 'Zimmerman letter' was intercepted by allied military intelligence and influenced the USA's decision to enter the war.

Before WW2 an English peer is believed to have given Japan information on aircraft carrier design, the defences of Singapore, and intelligence which may have helped plan the attack on Pearl Harbour.

The 'Cambridge four' of Philby, Blunt, Maclean and Burgess was recruited by the KGB in the early 1930s. No doubt they helped Stalin win World War 2 hands down (Philby et al., 2000).

Stalin was also helped by a group of Soviet Jews code-named MAX which fed the Germans the lie that, around the time of the battle of Stalingrad, the Russians were weakening. Nothing could be further from the truth and the Russians dropped powdered Tularemia bacillus on the unsuspecting Panzer divisions in Stalingrad, an act that may have been the turning point in the war (Alibek, 1999).

One of the greatest intelligence blunders of all time was the FBI in the USA ignoring several intercepted signals during 1941 that suggested the Japanese might attack Pearl Harbour (Hughes-Wilson, 1999).

Still recovering from the Great Depression which nearly destroyed the Union, the USA had no 'overseas' intelligence organization at that time.

At the end of WW2 Philby's information emboldened Stalin prior to the crucial Yalta conference. After WW2 he also helped thwart a number of covert CIA-MI6 Cold War operations against the USSR, for example that in Albania in 1949.

Assessments

The components of the equation $A^{**} = A + B + C + D + S$ (Equation 10.2) have much relevance to the two World Wars:

[1] *Initial attitude, A.*

Before World War I a number of nations including Germany, Russia and Austria-Hungary had increasingly aggressive foreign policies (Chambers, 1993).

Before World War II Hitler's plans for expansion into Europe were hatching, grievances remained from Japan's history of struggle against China, and there was a conflict of interests in the Pacific between Japan and the USA.

[2] *Behaviour, B.*

Hitler's celebrated 'night of the long knives' foreshadowed what was to come, perhaps, his ruthless ambition being the cause of World War II. His extermination of 6 million Jews was convincing proof that he was severely psychotic.

That Hitler was a bit cranky was witnessed on one occasion by the famous pioneer of thoracic surgery Ferdinand Saerbruch. He had been summoned by Hitler so that he could be sent to attend to the Turkish Minister for Foreign Affairs who was seriously ill (Sauerbruch, 1953).

Having earlier been warned about Hitler's temper, Sauerbruch was taken to a large room to wait for Hitler who arrived preceded by an enormous dog which bounded towards Sauerbruch. Used to dogs, Sauerbruch stood stock still and spoke soothingly to the dog.

Because of the dog's lack of aggression Hitler threw a tantrum which lasted several minutes. He raved that how could he win when those supposed to protect him behaved like this. Hitler threatened to have Sauerbruch arrested but Sauerbruch, as he had done with the dog, managed to calm Hitler down.

[3] *Contact history, C.*

The assassination of two people was a poor excuse for starting what became WW1 when, of course, the Serbian nationalist movement should have been dealt with directly by the Austro-Hungarian government, perhaps by negotiations in the first instance. Once war had been declared on Serbia, however, Germany seemed all too keen to join in and this was what led to a world war.

The history of the preceding century also set the scene for the war, involving as it did increasing political and economic rivalry and the establishment of increasing large military forces.

[4] *Differences, D.*

Hitler had a manic belief in the superiority of the Aryan races, whereas the Jews were defiled, and this was a major reason for his insane belief that Germany should dominate Europe, if not the world.

[5] *Societal attitudes, S.*

Hitler had a well-oiled propaganda machine led by Joseph Goebbels, head of the Ministry of Public Enlightenment and Propaganda, and German public followed blindly, if not enthusiastically:

The broad mass of a nation . . . will more easily fall victim to a big lie than a small one.
Adolph Hitler, *Mein Kampf* (1933), ch. 10.

Conclusion

The bottom line on both world wars and most others is:

All wars are planned by old men in council rooms apart.
Grantland Rice, *Two Sides of War* (1955).

Besides Hitler, there have been countless other despotic leaders throughout history, to the point at which one is reminded not only that 'power corrupts', but also that those who crave power the most are likely to be psychopaths.

Chapter 22

TERRORISM

Fighting terrorism is like being a goalkeeper.
You can make a hundred brilliant saves but the only shot
that people remember is the one that gets past you.
Paul Wilkinson (b. 1937),
British scholar and author on terrorism.
Daily Telegraph, London, 1 Sept. 1992.

A brief history of terrorism

Terrorism has a long history, for example:

➤ Secret societies in some ancient tribal cultures sometimes maintained their status through terror.

➤ A Shiite Muslim sect carried out terrorist campaigns against Sunni Muslims in the 12th century.

➤ In the 19th century the aftermath of the French Revolution saw occasional outbreaks of terrorist activity in support of revolution, culminating in the successful Russian Revolution of 1917.

➤ In the 20th century organizations in several countries including Croatia, Ireland, Macedonia, and Palestine often carried out terrorist activities in other countries. Sometimes these were government supported, as in the assassination of Archduke Francis Ferdinand of Austria in Sarajevo in 1914 which sparked World War I.

Northern Ireland

There has been conflict between Catholics and Protestants in Northern Ireland for centuries. The roots of the problem go back to the province of Ulster where the Roman Catholic earls of Tyrone rebelled against English rule circa 1600. They were forced to flee and most of the land was confiscated by King James I who gave it to Protestant Scotch, Welsh and English settlers.

Ulster was further colonized by Cromwell in the mid-17th century and in the early 20th century its opposition to Irish Home Rule led to the formation of Northern Ireland.

Since then there has often been conflict between Catholics and Protestants, this reaching a peak in the 1960s and 1970s when the Irish Republican Army (IRA) used terror tactics against Ulster Protestants and British military forces which resulted in 3000 people being killed before the 1994 cease-fire. Sinn Fein, the political branch of the IRA, was founded in 1902 and dominated the 1918 election. Its power diminished after 1926 but it participated in the peace talks on Northern Ireland in the 1980s and 1990s.

The Rev. Ian Paisley became the extreme voice of Protestant opinion in the sectarian strife of Northern Ireland, leading many demonstrations and repeatedly being imprisoned for unlawful assembly. He was elected to the House of Commons in 1970, was cofounder of the Democratic Unionist Party in 1971, and also organized the Third Force, a paramilitary group of Protestant fighters.

South Africa and the ANC

Nelson Mandela was one of the founders of the African National Congress which campaigned for democracy and thus equality for the black people of South Africa during the 1950s. Eventually the ANC abandoned its policy of non-violence and established a military wing with Mandela being made its leader in December 1961. He was arrested in August 1962 and imprisoned.

South Africa had a large biochemical warfare (BW) research program at that time, building up an arsenal of anthrax, botulinum, Ebola, Marburg and HIV virus. In fact, certain people in South Africa testified that many people in the antiapartheid movement were poisoned using BW material.

Latin America

Latin America has a long-standing tradition of political violence. So-called urban guerrilla movements were a new development, as terrorist activities shifted from country areas to the cities. One such group was Shining Path, a Peruvian Maoist terrorist group which used extremely brutal and indiscriminate tactics to destabilize the government, in turn provoking strong countermeasures.

In Colombia from 1948 to 1956 'La Violencia', a wave of urban and rural violence, cost 200,000 lives.

In the 1990's members of Colombia's cocaine cartel used terrorist tactics to force the government to reduce enforcement of anti-drug-trafficking laws.

During the 1990 election campaign 3 presidential candidates were assassinated. In August 1996 left wing rebels of the Revolutionary Armed Forces of Colombia (FARC) killed 80 soldiers and police in ten separate incidents.

In March 1998 FARC forces ambushed elite government troops in a remote southern jungle region, killing about 70 soldiers in the worst government defeat in the 35 years since guerrilla hostilities began. Government sources estimated that more than 41,000 Colombians, mostly poor farmers, fled their homes to escape the growing violence between guerrillas and paramilitary units.

Japan

In 1995 the religious cult Aum Shinrikyo released deadly sarin nerve gas in the Tokyo subway (Lifton, 1999), killing 12 people and injuring 5,500.

This small group isolated its converts and brainwashed them for long periods and had ambitious plans which included obtaining nuclear weapons (Lifton, 1999).

Socialist revolutionary terrorism

Throughout history people have risen up against oppressive monarchies, governments and occupation by foreign powers. The long-running Third Servile War or Gladiator's revolt led by Spartacus against the Romans just before the time of Christ is a well-known example.

Modern systematic terrorism evolved with the growth of revolutionary ideologies in the wake of the French Revolution, and proponents and opponents of revolutionary values engaged in terrorism after the Napoleonic Wars.

The Russian revolutionary movement before World War I had a strong terrorist element and Leon Trotsky employed terrorism as a principal instrument of policy. The political instability of the 1920s and 1930s which followed the Russian Revolution also included prevalent terrorist activity.

In West Germany the so-called Red Army Faction, better known as the Baader-Meinhof Gang, robbed several banks and raided US military installations. This group frequently cooperated with Palestinian terrorists, notably in the murder of Israeli athletes at the Olympic Games in Munich in 1972.

The Japanese Red Army terrorist group also cooperated with Palestinian terrorists.

The Italian Red Brigades carried out numerous acts of terror, in particular kidnapping and murdering former Prime Minister Aldo Moro in 1978.

To this day socialist terrorism occurs in parts of Africa, Asia, Europe, and South America, for example Maoists using terrorism in Nepal.

Right-wing terrorism

Japan was ruled by the militarist shogun almost continuously from 1192 up to 1867, when pro-imperial terrorism helped restore imperial government in Japan in 1868.

The political instability in some countries in the 1920s and 1930s which followed the Russian Revolution was often accompanied by terrorist activity from both extremes of the political spectrum.

More recently right-wing terrorism in support of authoritarian rule was responsible for the 1980 bombing of the Bologna railway station in Italy. In 1993 the historic Uffizi Gallery in Florence was one of the targets of a series of terrorist bombings attributed to the Mafia.

State sponsored terrorism

After the Russian Revolution the British secret service provided considerable covert support to the White Russian army resisting the revolution. When that failed they began counter terrorist activities against the new Russia, for example Lieutenant Agar's sinking of the Red Fleet cruiser Oleg in Kronstadt harbour in 1919 (Brook-Shepherd, 1998).

Fidel Castro was of such concern to the US that no less than 30 attempts were made on his life during the 1960s.

During the Vietnam War, North Vietnam backed a Communist campaign of terrorism and subversion in South Vietnam.

North Korea has carried out several terrorist attacks against South Korea, including a bombing in Rangoon in 1983 in which 17 people were killed, and the bombing of a Korean Air Lines passenger airliner in 1987 by North Korean agents.

Bombing of the Greenpeace ship Rainbow Warrior in Auckland harbour in 1985 by French secret service agents was also an example of state-supported terror.

Israeli and Palestinian terrorism

Jewish radicals such as the Stern Gang and the Irgun Zvai Leumi resorted to terrorism against Arab communities and other groups during their struggle for an independent Israel in the late 1940s.

The greatest Islamic grievance, of course, is the Israel issue. That much of Palestine was given by the UN to the Jews in 1948 was bad enough, but the territories later occupied by Israel after the 1967 war compounded this grievance greatly. The 1934 *Philips' New World Atlas* shows a country called British Palestine, a British mandate. The 1999 Encarta Encyclopaedia shows the very same area as being Israel. If that is not a cause for considerable grievance it is impossible to imagine what is.

Thus in the 1960s Israel's adversaries began to use terrorism much more systematically. In the 1970s the Black September group, so-named after the expulsion of Palestinian guerrillas from Jordan in September 1970, carried out many attacks.

The Palestine Liberation Organization (PLO) has conducted commando and terrorist operations both within Israel and in other countries right up until the present day. In response Israel have carried out actions against PLO and other targets outside Israel which can be considered as terrorism.

Islamic terrorism

Revolution in Iran in 1978 and the rise of Islamic fundamentalism saw terrorism spread globally thanks to new groups such as Islamic State, some examples being:

➢ In 1988 a bomb destroyed a Pan American Flight over Lockerbie, Scotland, killing all 259 people on board and 11 on the ground. Subsequently two Libyan agents were charged with the crime and one of them convicted.

➢ Fundamentalist terrorism directed against the socialist government of Algeria led to virtual civil war in the 1990s.

➢ Bombing of New York's World Trade Centre in 1993.*
➢ Bombing of US embassies in Kenya and Tanzania in 1998 with the loss of 224 lives.*
➢ Bombing of the USS Cole in 2000.*
➢ Attacks on the US by three hijacked planes on September 11, 2001 which cost almost 3,000 lives.*
➢ A car bomb attack in Bali on a bar popular with Westerners that killed almost 200 people in 2002.
➢ The Nov. 2003 Istanbul truck bomb attacks.*
➢ Chechen rebels took 800 people hostage in a theatre in Moscow. Russian troops gassed the building, resulting in 200 deaths.
➢ The 2004 Khobar massacre.*
➢ Attacks on trains and buses in Spain and England in 2004 and 2005.*
➢ June 2008 car bombing of Danish embassy in Pakistan.*
➢ Sept. 2008 truck bombing of Marriot Hotel in Pakistan.*
➢ The 2009 Khost CIA bombing killed 8 agents.*
➢ 2003-present: many bombings in Iraq.*
➢ 2010-present: Islamic State (IS) conflict in Afghanistan, Iraq and Syria with IS overtaking large regions.
➢ 2010-present: IS suicide bombings etc. around the world.
    * = known or believed to be due to al-Qa'ida.

Besides the globally active al-Qa'ida and Islamic State, there are many other terrorist organizations around the world, most of them Muslim, including:
➢ Gaza and the West Bank: Hamas and the PLO.
➢ Israel: Kahane Chai (Kach).
➢ Lebanon: Hezbollah.
➢ Iraq: QJBR (al-Qa'ida in Iraq).
➢ Afghanistan: the Taliban
➢ Bangladesh: Harkat-ul-Jihad al-Islami (HUJI-B)
➢ Sri Lanka: Liberation Tigers of Tamil Eelam (LTTE).
➢ India: Indian Mujahideen (IM).
➢ Japan: Aum Shinrikyo.
➢ Pakistan: Harakat ul-Mujahadin (HUM).
➢ South-East Asia: al-Jama'a al-Islamiya (JI).

- Uzbekistan: Islamic Jihad Union (IJU).
- Somalia: Al-Shabaab
- Uganda: Lord's Resistance Army.
- UK & Ireland: Continuity IRA (CIRA), Real IRA (RIRA).
- Greece: Revolutionary Organization 11 November.
- Turkey: Revolutionary People's Liberation Party/Front.
- Spain: Euskadi Ta Askatasuna (ETA).
- Colombia: FARC & the National Liberation Army (ELN).
- Peru: Shining Path (SL).

Al-Qa'ida

Osama Bin Laden, of course, had been on the side of the Americans in helping the Taliban fight the occupying Russian forces in Afghanistan in the 1980s (Nojumi, 2002).

In the 1990s, enraged at the presence of US troops in Saudi Arabia during the Persian Gulf War, he and his associates in al-Qa'ida turned their attention to the Americans with the bombing of several US embassies in the Middle East and Africa, culminating in the spectacular plane attacks of September 11, 2001.

An article in *The Australian* newspaper on 3 November 2004 reported that Bin Laden had vowed in one of his regularly released videotapes to send the US broke. He claimed that every dollar spent by al-Qa'ida on terrorist strikes had cost the US $1 million in economic damage. He estimated the US deficit at more than $US 1 trillion.

Al-Qa'ida's attacks often involve simultaneous suicide attacks on neighbouring targets. Its aim is removal of all foreign influences in Muslim countries and creation of a world-wide Islamic caliphate. As Salafist jihadists they oppose man-made laws yet ignore any religious scripture which might forbid the murder of civilians and bloody conflict.

Al-Qa'ida is intolerant of non-Sunnis and regards liberal Muslims as heretics and has carried out numerous sectarian attacks, for example the Sadr City bombings and the April 2007 Baghdad bombings, and such activities continue to this day.

Al-Qa'ida operates through unregulated banks and the 9/11 Commission report estimated that it needed $30M/year for its operations which include military training, finance, operations management, and a media division.

Al-Jama'a al-Islamiya

Established circa 1969, this militant Islamist terrorist organization is dedicated to establishing an Islamic caliphate in Southeast Asia. JI has cells in Thailand, Singapore, Malaysia, the Phillipines, Irian Jaya and Australia, and has connections with al-Qa'ida and the Moro Islamic Liberation Front.

JI was responsible for the 2000 bombing of the Jakarta Stock Exchange, the 2002 Bali bombing, the 2003 JW Marriott hotel bombing in Jakarta, the 2004 Australian embassy bombing in Jakarta, the 2005 Bali bombing, and the 2009 JW Marriott and Ritz-Carlton hotel bombings in Jakarta. JI was also responsible for dozens of bombings in the southern Philippines, usually with the help of the Abu Sayyaf Group (ASG).

Several JI leaders have been captured in the last decade.

The Taliban

This fundamentalist Islamic political movement spread into Afghanistan where it formed government in 1996 but gained diplomatic recognition only from Pakistan, Saudi Arabia and the United Arab Emirates.

The Taliban strictly interpret Sharia law, limiting the rights of women. The top leadership group is the Quetta Shura based since circa 2001 in the city of Quetta in the Balochistan province of Pakistan.

Members of Pakistan's Inter-Services Intelligence (ISI) are believed to have attended meetings of the Quetta Shurah and supported the Taliban.

In 2009 the Pakistani government acknowledged the existence of Quetta Shurah for the first time and since that time several of its members have been detained at various locations in Pakistan.

Islamic State

The Sunni terrorist organization Islamic State (IS), also known as Islamic State in Levant (ISIL), have been the major revolutionary terrorist group in recent years, having overtaken much of Iraq and Syria.

IS has committed countless atrocities, beheading and burning people alive, and making propaganda videos of such actions. Such propaganda has succeeded in recruiting young Muslim men and women globally, the women being used for suicide bombings or as wives and household and sexual slaves.

Despite many Saudi Arabian bombing raids in Syria, and US drone attacks in Iraq and elsewhere, IS continues to capture major cities in Iraq and Syria, causing concern in the West which is likely to ramp up its efforts to curb IS.

The USA - the enemy within

In US there are many sectarian and religious militia groups such as the Klu Klux Klan, Aryan Nation, Posse Comitatus, The Order, The Texas Militia and many others (Dees, 1996; Jones and Israel, 1998; Snow, 1999).

In the southern US, the Ku Klux Klan was formed after the defeat of the Confederacy in the American Civil War to terrorize former slaves and representatives of the Reconstruction administrations imposed by the federal government. It still remains active, but less so then hitherto.

The 1995 Oklahoma City bombing, in which 168 people were killed, was the most spectacular act of terrorism on US soil before the September 11 attacks. The FBI charged Timothy McVeigh and Terry Nichols with the bombing but only McVeigh was convicted.

McVeigh's chief defence counsellor found that McVeigh and Nichols had had contacts with Aryan Nation, a group with neo-Nazi sympathies, and that Nicholls had been to the Philippines several times where he had been in contact with Ramzi Yousef who was responsible for the 1993 bombing of the World Trade Centre, and for the plot to destroy Philippines Airlines Flight 434 in 1994.

Another supposedly lone bomber in the USA was Theodore Kaczynski, known as the Unabomber.

Not only must the US expect further attacks from external organizations like al-Qa'ida, there is also the possibility of attacks organized by one of its militia groups:

> *I suspect Americans will begin engaging in terrorism*
> *on a scale the world has never known.*
> William Pearce, author of *The Turner Diaries* (1978)
> and leader of the National Alliance, a US neo-Nazi group.

Assessments

The components of the equation $A^{**} = A + B + C + D + S$ (Equation 10.2) have much relevance to terrorism:

[1] *Initial attitude, A.*

The term fundamentalism is used to describe conservative trends in various religious denominations, notably Islam, Judaism, and Hinduism.

Fundamentalists oppose governments they consider too liberal, or try to win political office in order to represent fundamentalist views. In Israel, for example, the Likud party has a strong power base amongst Jewish fundamentalists who believe the Jewish scriptures justify Israel's possession of land claimed by the Palestinians.

All too many Muslim fundamentalists, however, hold impractically extreme views not in keeping with the modern technological world.

[2] *Behaviour, B.*

Terrorism is to be abhorred at all times but yet Islamic terrorism continues around the world to the point at which most non-Muslims regard Muslim fundamentalists as primitive, unpleasant, and dangerous, and have little better regard for Muslims in general.

Response to Muslim terrorism, however, has often been ill-conceived. The second invasion of Iraq, for example, did more good than harm and peaceful and patient means of obtaining democratic government in that country should have been used.

[3] *Contact history, C.*

As the many examples of it given earlier in this chapter suggest, terrorism seems to have become commonplace in many parts of the world in the last 50 years or so.

Violence begets violence, and the US-led invasions of Iraq and Afghanistan were to deal with Islamic terrorism at its source by attempting to 'stabilize' those countries.

[4] *Differences, D.*

Fundamentalist and radical leaders are, of course, at pains to differentiate themselves from mainstream society. Those who do not follow their extreme dictates they denigrate, often with long speeches that seem nonsensical to all but their 'disciples' who, all too often, are used to carry out acts of terrorism aimed at eventually empowering the leaders politically by weakening any political opposition.

[5] *Societal attitudes, S.*

In non-Muslin countries, many journalists and politicians have linked Islamic fundamentalism to violence and terrorism. In fact, Islam preaches tolerance, but also requires its followers to protest against what they see as political and moral abuses of their societies. Unfortunately, all too often such protest has been of the violent kind and, most culpable of all, there is all too little complaint from other Muslim leaders or the general Muslim community.

Conclusions

Islamic terrorism remains a major and costly problem in the world today. In the countries from which it originates it is bad for business, especially tourism, of course. Elsewhere it considerably increases government military and police expenditures, also increasing costs in many industries such as the airline industry.

Worldwide there were 11,604 terrorist attacks in 2010, 5% more than the year before. Since then Islamic State (IS) has conducted terrorist activities on an unprecedented scale, particularly in Iraq and Syria.

There are also still hundreds of people active in al-Qa'ida and it still exerts much influence, particularly in Afghanistan, Iraq, Pakistan, and Yemen.

A former leader of the CIA bin Laden team during the 1990s said in 2011 that, far from winning the war against terrorism, the West was losing and did not understand the conflict (article in *The Times* by Tom Coghlan in May 2011).

He concluded: *It is support for Israel, support for the Saudi police state, it's our presence in the Arab peninsula, it's support for the Russians in the Islamic Caucasus. There is no more effective recruiter for al-Qa'ida than the status quo of American foreign policy.*

The first three points are those which Bin Laden made when he openly declared war on the US in 1998.

That there has been no resolution of the 'Palestine question' after so long is shameful and firm UN resolutions are needed to force an ever-intransigent Israel to more equally share the area that was Palestine for most of the last two thousand years and right up to 1948. If Israel chose to ignore such resolutions then the West should withdraw all support for Israel, no matter what the consequences.

Conversely, since Korea was divided in 1945 it has remained a problem and, perhaps, the country should be reunited in some way.

On terrorism, civil war etc., the bottom line on such problems is that they are often caused by the stirrings of a few radical outcastes with nothing better to do, Bin Laden perhaps having been an example. That they sometimes have such influence on the gullible, in turn resulting in enormous loss of life, is tragic and the human race has to wise up to the propaganda and lies it has been fed from pulpits, lecterns, soap boxes, and by the media for millennia.

A recent example of this was the bombing of the 2013 Boston marathon by two young Muslim men who had been influenced by the ravings of radical Muslim clerics, little Hitlers that this world needs to rid itself of as soon as possible. As it is, however, is it likely that the Muslim religion will come to be regarded as somewhat evil for the rest of human history in the same way as the Nazis will be.

At present, however, there seems no end in sight of "World War 3", that is, the continuing spate of Islamic terrorism that afflicts much of the world (Mohr et al., 2015).

Chapter 23

REVOLUTION

Revolution is not a bed of roses,
it is a struggle to death between the future and the past.
Fidel Castro, Second Anniversary of the Cuban Revolution,
Speech in Havana, January 1961.

Introduction

There have been many revolutions in history, one of the earliest being the Gladiator's War or Third Servile War (72 – 71BC) led by Spartacus. One with a comparable cause was the Peasants Revolt of June 1381 in England which was precipitated by oppressive taxes and other grievances.

The English Civil Wars, sometimes referred to as 'The English Revolution' or 'The Puritan Revolution', were summarized in Chapter 20.

In the last century almost all the European colonies around the world have all gained independence, some of these by revolutionary means. Similarly, the so-called Revolution of 1989, which began with demolition of part of the Berlin Wall by civilians in November 1989, freed East Germany from the USSR and began the dismantlement of the USSR.

The American Revolution

A prelude to this was the Boston Massacre of 5th March 1770 when British troops killed five people after firing upon a crowd protesting against British regulations and troop presence.

Another was the Boston Tea Party in 1773 when, as a protest over British taxation, 342 chests of dutied tea were destroyed by workers disguised as Indians. Britain's parliament responded by passing the Intolerable Acts bill in 1774 to punish Massachusetts, leading to the establishment of the First Continental Congress (1774).

In April 1775 fighting broke out between colonial militia, known as the Minutemen, and British troops at the Battles of Lexington and Concord in Massachusetts.

Colonial forces captured Fort Ticonderoga in May 1775 but lost the battle of Bunker Hill.

In June 1775 The Second Continental Congress elected George Washington to command the Continental Army and in July the congress issued the Declaration of Independence.

The British evacuated Boston in May 1776 but defeated Washington's troops in several skirmishes in the New York area.

Washington's surprise attacks at Trenton (25th Dec. 1776) and Princeton (Jan. 1977) were small victories but they gave encouragement to his cause. He won the Battle of Saratoga in upstate New York in June 1977, this battle convincing the French to join his cause, bringing much needed financial and military support, including a fleet.

In September 1777 the British won the Battle of Brandywine in Pennsylvania. In 1778 British forces invaded South Carolina and moved north but were forced to surrender to the colonial and French forces in Virginia in 1781. After two years of negotiation the Treaty of Paris was signed in September 1783.

The French Revolution

Causes included a large underfed population, loss of support for the feudal system, an expanding bourgeoisie excluded from political power, and a fiscal crisis deepened by participation in the American Revolution.

The revolution began with the storming of the Bastille on July 14th 1789, resulting in a reformation of the government and wide-ranging political, social and economic measures, including the abolition of feudal, aristocratic, and clerical privileges, and confiscation of Church property to pay off public debt.

The Constitution of 1791 established a short-lived constitutional government and the king tried to flee the country but was apprehended at Varennes.

In April 1792, unjustified fears of invasion by Austria having been raised, France declared war on Austria and Prussia, beginning the French Revolutionary Wars. A succession of defeats of the French army followed.

After an insurrection on August 10th 1792 France was declared a republic. The following month the September Massacres occurred when rioting crowds in Paris, panicked by advancing armies, broke into prisons and massacred thousands of people.

Louis XVI and his queen were executed in January 1793. Then the ruling party, the republican Girondins, was overthrown by the radical Jacobins led by Robespierre, beginning the dictatorial Reign of Terror.

Robespierre was executed in 1794 and, with military force used to suppress opposition, the government of the Directory was formed in 1795. This was overthrown by Napoleon Bonaparte in the Brumaire Coup in 1799, leading to the First Empire (1804 – 1815) which spread the Revolution's ideas of 'Liberty, Equality, Fraternity' and popular sovereignty.

The Fenian movement

The Fenian movement began in 1858 and was named after the Fianna, a legendary band of Irish warriors in the 2nd and 3rd centuries. The movement was a secret oath-bound society which planned a revolution to achieve independence for Ireland.

The movement grew in Ireland as the Irish Republican Brotherhood, and amongst Irish Nationalists in the United States as Fenian Brotherhood.

The Fenian movement also had branches in England, the British dominions, and several other countries.

The US branch smuggled money and arms to the Irish branch, though informers caused much of this to be intercepted, and many of the Fenian leaders in Ireland were arrested.

Hoping to pressure England into granting Ireland independence, the US Fenians attempted to invade Canada in 1866, most of the invasion force being stopped by US authorities, but a small force did cross the border near Buffalo in June, but was repelled by Canadian volunteers and forced to surrender to an American gunboat in the Niagara River. The Fenians made two other failed attempts to invade Canada in 1870 and 1871.

In 1866 and 1867 the Fenians attacked police stations in Ireland, and set off bombs in England, but the rebellion was put down and hundreds of suspected rebels were imprisoned.

The Fenians ceased to exist circa 1885 but their ideals were adopted by Sinn Fein in the early 20th century.

The Russian Revolutions

The Revolution of 1905 was a series of nationwide strikes, demonstrations and mutinies. 'Bloody Sunday' (9th Jan.), a massacre of demonstrating workers by soldiers, heightened the tensions and Tsar Nicholas II was forced to legalize political parties and allow elections.

In the Bolshevik-led October Revolution of 1917 armed workers (Red Guards) arrested members of the Provisional Government and they were replaced by the Soviet of People's Commissars, chaired by Lenin who had exploited the crisis situation in Russia resulting from war with Germany to foment revolution.

The Russian Civil War (1918 – 1922) followed in which Anti-Bolshevik forces (Whites) were supported by Britain, France, the USA, and Japan. The Red Army eventually prevailed and, though Poland, Finland and the Baltic states were given independence, Armenia, the Ukraine and Georgia remained under Soviet control.

The Revolution of 1918

In the wake of defeat in WW1 Germany's monarchy fell because of growing social disorder. On November 9th the leader of the Social Democratic Party of Germany (SPD) formed a socialist government which met in Weimar on 19th January 1919 to draft a constitution.

The SPD had relied upon monarchist and right-radical military forces to restrain the radical left, however, restricting major socio-economic and administrative changes, some feel opening the way for the subsequent rise of the Nazi Party which had been formed in 1919.

The Chinese Revolution

This broke out on October 10th 1911 in central China when an anti-monarchist army unit mutinied. Dissent spread and by the start of 1912 delegates from 16 provinces had elected a provisional president of a Chinese republic. Fearing foreign intervention to protect their economic interests, he offered the presidency to the commander of the royal army who became President of a unified republic after the abdication of the young emperor.

The revolution, however, brought little social change.

The Chinese Civil War

Immediately after Japan surrendered in August 1945 communist challenges for supremacy of China re-emerged. The US brokered a treaty on 14th January 1946 but soon hostilities resumed, by July 1946 stopping US supplies to the nationalist forces.

The still better equipped nationalist forces took the communist capital, Yan'an, on 19th March 1947. Gradually the communists moved from rural-based guerrilla campaigns to full-scale battles, recapturing the city a year later.

In a decisive series of battles in late 1948 and early 1949 the nationalist forces lost 500,000 men. The communists then captured Beijing and Tianjin (Jan.), Nanjing (April), and Shanghai and Canton (Oct.).

The People's Republic of China was formally proclaimed by Mao Zedong on 1st October 1949, the nationalists withdrawing to Taiwan on the 7th of December.

The Cuban Revolution

Cuba revolted against Spanish rule in the Ten Years' War (1868-78), and again in 1895. The US took control after the Spanish-American Wars of 1898, when the entire Spanish fleet was destroyed near the seaport of Santiago de Cuba, but granted Cuba independence in 1902.

The US invested heavily in the sugar, tourism and gambling industries until circa 1950 but inequalities in the distribution of wealth festered popular discontent.

Fidel Castro was the son of a prosperous sugar planter. He became a lawyer, worked on behalf of Havana's poor, and was a candidate for Cuba's legislature when General Fulgencio Batista overthrew the government in 1952.

Castro led a failed rebellion against Batista in 1953 and was captured and sent to prison. He then went to Mexico where, with Che Guevara and others, he continued plans to overthrow Batista.

Castro led an armed expedition back to Cuba in 1956 where most of his men were killed, a dozen survivors hiding in the mountains from where they organized guerrilla groups throughout the island.

On January 1st 1959 Batista fled the country and Castro nationalized commerce and industry and expropriated US-owned land and businesses.

Under Castro all opposition was ruthlessly suppressed but health services and literacy were greatly increased.

The US made many attempts to assassinate him and the failed Bay of Pigs invasion led to the Cuban Missile Crisis which raised the threat of imminent nuclear war between the US and Russia.

For three decades Cuba received considerable economic support from the USSR, in return sending troops to prop up Soviet client states in Angola and Ethiopia.

With the disintegration of the USSR circa 1990, Cuba's economy suffered considerably, resulting in relaxation of controls over business activity.

Assessments

The components of the equation $A^{**} = A + B + C + D + S$ (Equation 10.2) have much relevance to revolution:

[1] *Initial attitude, A.*
Revolutions may result when governments are seen to be incompetent, corrupt and oppressive. They have a 'democratic' basis and are more likely to succeed when the majority of the people are in support of it.

[2] *Behaviour, B.*
Civil unrest initially exhibits itself as protest marches and demonstrations outside government buildings.

When such demonstrations are disallowed, or when people are killed by police or troops during such protests, an escalating cycle of violence often results.

[3] *Contact history, C.*

When, over a number of years, civil discontent grows and governments are seen to refuse to meet civil demands, if not suppress them, perhaps with violence, then a growing number of people become increasingly frustrated.

When the 'contact history' becomes too negative tensions and pressures in society may reach a breaking point and revolution ensues.

[4] *Differences, D.*

Most revolutions have been the result of excessive differences in society, with a favoured few being seen to get richer and richer while most of the population suffers increasing levels of poverty.

[5] *Societal attitudes, S.*

It is particularly when oppressive regimes are seen to take an unsympathetic attitude to the complaints of the people that the peoples' attitude towards those regimes worsens and their resolve to replace them increases.

All that is needed is for a small group of revolutionary leaders to emerge who, with promises of improvement, persuasively seek supporters and organize protests which are sufficiently alarming to the authorities to consider reforming the government and allowing free elections that may result in some of the changes the populace desires.

Conclusions

Revolutions usually occur in times of economic difficulty which, of course, most affect common working people. When large numbers of them lose their jobs, of course, that can only make revolution still more likely.

Then dissident groups will quickly proliferate and grow if persuasive activists with an attractive message and goal lead the 'cause'. Marxism, for example, was a goal that inspired a number of revolutions in the 20th century.

PART 4: CONCLUSIONS

Chapter 24

THE ATTITUDINAL MODEL OF CONFLICT

*. . .there were no more than twenty-six days ... in which there was
no war somewhere in the world ... on any given day ... there is an
average of twelve wars going on somewhere in the world.*
Anthony Sampson, *The Arms Bazaar* (1978),
referring to the results of a study of the years 1945 - 1978.

Hate has no medicine.
African (Ovambo) proverb.

Introduction

The Atlas of 20th Century History (Natkeil, 1982) is almost
entirely about human conflict, suggesting that for humans
conflict is something of a habit, as it is for many other animal
species.

Today we only have to turn on the TV and, of course,
most of the news of the world is bad news: bad economic
news here and there, wars in a few other places, locally
perhaps a drought or bush fire, and so forth. The sports
segment gives little relief from my point of view, showing as
it does highly competitive people fighting over a ball.

The good news? That should perhaps be a short segment
of a couple of minutes like the weather, at best perhaps
some new medical discovery that might save lives.

This would remind us that, whilst wars, famines,
widespread poverty and other disasters are the norm, the
exceptional positive outcome, for example the (accidental)
discovery of penicillin is the exception. Some of the reasons
why this is so are discussed later in this chapter.

Causes of conflict

The thirteen chapters of Part 3 discussed a wide range of areas of human conflict. The major causative factors of conflict in each of these areas may be summarized as follows (chapter numbers in parentheses):

The War of the Sexes (11): the traditional 'male-breadwinner' role was exploited by feminist activists as inequality and injustice. The result: 50% divorce rates in the West.

Bullying in schools and the workplace (12, 13) and urban crime (14): in part a result of societal conditions, these may also be related to alpha male behaviour which is discussed later in this chapter.

Tribal and territorial conflict (15): this relates to man's 'natural' way of living in family groups within some well-defined community and area.

Imperialism and World Wars (16, 21): usually caused by ambitious leadership, as discussed later in this chapter. Here propaganda is important, as also discussed later in this chapter.

Religion (17): here relatively 'artificial' differences are a major factor that often leads to bitter conflict. Again propaganda is important.

Ethnicity (18): here both genetic and cultural differences set people apart and conflicting territorial claims may also be a factor.

Conflicting Societal Groups (19): groups differentiate themselves in some way, sometimes causing conflict.

Political (20): 'hard times' and social injustices are often the cause of conflicts over governance.

Terrorism (22): small, hidden, factions claiming major grievances resort to this.

Revolution (23): here a major proportion of the population protests wrongs in society, perhaps resulting in conflict.

Assessments

If the simple attitudinal analysis of Tables 10.1 and 10.2 is undertaken for each of the areas of human conflict in Part 3 of this book, totals for a hypothetical person for each of the five sections might be as shown in Table 24.1.

Table 24.1. Totals for the equation: $A^{**} = A + B + C + D + S$
A =initial attitude, B =behaviour, C =contact, D =differences, S =societal attitudes. Max/min for A, B, C, D, S = 10/-10.

Conflict type	A	B	C	D	S	A**
Gender	0	+4	-2	-8	-2	-8
School bullying	-2	-2	-1	-3	0	--8
Work bullying	-2	-2	-2	-5	0	-11
Tribal/territorial	-4	-3	-3	-2	-4	-16
Imperial	-6	-6	-5	-6	-5	-28
Religious	-4	-2	-4	-6	-6	-22
Ethnic	-4	-4	-4	-6	-4	-22
Societal groups	-2	-2	-3	-5	-2	-14
Political	-3	-1	-1	-4	-6	-15
World War	-6	-8	-8	-4	-8	-34
Terrorism	-5	-6	-6	-5	-6	-28
Revolution	-5	-6	-3	-4	-4	-22

Total scores A^{**} for gender conflict, and school and workplace bullying, are from -8 to -11 or 'mildly negative' scores because conflict in these areas is on a minor scale.

Scores for tribal/territorial, political, and societal groups range from -14 to -16, or 'medium negative' scores.

Scores for imperial, religious, ethnic, terrorist, and revolutionary conflict range from -22 to -28, or 'high negative' scores, reflecting the severity of conflict often involved in these areas.

Finally, the score for world war is -34 because of the escalation of the level of conflict that occurred in the two world wars of the last century.

Psychopathic leaders

Table 24.2 shows Cattell's personality factor scales, the letters being named, like vitamins, in the order in which he became convinced of their existence. Where a letter is missing, for example D, this is because the factor in question was eventually found to be unimportant. There are four 'Q' factors because these were thought to be factors often found in self-report questionnaires (Larsen & Buss, 2002).

Table 24.2. The 16 Personality factor scales.

	Factor	Trait
1	A	Interpersonal warmth: easy to get along with
2	B	Intelligence: information processing efficiency
3	C	Emotional stability: tolerates stress well
4	E	Dominance: assertive, aggressive etc.
5	F	Impulsivity: doing without much aforethought
6	G	Conformity: follows group standards
7	H	Boldness: adventurous, not shy
8	I	Sensitivity: artistic, insecure
9	L	Suspiciousness: critical, irritable, paranoid
10	M	Imagination: creative, a thinker
11	N	Shrewdness: thinks things through first
12	O	Insecurity: worrier, moody
13	Q1	Radicalism: against tradition, likes the new
14	Q2	Self-sufficiency: loners, like working alone
15	Q3	Self-discipline: controlled, organized
16	Q4	Tension: anxious, frustrated, hard to calm

Factors A, B, C, M, N and Q3 are the factors that we should like our leaders to have.

History is long, however, whereas leaders come and go, often quickly in the case of elected leaders, Italy being perhaps the best example over the last 50 years, having had 50 leaders in that time.

All too often, therefore, our leaders exhibit factors E, F, H, and L, and perhaps could be likened to the psychopathically competitive, dominant, and hostile alpha males in the animal kingdom. This, of course, corresponds to type A personality syndrome, a cluster of traits including ambition, impatience, competitiveness, and hostility (Larsen & Buss, 2002).

Such people are more likely to have been bullies in the classroom, also being somewhere near the bottom of the class, the 'nerds' at the top being those they might have bullied and also those more likely to make an important scientific breakthrough later in life.

The Gaussian distribution of intelligence spreads wider for men than for women (Mohr, 2012c, 2018), those at the lower IQ end often being the criminals in society when they grow up, here criminal including lying and war-mongering leaders.

Then, as discussed in Chapter 9, hierarchical organizations empower those who rise up in them and then, as all history shows, 'power corrupts'. Indeed, it seems that something comparable to the behavioural changes of Transactional Analysis (TA) occurs (Campos & McCormick, 1974).

In TA it is postulated that we can switch, according to circumstances, from behaving in child, adult and parent modes. When someone is made boss they change into 'boss' mode, comparable to TA's parent mode, whilst the lowliest workers or slaves must remain in child mode, at least while they are at work. When they get home perhaps they can switch to parent or 'boss' mode if they have children.

Thus, those who rise high in hierarchies are, of course, ambitious and competitive, but hostility may only be added to their behaviour when they become leader. Then they are able to delegate the dirty deeds of conflict and war when it is never they who are said to be at war, but the royal 'we are at war', really meaning the slaves in the army who do the actual fighting.

Thus, as US sportswriter Grantland Rice summed it up so well: *All wars are planned by old men in council chambers far apart.*

As this statement suggests, however, it would be a better outcome if the leaders engaged directly in conflict, whether in a council chamber or duelling at a rifle range where they could each play the role of target at opposite ends of the range.

Propaganda and 'brainwashing'

As discussed in Chapter 5, modern advertising can rightly be regarded as 'brainwashing', no doubt why it is used increasingly and at great expense in electoral campaigning in modern Western democracies.

Thus, whether the subject is what soft drink to consume, what God to believe in, who to vote for, or who is the enemy we should fight, we are preached to from 'on high' with a hail of one-way bullshit that slowly convinces us one by one what to do.

The reception-yielding model of Figure 6.2 is important here, of course, for those most easily persuaded in turn influence others to imitate them, this being 'social learning', this being how so many young children still take up smoking, and how so many young men in the West end up drinking beer. Why? Because, as the quotation that opens Chapter 5 suggests, big business wants their money. It is a form of psychological robbery really, not the old-fashioned 'your money or your life' of stagecoach robbers, but 'your money for life' because you become a lifelong consumer.

In the case of human conflict the three step 'CAB' process of persuasion shown in Fig 6.1 is involved twice, firstly to persuade people to adopt a particular cause, religion or side of a 'political fence', secondly to persuade them to give money to and, if necessary, fight for that cause. Unfortunately, throughout history leaders have all too often been able to both convert people to their cause and convince them to fight for it.

Social inequity and prejudice

Social inequity has, of course, often been a cause of human conflict, for centuries Europe's feudal system requiring vassals to fight for their lords whenever required.

In modern times things have not changed much and now rampant Capitalism ensures that about a third of the world's population remains undernourished. In the most affluent countries it allows the highest paid executives to earn up to a thousand times as much as the lowest paid worker who actually produces something tangible, that is a saleable product. Thus the richest 1% of the population control up to 70% of the wealth, no real advance whatsoever from feudal times. Still the young from poorer backgrounds are those more likely to join the armed services, perhaps simply to get a roof over their heads, and certainly this is very much the case in the poorest countries such as most of those in Africa.

It is economic injustice and inequality that has been at the root of many a revolution in history and such injustice is perpetuated by absurd modern 'econobabble' such as the 'trickle-down effect' being used to justify decreasing taxes for the richest people (Wheen, 2004).

Similarly, ethnic prejudice and thence socioeconomic inequity has also been the root cause of many conflicts in human history.

The attitudinal model of conflict

The contact hypothesis says that, under the right conditions, inter-group contact reduces conflict, and was discussed in some detail in Chapter 8, and Forbes' 'three-value' model of ethnic conflict was also discussed (Equations 8.1; Forbes, 1977). In Chapter 10 a broader 'five-value' attitudinal model of conflict was given:

$$A^{**} = A^* + f S = A + x B + y C + z D + f S \qquad (24.1)$$

where A = initial attitude, A^* and A^{**} = 'overall' attitude
B = attitudes towards behaviours of the second party,
C = contact history between the two parties,
D = degree of difference between the parties considered
[note that positive values of D = similarity],
S = view of society's attitudes towards the second party
[a contribution comparable to the subjective norm SN of Equation 7.2.],
and f, x, y, z are scaling coefficients that indicate the relative importance of the terms.

To complete the model a simplification of Equations 8.2 and 8.3 can be used to include the effect of contact upon group differences:

$$C^* = C + d D, \text{ where } d = \text{scaling factor} \qquad (24.2)$$

$$D^* = D + c C, \text{ where } c = \text{scaling factor} \qquad (24.3)$$

so that 'positive differences' (i.e. similarities) increase positive contact, and positive contact increases 'positive differences' (i.e. similarities), the positive and negative scoring used here (e.g. see Table 10.1) being similar to that used for the 'five-factor' model of personality (Larsen & Buss, 2002).

Note that Equations 24.2 and 24.3 involve a 'positive feedback loop' and this is discussed further in Chapter 28.

Like the information integration model of attitude formation discussed in Chapter 7, the attitudinal model of conflict also has an 'initial attitude' component A. As noted in connection with Table 10.1, weighting factors can also be associated with the some of the items used in evaluating the components A, B, C, D and S of the attitudinal model of conflict.

It is assumed that the attitudinal model applies to typical members of groups and that conditions such as equal status contact are necessary for positive outcomes (see the 1st section of Chapter 8). The same can be said of conferences between group leaders. In times of conflict, however, such meetings do not usually occur and, indeed, the important decisions of starting a war are usually made secretively, exactly why 'secret services' are needed.

Attitudes regarding responses to hostile actions of a group may be measured as in Table 10.3 and the results will, of course, depend on the general attitude towards the group given by Equation 24.1.

The responses considered in Table 10.3 are 'negative' ones. Negotiation and conciliatory measures should always be considered as a first priority, however, and an example of assessment of attitudes toward these is given in Table 28.1.

The economics of conflict

Casselli and Coleman (2012) propose an economic model of ethnic conflict that applies, to some extent at least, to the motivations for imperialism and empire building. They propose that, for two groups A and B with populations N_A and N_B, if there is a common resource of value T\$ then the per capita value of that resource is the same for both groups, that is:

$$A\$ = B\$ = T\$/(N_A + N_B) \tag{24.4}$$

If, however, group A resorts to costly conflict to take over the resource the per capita value resulting (for group A) is:

$$A\$ = (T\$ - C\$)/N_A \tag{24.5}$$

where C\$ is the cost of the conflict.

This model applies better to empire building where historically powerful occupying forces take over local resources entirely at relatively little cost, and sometimes with minimal conflict.

Wars of any scale, however, are very expensive and, furthermore, are often fought over ethnic/religious or political grounds when there is no financial gain T\$.

Any crude model involving an equation or two, however, does serve to clearly bring to attention the costs of conflict and, perhaps, suggest better alternatives than short-sighted greed and conflict.

Great Britain, for example, had a large empire at the start of the 19th century but the average working man in England is now probably worse off as a result. During the days of empire huge costs were incurred keeping foreign forces and administrations in place with little return but for endless animalistic chest beating about the greatness of the empire. Had the costs of empire been wisely invested and not frittered away, however, England would not be the economic ruin that it is now.

Conclusions

In his book on eugenics David Galton noted (Galton, 2001):

> *It has been said that the history of society is a record of*
> *the struggle of poverty against wealth (de Tocqueville);*
> *others have seen it as a struggle*
> *of liberty against despotism (Schiller),*
> *or of the proletariat against the capitalist class (Marx).*

Divisive factors such as ethnicity (including race) and religion have also played a part, of course, and thus the simple 'attitude/behaviour/contact/differences' model of Equations 24.1 – 24.3 is a crude but useful means of trying to quantify inter-group attitudes and their potential for conflict by evaluating the terms as in Tables 10.1 - 10.3.

Throughout history, however, the greatest problems have been a result of the hierarchical nature of our societies and the lousy leaders who all too often rise up to brainwash us with propaganda and lead us into wars.

Thus, monarchy, democracy and socialism have failed us. Democracies are in practice oligarchies, and thence capitalist and economically competitive and exploitative, frequently giving grounds for conflict. Socialism, on the other hand, in practice tends to allow too little freedom.

About a century ago, the world had only about 50 or 60 nations. Now, thanks to 'decolonization', the number is about 200 and growing.

It does, indeed, seem that people want independence, and rightly so. Normal people also want peace though there will always be disagreement and conflict between individuals occasionally. Conflict on a larger scale should be avoided as far as possible and in the final chapter a modest attempt is made to suggest how we might reduce human conflict in an overpopulated and thus increasingly stressed world.

Chapter 25

DEMOCRACY & SOCIALISM

A democracy exits whenever those who are free and are not well-off, being in the majority, are in sovereign control of government, an oligarchy when control lies with the rich and better born.
Aristotle, *The Politics* (343 BC).

Just as Darwin discovered the law of evolution of organic matter, so Marx discovered the law of evolution of human history.
Friedrich Engels, said at the funeral of Karl Marx (1883).

Introduction

Again and again throughout human history people have revolted against corrupt regimes, an example being the 'Third Servile War' led by Spartacus against the Romans (73 – 71BC).

Furthermore, more often than not, sooner or later members of collective governments have tired of their leader and sought a replacement, and have almost invariably succeeded in doing so ultimately.

The following chapter gives just a few examples of man's struggle throughout history for fairness in government.

Discussion of democracy and socialism is given particular attention, these being the two somewhat opposing forms of government of most note in the world for the last hundred years or more.

Democracy

The city states of classical Greece and Rome were direct democracies in which the people directly spoke and voted at meetings, though in both cases this was limited to men and then only property holders in Rome.

Aristotle's remark about oligarchy which opens this chapter is an important reminder that, as then, we do not have *real* democracy today.

The populations of the Greek city-states of his time rarely exceeded 10,000 people, all the 'citizens' of which voted with black and white stones on the questions of the day in open forum.

Aristotle's complaint was that it was only the men and not women or slaves who were allowed this privilege and slavery, of course, can hardly be equated with democracy.

As noted in Chapter 2, Rome's Senate eventually allowed both patrician and plebeian members, but then only when the plebs had become property holders.

In the modern era we invariably have representative democracies, though some degree of direct democracy is usually available through referendums. The latter are usually rare, and usually unsuccessful, but in Switzerland they may be initiated by a petition of 50,000 voters.

The Westminster System

In most of the world today we do not have anything like real democracy. We have, in fact, Westminster type *parliamentary democracy,* a very brief history of which is (Mackenzie, 1950):

Pre 1066 (Saxon times). The barons and King met each year at Easter, Whitsun and Christmas.

1258 (in the reign of Henry III). A meeting of the barons of England at Oxford was the origin of the *House of Lords.*

1264. Simon de Montfort, on the King's behalf, organized a meeting of two knights from each county.

1265. Two citizens from each county were included in the latter meeting, constituting the origin of the *House of Commons*.

In the reign of Elizabeth I the puritans became the first party and were the opposition to the crown.

In the reign of Charles I the cavaliers and roundheads emerged as two opposing political forces.

1681. The origin of the names *Whig* and *Tory*.

This system has evolved in England, Australia and New Zealand into the two main parties being a conservative party, which supports the capitalist ruling class, and a Labour Party which traditionally supported the workers or modern-day slaves.

The Conservative Party is said to be *right wing* and the Labour Party *left wing*, a fine example of the power of emotive language.

Now, however, big business has considerable influence on both parties and the policies of the Labour Party are often more conservative than those of its opposition conservative party.

The result is a revolving door parody of democracy in which stooges become our leaders for relatively brief periods but their policies are greatly influenced by the business sector and the economic imperialism of traditional allies in war, in Australia these being the US and UK.

In this parody the 'fat cats' of the public service wield more influence in policy-making than do average members of parliament (Self, 1977).

Socialism

There have been a variety of socialist ideas, for example:

(1) Saint-Simon (1760 – 1825) who envisaged a just society directed by a technocratic elite.

(2) Utopian Robert Owen (1771 – 1858) built a model factory town in New Lanark, Scotland.

(3) Utopian communal experiments such as Brook Farm, Massachusetts (1841 – 1847) were tried in the USA.

(4) Bakunin (1814 – 1876) was a prominent anarchist who spread his views throughout Europe. Anarchists oppose any form of government, believing that individuals should be free to express themselves without any external control.

(5) Marx (1818 – 1883) posited the inevitable triumph of socialism in the industrial countries through a historical process of class conflict.

It is important at the outset to note that *socialism* refers to the 'means of production' being owned by the state whereas *communism* refers to the means of production being owned by the people. The two terms are often confused but in a complex and highly technological modern society it is doubtful that communism is practical. It is doubtful, for example, that the very large companies required in some industries, many of these now transnational ones, can be owned and run by the 'people', taking people to mean those in a particular community.

What is clear, however, is that the 1848 Marx-Engels manifesto was anti-capitalist and this was the real spirit of the 1917 Russian revolution, a spirit which many believed would eventually spread globally. This revolution created a socialist state with a long term view towards forming a communist society.

Marxists argue that the capitalist *class* accumulates increasingly more capital or a 'surplus value' in fact created by the workers. The working class, therefore, are left to accumulate misery or, as Marx put it:

> *In proportion as capital accumulates, the lot of the labourer be his payment high or low, must grow worse.*

Critics of this view will point out that in practice state ownership leads to totalitarian government which makes the people worse off, rather than better.

Marxists will also argue that in capitalism monopolies or oligopolies must eventually develop, in turn influencing the political system so that something akin to totalitarianism can result.

In defence against this view critics of Marxism will argue that it is better to reform the capitalist system, not replace it, for example by introducing antimonopoly laws.

Theoretical arguments aside, revolutions have always occurred when there are high levels of unemployment and poverty.

Capitalism, however, relies upon a substantial pool of unemployed to keep the price of labour down (Sweezy, 1946). As a result, some studies found little reduction in poverty in the USA in the years 1947 - 1960 (Townsend, 1970) whereas socialism has reduced poverty and famine in China dramatically (Maxwell et al., 1977).

Russia

The French revolution that began in 1789 disposed of the French monarchy but was finally ended in 1799 when Napoleon took over the government and most of the revolution's reforms were abandoned so that, for example, again only those who paid a certain amount of taxes were allowed to vote.

The Russian revolution of 1917 was a massive event that drastically changed Russia. It also had the UK and US concerned and the British secret service provided considerable covert support to the White Russian army resisting the revolution. When that failed they began counter terrorist activities against the new Russia, for example Lieutenant Agar's sinking of the Red Fleet cruiser Oleg in Kronstadt harbour in 1919 (Brook-Shepherd, 1998).

Though the USSR has been more or less dismantled, some aspects of its system remain whilst socialist systems operate elsewhere in the world. Moreover, the communist party in Russia, for example, still has a good deal of support.

Hence some discussion of the USSR system as it was is still worthwhile, principal features of that system being:

[1] In the USSR policy was based on five year plans. Critics would argue that this was too inflexible and did not allow for adjustments. But business plans might typically be five year ones and allow for adjustments, so this argument is invalid.

[2] Without a free market coordination was difficult. Supposing we wished to increase steel production, for example, then we needed extra plant to make it and in turn extra steel to make the plant, but where could we get if from? In other words it is difficult to be self sufficient as a single entity despite a perhaps massive size.

Again the argument is invalid, there being nothing to stop a country like Russia from having two steel organizations, typical of the common duopoly situations in the USA.

[3] Circa 1970 investment in the USSR ran at about 30% of GNP (about the same figure as Japan at the time and twice that for the USA), this funded by a 30% general sales tax (GST). This high level of investment was aimed at building industry but resulted in excessive restrictions in consumption and chronic shortages in goods.

Such a rate of expansion, however, was never going to be permanent and therefore must have been a positive developmental stage, a period of shortages for the general public being far less of a problem than the sacrifices involved in war, economic or otherwise.

[4] In the USSR system there was effectively no such thing as unemployment as everyone could be given a job, however unproductive.

[5] Reform in 1988 resulted in the establishment of a congress of 2,250 People's Deputies elected throughout the USSR. The 542 members of the upper chamber of the congress, the Supreme Soviet, met twice a year for 3 – 4 months to decide on legislative issues.

[6] The Supreme Soviet also had two chambers, one with a national focus, one with a regional focus, and was headed by the President whose incumbency was limited to two five-year terms. The Presidium, made of executive members from both chambers of the Supreme Soviet, operated continuously.

[7] The work of the government was, however, directed by the Communist Party of the Soviet Union (CPSU). Locally, party officials served as secretaries in their district, city, province, or region. Delegates from party organizations throughout the country formed the Communist Party Congress which met at least once every five years to elect a Central Committee from its members, and at least twice a year to draft policy passed on to the Politburo, the twenty members of which formulated party policy at general assemblies (plenums). The Politburo's decrees were sent to the Supreme Soviet for enactment into law.

The Central Committee and the Politburo were supported by a large permanent staff of bureaucrats called the *apparat* whose senior members formed the Secretariat. The entire CPSU was headed by its General Secretary, often the President (Yeltsin, 1990).

Since the dissolution of the USSR Russia has established a free market economy but the government has much more control over the economy and business than in such countries as the US and UK.

Capitalism

While so-called democracy prevails in most of the world, the reality is that, with the world's markets becoming increasingly global, transnational companies and thence unrestrained capitalism provides the power and influence that runs the politics of most countries.

In the 1930s John Maynard Keynes proposed that a multiplier effect existed such that small increases in government spending in the community have a much greater effect upon the productivity of the nation.

This *fiscal* approach was widely adopted by many countries in the West to stimulate flagging economies.

Milton Friedman and other economists favour the free market or *monetarist* economic philosophy. This stems from the 17th century and is based on the equation (Wonnacott & Wonnacott, 1979):

$$MV \text{ (aggregate demand)} = PQ \text{ (aggregate supply)}$$
where
M = the amount of money in circulation (per year)
V is its velocity of circulation (in transactions per year)
P = the price of goods in circulation
Q = the quantity of goods in circulation (per year)

Here V is the only relatively stable quantity and is based on the fact that, when you buy a product, the money you pay for it will be passed on quite soon as wages for somebody in the company you bought the product from. Then that person spends their wages on food and other necessities, and so on. Typically V takes a value of around 4 in modern economies.

This little or no government monetarist approach has led to more rampant capitalism than ever before. As a result an 'establishment' that effectively rules capitalist countries is formed (Blondel, 1963).

This establishment deplores the mildest hint of socialism and thence government ownership of industry, or even influence over industry. *They* tell government to reduce company taxes further and to cut back on government spending to do it and governments continue to heed them.

Effectively running military-industrial countries like the UK and US as they do, the barons of capitalism have ensured that their governments fight the evil threat of socialism, for example leading to the British secret service providing considerable covert support to the White Russian army resisting the 1917 revolution.

Some evidence of such policies was given by the first president of the National Civic Federation in the USA when he wrote in 1909: "Our enemies are the socialists and other labor people and the anarchists among the capitalists."

In the 1970s David Rockefeller funded the Trilateral Commission which in 1975 funded a meeting of multinational corporate executives to consider the "excess of democracy" afflicting advanced capitalist countries and to "rationalize the US economy through capitalist dominated planning and in conjunction with other leading capitalist nations to reassert US authority on a world scale" (Crough et al., 1980).

Proposals for change

Some authors suggest that inequality in capitalist societies should be reduced by reducing the inheritability of wealth by increasing death duties (Broom et al., 1980).

This is an unpopular proposal to both the rich and the middle class. As a result the Australian state of Queensland abolished death duties many years ago and other states only apply them to large fortunes.

Marxists aim to equalize incomes, penalizing effort as well as inheritance (Jencks et al., 1975).

A more original and interesting proposal was made by Peter Jay (1981), a former economics editor of *The Times*:

> *- - that the enterprises which create the wealth, the firms, the corporations, should belong to, be owned by, should have their directors exclusively appointed by, and their net assets and their residual earnings should belong to, and exclusively to, the people who work at them.*

Jay suggested that it is an accident of history, not a law of economics, that the entrepreneur has tended to be the person who supplied the risk capital. He proposed that in modern economies worker-owned companies should be able to raise debt finance from banks and equity finance from shareholders in the usual way.

Capitalists are happy to have their workers become shareholders, of course, because shareholders do not have to be paid dividends in bad times whereas banks always require interest to be paid on loans.

Jay's proposal goes a lot further and might eliminate the absurd salaries, share and rights bonuses, and retirement packages we see today. Indeed, it would only seem fair that *all* workers for a corporation should receive share issues as a non-taxable part of their income.

A criterion that the modern welfare economist employs in deciding whether a given change is 'efficient' was developed by Vilfredo Pareto (Buchanan & Tullock, 1962). This relies on the ethical postulate that the 'welfare' of a group of individuals is said to be increased if:

[1] Every individual in the group is better off, or if

[2] At least one member of the group is better off, without any member of the group being made worse off.

This is illustrated for the case of just two individuals X and Y in Figure 25.1 where the axes measure 'welfare' or 'utility' of the individuals and any point on the line $X_m Y_m$ is a Pareto-optimal state. Any movement from such a point to another point on or outside the curve must reduce the utility of one of the individuals.

If we assume some initial position A, then moving to any point on the curve between B and C is clearly Pareto-efficient because both parties are better off. Moving to point D, on the other hand, is not Pareto-efficient because Y will be worse off.

Here it should be noted that a person is deemed better off when they move from one position to another freely of their own choice, that is, 'better off' is subjectively evaluated. A common example might be people who reduce their working hours and salary in order to improve their overall quality of life.

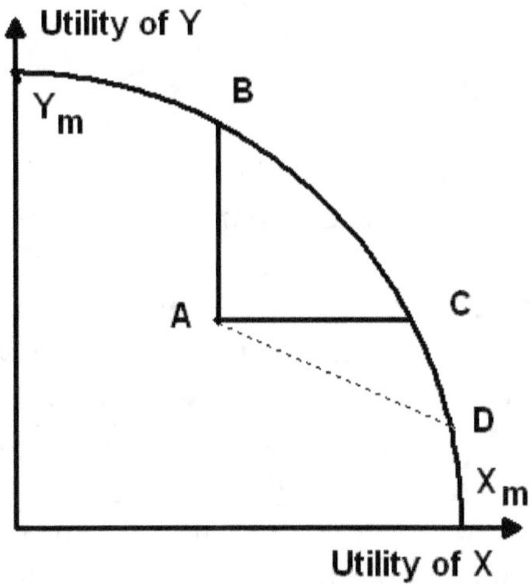

Figure 25.1. Illustration of Pareto-optimal states.

There are clearly many changes that can be made to either of the capitalist and socialist extremes that might result in a compromise that might improve the overall position of people. That monarchies no longer play an active role in government in the world is an example that significant change is indeed possible.

Russia and China

The Soviet Union, like any large hierarchical organization, was not without corruption, members of the Party elite having access to special cars, airplanes, department stores and vacation sites (Yeltsin, 1990).

The imminent collapse of the Soviet Union was not without tensions, for example an attempt on Boris Yeltsin's life in 1989 which was probably carried out by the KGB, making one think, of course, of Vladimir Putin, ultimately president after Yeltsin's 1991-1999 term.

Not surprisingly, therefore, Yeltsin's autobiography says: "I can foresee that a fierce, hard struggle lies ahead over the future of the army and the KGB" (Yeltsin, 1990).

Yeltsin also decried the "state's monopoly of property ownership," saying: "Only when the land is worked by the people who own it will the country be fed."

On politics he said: "My view is that we still need to grow and mature toward a real, civilized, multiparty system." It is now safe to say that Russia's system has changed and some aspects of socialism, such as centralization of power, have been much reduced. Before the USSR was dismantled, however, there had long been changes such as a greater tendency to pay highly skilled workers more, less interventionist government, and slow opening up to outside (and hence not state) capital.

Nevertheless, with people from the 'old guard' like Putin still in control Russia is still only perhaps halfway democratic, the government still being somewhat authoritarian. An example of this, perhaps, there is only 13% personal tax, the mining industry paying a large share of the government's tax take.

China does not appear likely to suffer the same fate as the Soviet Union which was ethnically diverse and only about half Russian, ultimately leading to ethnic divisions and dissolution. In contrast, China is about 93% Han Chinese with much greater ethnic cohesion (Calder, 1997).

In addition, because of China's "mass-based agrarian revolution and Mao's emphasis on egalitarianism" its government has been more responsive to the feelings of the populace, whereas the Soviet leadership was more dictatorial (Calder, 1997).

China, of course, is not immune from corruption. Some claim, for example, that corruption by government officials is rife, some having siphoned off large amounts of money to remote banks, eventually investing the laundered money in the US and elsewhere.

One of the Chinese companies involved in this activity, Longtop Financial had Deloitte as their auditor for six years but, after recent forensic investigations, Deloitte felt forced to quit.

China, having experienced massive economic growth in recent decades, is now the biggest holder of US debt, so that the aforementioned corruption (according to Deloitte) may, in fact, be part of how that came about, perhaps with some degree of official encouragement from the Chinese government at large.

Convergence of the systems

Not long ago some economics texts asked the question about socialism and capitalism: "Are the systems converging?"

In the USA and like countries there is some disenchantment with the two-party system that may begin to crystallize somewhere. In Australia, for example, three independents and the Greens party currently (2013) hold the balance of power in both the legislative lower house of representatives, and the upper house or senate which is required to approve legislation from the lower house.

In Westminster the Tories vs. Whigs farce has changed to Tories versus New Labour, with the Liberal-Democrats on the fringe as usual.

A former Australian finance minister wrote in his 2011 book *Dumbing Down Democracy* that politicians now consider appearances far more important than outcomes, lamenting that the resulting "sideshow syndrome" was eroding informed democracy as the basis of decision-making.

Thus we conclude that the politico-economic systems of both the 'east' and the 'west' will doubtless continue to change slowly. Whilst current trends are towards freer capitalist markets it is certain that this trend may be slightly reversed at some point.

Socialist parties remain strong in many countries in Europe, for example Belgium where the Belgian Worker's Party was founded in 1885, gaining 27 seats in the 1983 election. After WW1 the party abandoned its revolutionary Marxist stance and became a regular coalition partner in Belgian governments, often leading them in the 1950s and 1960s. The socialists had 37% of the vote in the mid-1950s but their popularity has since declined, though they still remain a significant force in Belgian politics.

The communist party in Russia might currently have less than 50% of the vote but that might not last. Thus Russia could be counted as roughly 7 or 8 on the 'commie scale' at present, as could China, with India perhaps about 6. Then, of course, Vietnam and North Korea are strictly socialist.

Some countries in South America and much of Africa, on the other hand, are in a state of economic collapse, as usual, and God only knows what 'colour' their politics is. In some cases not simply 'red' to whatever extent, but often the politics of chaos one supposes.

Conclusions

The French and Russian revolutions, of course, involved a good deal of conflict. As noted earlier in this chapter, the latter provoked espionage on the part of the UK government aimed at supporting the White Russian army's resistance to the revolution.

Since World War 2, after Stalin had annexed much of Europe, the Cold War between the USSR and the US and UK led to a very wasteful and costly arms race. Indeed, the US and USSR may have come close to nuclear war during the Cuban Missile Crisis.

The UK and US have also fought numerous wars against communism, including:

(1) The UK fought against communist revolutionaries in Malaya circa 1950.

(2) The US fought a bitter war in Korea in the early 1950s.

(3) The costly Vietnam war which the US ultimately lost comprehensively.

In addition, the US and its allies have surreptitiously overthrown "dictators," many of them of socialist inclination, in several countries around the world.

Finally, as always, conflict continues around the world, most noticeably at present continuing terrorism by Muslim extremists.

Indeed, there is no end to this in sight, in part because no end to the conflict between Israel and the displaced Palestinian peoples is in sight.

In addition, it is not hard seeing "the world's only super power", the USA, one day becoming involved in conflict with China. Indeed, the CIA has conducted simulated economic war games against China in which the US lost, China's growing economic power being, of course, in part at the expense of the USA and thus a source of grievance to it.

Chapter 26

DECLINE & FALL OF
THE WESTERN EMPIRES

*Twenty-two acknowledged concubines, and a library
of sixty-two thousand volumes attested the variety of his
inclinations, and from the productions which he left behind him,
it appears that both the one and the other were designed
for use rather than ostentation.*
Edward Gibbon on Emperor Gordion the Younger,
The Decline and Fall of the Roman Empire (1776 - 88), ch 7.

To accept civilization as it is practically means accepting decay.
George Orwell, 'Inside the Whale',
Inside the Whale and Other Essays (1940).

Introduction

As discussed in earlier chapters, man's history of large scale conflict has almost always been for the purpose of building states and empires, or the defence of territory.

In this chapter we shall concentrate mainly on the decline of the Western Empires, the 9th edition of the Concise Oxford Dictionary defining 'west' as:

west **n.** 2 (usu. the West)
a European in contrast to oriental civilization.
b hist. the non-Communist states of Europe and N. America.
c non-Communist states or regions in general.
d the western part of the late Roman Empire.
e the western part of a country, town, etc.

The European Empires

The great Roman Empire followed hard upon the heels of the substantial empire created by that great warrior Alexander the Great which stretched from Gibraltar to the Punjab.

We remember the Roman Empire for its might, its dominance of much of Europe and beyond, and its brutality in dealing with those it conquered, for example mass crucifixions. It will also be remembered for its widespread use of slavery and for its corruption.

In the last few hundred years most European countries have colonized other countries, including:

(1) Dutch conquests included the Dutch East Indies and part of North America where they named their colony in the Hudson River valley New Netherland. The first township was Fort Orange in Albany in 1617 and New Amsterdam followed in 1624 and was renamed New York by the English in 1664.

(2) France's First Empire was established by Napoleon Bonaparte who conquered much European territory, only to be ultimately defeated by the forces of Wellington and Blücher and banished to die in St Helena.

(3) The Spanish Empire controlled much of South America but Napoleon's invasion of Spain in 1808 was followed by the Spanish-American wars of independence which saw Chile, New Granada, Peru, Quito and Venezuela gain independence.

The Spanish-American War of 1898 saw Spain lose the rest of its empire - Cuba, the Philippines and Puerto Rico to the USA.

(4) The union of the crowns of Spain and Portugal in 1580 led to a weakening of the Portuguese Empire. Its most substantial colony Brazil became independent in 1822, the last vestige of its empire, Macau, being handed back to China in the early 1990s.

(5) The German Hapsburg Empire existed from circa 1100 to 1918 and Hitler's efforts to create a new German empire resulted in WW2. In the end, however, it was Stalin who ended up taking half Europe.

(6) England's first major quest for empire was the crusades of Richard I circa 1190 - 94. Later England often controlled much of France.

The British Empire was certainly the greatest of them all in terms of global spread, reaching its peak in 1919 with control over German and Ottoman territories in Africa and the Middle East.

In the three decades following WW1, however, England had difficulty controlling its huge empire. The dominions gained independence in 1931, and the Middle Eastern mandates were effectively lost before WW2. India gained independence in 1947 and the other Asian colonies followed soon thereafter, Malaya gaining independence in 1957.

Often said to be "the empire on which the sun never sets," like so many before it the British Empire gradually declined and finally vanished.

Thus the first author well remembers statements by two of the first people he met at Cambridge University when he went to do his PhD there:

(a) The Head of Engineering: "It's not like the old days."

(b) An ex-army night security guard in the computer centre: "What this country needs is another war to get it going again."

(7)The USSR, already a large empire, annexed much of Europe after World War 2, leading to decades of 'Cold War' with the USA and its allies, particularly the UK.

The USSR had considerable influence over many countries around the world, having control in some of them, for example Afghanistan from 1978 to 1992.

Weakened by decades of economic isolation, however, the USSR disbanded in 1991.

The American Empire

The Spaniards reached Florida in 1513 and New Mexico in 1540, the French began exploring the Mississippi River valley in 1673, and the Russians reached Alaska in 1741. It was the British, however, who were the most successful colonizers in North America, in 1607 Jamestown becoming their first permanent settlement and the foundation of the Virginia colony. Georgia was the 13th colony, founded in 1763 by James Oglethorpe as a refuge for debtors and convicts.

Discontented with British mercantile and revenue policies the colonials began their fight against British control in 1775 and on July 4, 1776, The Second Continental Congress, acting for the 13 colonies, declared independence and created Articles of Confederation to govern the new nation.

Victory over the British came in 1783, and the resulting Treaty of Paris established US boundaries, except for Spanish Florida, west to the Mississippi River.

The Louisiana Purchase from France in 1803 added the western half of the Mississippi River basin, nearly doubling the size of the nation. Thenceforth the movement into the lands west of the Appalachians became a flood, and US victory in the Mexican War (1846-48) added all or part of the future territory of seven more states, including California and Texas.

In 1867 Russia sold Alaska to the US for $M7.2.

The short Spanish-American war of 1898 saw the USA on the road to imperialism. In response to the sinking of one of its battleships in Cuba the US blockaded Cuba and declared war on Spain on April 24 and by the end of the year Spain had ceded Guam, the Philippines and Puerto Rico, and granted independence to Cuba.

In 1915 US troops landed in Haiti, making it a virtual US protectorate until 1934, when they were pulled out.

In 1916 the US bought the Virgin Islands from Denmark and established military government in the Dominican Republic.

At the conclusion of WW2 the US took over control of Japan and parts of Germany and Korea, in the early 1950s becoming involved in the Korean war. The US then began to support anti-Communist forces in South Vietnam, eventually becoming bogged down in a long and unsuccessful war campaign until 1975.

The US and UK have had much involvement in the Middle East since the 1930s where their oil companies obtained substantial leases. With the troublesome creation of Israel in what some Atlases of the time termed British Palestine, that involvement continues and promises of a 'two-state solution' remain just promises to date.

In 1983 the US invaded Grenada to put down a Marxist government. In 1989 it invaded Panama to overthrow Manuel Noriega's government.

In 1991 the first Iraq war was fought, liberating Kuwait from partial occupation. In 1992 the US led UN-sanctioned forces into Somalia, the forces withdrawing in 1995. In 1994 US forces took control of Haiti, a UN force taking over in 1995 and US forces withdrawing in 1996.

In 1995 the US joined UN forces in the war in Bosnia and Herzegovina.

The US having inflicted no-fly zones on Iraq for years, the second Iraq war was quickly won in 2002, US occupation of Iraq continuing for nearly a decade.

The long conflict with the Taliban in Afghanistan followed and continues with withdrawal of most frontline US forces scheduled for 2013/14.

In 2011 the US played a major role in supporting rebels in Libya trying to overthrow the long-time leader Muammar al-Quadaffi, also promoting unrest in a couple of other Middle Eastern states with a view to change in leadership in order, US officials say, to "promote democracy."

US power and influence peaked sometime after World War 2, but the Cold War, wars against the 'Red Peril' in Korea and Vietnam, and covert campaigns to remove socialist governments in South America and elsewhere were costly. At the end of what many called "The American Century", therefore, the present century was being called the 'The Asian Century."

As for yet another mistaken war, super spy Kim Philby said regarding Russia's unsuccessful 8-year military involvement in Afghanistan: *My advice was not sought on Afghanistan. If it had been I would have said, look what happened to the British there, those interminable wars. So I would have said keep out at all costs* (Knightly, 1988).

Increasing US debt

The US has been running budget deficits for many years now but with the GFC in late 2008 things have become particularly serious. For a country that has fought so long and so hard against the 'red peril' to have to bail out two of its big three car makers, as well as a couple of its largest banks after the collapse of another, is serious indeed. Now, a few years later, the dust has settled a little and share markets have recovered much of the value lost with the GFC crash, but the US is only now beginning to try and come to grips with the task of paying back its mounting national debt which is continuing to increase.

We took little notice of Japan reducing its official interest rates to zero in the early 1990s, but they still remain in that state and, with the massive tsunami and earthquakes of early 2011 Japan's situation has worsened.

The US being forced into zero official interest rates by the GFC really is a remarkable phenomenon that perhaps indicates the beginning of the end of its short reign as the "world's only superpower."

After the GFC the US unemployment rate topped 10% for a while, and still remains near that highly unsatisfactory figure.

Here it should be remarked that Western economists generally hold that 5% unemployment is 'about right,' though this really corresponds to the 'Marx pool' of unemployed required to keep wages in check and maintain high company profits and CEO salaries (Sweezy, 1946). In addition, the tax burden of higher welfare costs falls mainly on the workers, not big biz.

Indeed, it is possible that the US may never recover fully and that still more of its major companies will be sold off to overseas investors. In addition, one of the big three car companies may have to be shut down or sold off. As a step toward that outcome, perhaps, Fiat became the major shareholder in Chrysler (53.5% holding) in July 2011.

Indeed, the decline of manufacturing in the US is reminiscent of the gradual disappearance of the British motorcycle and car industries since the 1960s, very little of these industries remaining now.

Already, in fact, it is clear that the US can no longer afford to go it alone with its endless sequence of wars. In Vietnam it had some international support but in Afghanistan it was crying out for help and continues to do so in Libya and elsewhere.

It was the famous economist John Maynard Keynes who likened war to digging a hole and pouring money into it and, indeed, it was only shortly after WW2 that the sun finally set on the great British Empire.

America's 'space race' with Russia was costly, of course, particularly in the 1960s. With America's space shuttles now scrapped, Russia is the "master of space" ('Shuttle send-off leaves Russia as master of space", Wall Street Journal article in *The Weekend Australian,* July 9-10, 2011).

The US might not be down and out for the count economically just yet, but its global dominance is gradually diminishing year by year.

The rise and rise of China

The industrial revolution that began in China two or three decades ago, resulting in GDP growth rates circa 10% for the past decade or more, has transformed much of the country. China's economy is now the world's second largest with the USA, although still largest, facing debts from which, like England before it, it may never recover from.

Cheap Chinese products totally dominate the cheap section of the market and 2$+ shops selling cheap household items are now seen scattered throughout the world's cities. No fluke, of course, these are usually run by Chinese people.

Such products exemplify the inverted supply and demand law proposed by Mohr (2012a, 2012b, 2018a), high volume of production along with little or no advertising costs lowering prices enough to stimulate demand.

In the middle price range Chinese goods also take a large share of the market, just one example being Lenovo's takeover of IBM's PC business several years ago.

With the recent appearance of Chinese cars on the world market China is entering the top price section of the general consumer product market at a time when some other car manufacturers, particularly the US companies, are having trouble surviving, for example cash-strapped Ford selling Volvo to the Chinese.

Other Asian countries are also doing well. Korea's LG has dominated the market for microwave ovens for decades and its car makers are doing increasingly well.

India is also on the rise and, like China, is set to become a major player in world affairs before long.

Conclusion

Having expanded from a small colony to a large and powerful country, and said since the dissolution of the USSR to be "the world's only superpower," the USA has military and intelligence gathering bases all over the world and is usually involved in military conflict in one or two countries at any one time, either as an active participant or in a logistically supportive role. In Vietnam 3 million civilians were killed, in Iraq one million, and the carnage now continues elsewhere.

All this has come at a cost. California went broke and the US ran budget deficits for many years and its economy was heading for a fall. Toxic loans problems brought some of the country's banks and two of its three major car companies to their knees begging for government bail outs in late 2008, leading to the "Global Financial Crisis" (GFC).

As a result several European countries are in trouble economically, in particular England, Greece, Ireland, Italy, Portugal and Spain, along with some of the former USSR countries.

Like Japan had since the early 1990s, the US had near zero official interest rates for several years after the 2008 GFC, and in April 2011 a major rating agency put the US's AAA credit rating "on watch" for two years with a view to a possible downgrade.

An article in the *Herald-Sun* on Sat. Dec. 8, 2012 on the US 'fiscal cliff', a series of tax hikes and spending cuts to hit in 2013 noted: *Many of the austerity measures are rooted in last year's debt-ceiling crisis, which prompted Standard & Poor's to downgrade US Government bonds for the first time in the nation's history.*

The governor of Australia's reserve bank has said that the rise of China was "a transformative event for the global economy," pointing out that China produces almost half the world's steel and 9 times more than the US, and that it has more of the world's top 100 banks (12) than any other country.

He went on to say the integration of China and India into the global economy has "a good way to run yet" and that China would outsize the euro-zone economies within 5 years and approach the US in economic strength terms within a decade (Michael Stutchbury, *The Weekend Australia* April 16-17, 2011).

It seems certain that, like the warmongering UK before it, the warmongering US is in decline and Asia, led by China, will increasingly dominate the world economy in decades to come and, indeed, the 21st century has already been referred to by some as "The Asian Century."

Globally, however, the problems of overpopulation, resource depletion, global warming, and desertification are likely to limit the prospects of future prosperity for all but the richest people in the world.

In the decline of empires, not only costly wars, but also poor economic policy will play a part.

In China, for example, obsession with growth has led to the building of whole cities of empty high-rise apartment blocks that few can afford, suggesting that China's growth will slow, in part because it will gradually have to increase wages, thereby reducing the competitive advantage of its manufacturing industries.

The bottom line, however, is that the last of the great Western empires, that of the USA, has been in decline for more than a decade and that Asia, and particularly China, and to a lesser extent India, are becoming much more powerful economically.

If the world's population reaches an expected circa 10 billion by about the middle of the century, however, it seems certain that the long-term prospects for the human race are poor (Mohr, 2012b; Mohr et al., 2018a) and with increasing crowding and resource depletion human conflict may also increase.

Chapter 27

FUTURE CONFLICT

In 1956 Professor W.A. Lewis calculated that if the world population were to double every 25 years (a rate of increase currently observable in some parts of Africa and Asia), it would reach 173,500 thousand million by the year 2330, at which time there would be standing room only, since this is the number of square yards on the land surface of the earth.
John Carey, *The Faber Book of Science* (1995),
'The Menace of Population.'

The human race will be the cancer of the planet.
Sir Julian Huxley, British biologist (1887 - 1975), attributed.

The seeds of conflict

Human population has grown exponentially since the industrial revolution began in Europe in the middle of the 18th century. The two quotations above remind us that, not only will we begin to suffer overcrowding before very long, but we are also damaging the planet as well (Mohr, 2012b; Mohr et al., 2018a).

With this massive growth in population, and thus increasing scarcity of fast vanishing resources, comes increasing risk of conflict. Now, with about a third of the human population undernourished, and with the disparity between the rich and poor growing ever wider, the seeds of conflict continue to be sown.

In the second half of the last century there were more than 100 wars fought in more than 60 countries (Bell & Hall, 1991) and it seems likely that this carnage will continue.

Now we have economic warfare in progress which may eventually spark armed conflict between such economically competitive countries as China and the USA (Clark 1967).

In addition, extremist Islamic terrorists still talk of building a global Islamic empire or caliphate and continue to orchestrate terrorist attacks around the world.

The main concern, of course, is that sooner or later future wars will involve nuclear and biological weapons.

Too many people

The world's human population is, in the authors' opinion, now at least twice that which can be sustainable for the long term.

Table 27.1. Human population since 10,000BC, N = population in millions, Year = thousands AD.

N	1	5	27	50	200	300	400	500	600	750	1000
Year	-10	-5	-2	-1	0	0.5	1	1.5	1.65	1.75	1.8

Table 27.1 shows human population (millions) since 10,000BC, when we reached our first million. It then took 10,000 years to reach 200 million, but only another 1000 years to add a further 200 million, 10 times the rate of increase.

Table 27.2 shows the date at which the human population reached 1 billion, 2 billion etc., including UN projections for when it will reach 8, 9, and 10 billion.

Table 27.2. Dates for population in billions, * = United Nations Population Fund estimates, 31/10/2011.

N	1	2	3	4	5	6	7	8*	9*	10*
Year	1800	1927	1960	1974	1987	1999	2011	2025	2043	2083
+ yrs		127	33	14	13	12	12	14	18	40

As shown in Table 27.1, it was 11,800 years after 10,000BC before we reached 1 billion, that is, about 50,000 years since Homo sapiens sapiens first left behind evidence of religion, recorded events, and art.

Then, as shown in Table 27.2, it was only another 127 years until a further billion people were added, reducing to a minimum of 12 years to have added another billion people in both 1999 and 2011. Needless to say, a further billion people in 12 years is like the speed of light compared to a tortoise when we compare it to 50,000 years to reach the first billion.

This reflection does, indeed, remind us that some authors have compared our population to that of a deadly viral or bacterial infection spreading over the planet, one that gobbles up resources and spoils and pollutes the planet at an increasingly rapid rate.

Ironically, our population began to exponentiate more rapidly with the coming of the industrial revolution in Europe (Cipolla, 1974), since then many improvements in living conditions such as sewerage, and medical advances such as antibiotics, having reduced mortality rates and increased longevity considerably.

In table 27.2 it is assumed that the rate of population increase is slowing, and this indeed is the case. Thus some "experts" predict our population will peak at between about 9 and 10 billion somewhere between 2050 and 2100.

There are those that doubt that the planet can support 8 billion people, the present authors feeling that half that number is all that we could hope to sustain with a truly modern standard of living rather than a subsistence one.

Alarmingly, population growth is more rapid in the poorest, most backward countries, and thus from 1990 to 2008 Africa's population increased by 55%.

In the period 1990 to 2010 India's population increased by 40.2%, Bangladesh's by 41.3%, Nigeria's by 62.4%, and Pakistan's by 55.3% (in March 2013 their respective populations were 1.27B, 154M, 170M, 182 M).

In March 2013 India's population density was 386.5 people per square kilometre, compared with 1068 /sq. km in Bangladesh, 226.7/sq. km in Pakistan, 183.7/sq. km in Nigeria, 141.5 /sq. km in China, 32.3/sq. km in the USA, or about 3/sq. km in Australia.

It is estimated that in 2050 Africa's share of the human population will be 20.8%, up from 13.8% in 2005, whereas in the same period Europe's share of population will have declined from 11.3% to about 5%.

Africa is a dry but populous continent, and in recent decades there have been mass migrations of conflict ridden and starving people from some of its poorest countries such as the Central African Republic, Chad, Nigeria, and the Sudan (particularly the Darfur region), such countries having a life expectancy of only about 50.

For decades there also been mass migrations from other countries that have suffered conflict and regime change, Vietnam being an example in recent decades.

The result is thousands of 'boat people' trying to arrive in freer and more prosperous places such as Australia and Europe. Ultimately, the stresses of exponentiating population and diminishing resources can only lead to an escalation of conflict around the world.

The global arms industry

The arms industry is one of the world's two largest, along with the illegal drugs trade.

During World War 2 the US made a fortune out of the lend-lease program which sold weapons to 35 countries including the UK, China, the USSR, the Netherlands, Belgium and the Free French. By the end of the war lend-lease appropriations had totalled $48B.

In departing from office President Dwight Eisenhower coined the term 'military-industrial state', warning against the "military-industrial complex" having too much influence, a situation that has come to pass (Wheen, 2004).

The US remains the world's largest manufacturer of military equipment and weapons. In the period 1970 – 76 the US made arms sales to almost 100 countries. In 1976 some of their best customers were Australia ($0.41B), Germany ($0.21B), Iran ($1.3B), Israel ($0.92B), Jordan ($0.43B), Korea ($0.63B), Saudi Arabia ($2.5B), Switzerland ($0.45B), and Taiwan ($0.22B) (Sampson, 1977).

The UK is the second biggest arms dealer in the world, Israel being one of its main customers. Indonesia used UK-supplied weapons, including rockets from Hawk aircraft, to attack East Timor in the 1990s, killing a third of the population. An Indonesian source confessed to using torture on citizens (Thomas, 2006).

Then, of course, there is the second-hand arms business, an example being Israel selling 100,000 AK-47s, 300,000 artillery shells, thousands of tank engines, and ten aging Hercules aircraft to Iran, the total for the deal being a billion dollars (Ben-Menashe, 1992).

Farcically, it was converted Bell helicopters that were sold to Iraq by Cardoen, a well-known Chilean arms dealer, and then used for biochemical warfare against the Kurds (Clarkson, 1998). Cardoen also began building a chemical weapons plant outside Baghdad, one reason why the USA began the first Iraq war.

Nuclear warfare

The atom was first split at the Cavendish Laboratories in Cambridge in 1931 (Mohr, 2012a). This led to the Manhattan project in which the first atomic bomb, a 20-kiloton implosion-type device, was tested in New Mexico on July 16th 1945.

On August 6th 1945 a 13-kiloton gun-type bomb was dropped on Hiroshima, killing from 70 to 100 thousand people and injuring as many again. Three days later a 22-kiloton implosion-type bomb was dropped on Nagasaki, killing about 40,000 people, the smaller number of fatalities being because of the hilly terrain.

In Hiroshima there was complete destruction for a radius of about a mile, severe damage for a radius of about 1.5 miles, and minor damage occurring up to a radius of four or five miles. There were massive amounts of fallout, thousands of tons of radioactive soil and dust flying up to 100,000 feet into the atmosphere and spreading over a radius of more than 100 miles.

Table 27.3. US & Soviet Nuclear Armaments (Bethe, 1991).

	US	USSR
Delivery vehicles		
Intercontinental Ballistic Missiles (ICBMs)	1,050	1,400
Submarine Launched Ballistic Missiles (SLBMs)	630	950
Bombers	350	140
Total	2,030	2,490
Warheads		
ICBMs	2,150-2,250	5,500-6,400
SLBMs	4,750	1,750-1,900
Bombers	2,500-3,500	280-550
Total	9,400-10,500	7,530-8,850
Equivalent megatons		
ICBMs	1,300	5,900
SLBMs	800	1,200
Bombers	3,500	900
Total	5,600	8,000

Table 27.3 shows strength of the USSR and USA nuclear arsenals circa 1990. Note that in table 27.3, 2 megatons = 1.59 equivalent megatons. The latter is the best measure of the area that can be destroyed, whereas megatons are the best measure of fallout.

Circa 1990, China had circa 350 nuclear warheads, the UK circa 150, and France circa 200 (Bell & Hall, 1991).

Hydrogen or fusion-type bombs are far more destructive than fission bombs. In 1952 the US tested a 10.4 megaton hydrogen bomb and in 1961 the USSR tested a 58 megaton hydrogen bomb.

Relatively new, neutron bombs are designed to kill people, not destroy infrastructure. They release ten times as much radiation as atomic bombs and can be fired by artillery, as well as carried in missiles or dropped from aircraft.

Since 1945 there have been at least 15 occasions when the use of nuclear weapons has been seriously considered (Bell & Hall, 1991), for example:

> In 1946 the US threatened to use fission bombs if the USSR did not withdraw troops from Azerbaijan.

> At least 5 misreadings of radar led to consideration of the nuclear option.

> The US has considered limited nuclear war 7 times.

> The 1962 Cuban missile crisis and the 1973 Yom Kippur war.

In the Cuban missile crisis of 1962 the US and USSR came very close to all-out nuclear warfare. Indeed, according to the documentary movie *The Fog of War* by Errol Morris, Castro had recommended that the USSR launch its nuclear arsenal on the USA, knowing full well that Cuba would be wiped off the map.

Circa 1990 only 5 countries had nuclear weapons, now that number is about a dozen, making eventual nuclear warfare increasingly likely.

Biological warfare

Biological warfare (BW) dates back to Roman times when dead soldiers were thrown into the water supplies of cities under attack.

During air raids during the 1930s the Japanese dropped porcelain canisters of fleas infected with plague on the Chinese. These and other primitive biological weapons killed thousands in rural areas of Manchuria (Alibek, 2000).

During WW2 the Russians dropped tularemia on the stalled German Panzer divisions freezing on the outskirts of Stalingrad (Alibek, 2000).

It is well known that Sadam Hussein used chemical weapons on the Kurds in Northern Iraq in the late 1980s, and other countries in the Middle East, including Israel, have engaged in biological weapons (BW) research.

Table 27.4. Soviet & US peak BW agent production levels in metric tons per year (Miller et al., 2001).

Agent	USA	Soviet U
staphylococcal enterotoxin B	1.9	0
tularemia	1.6	1,500
Q fever	1.1	0
anthrax	0.9	4,500
Venezuelan equine encephalitis	0.8	150
botulinum	0.2	0
bubonic plague	0	1,500
smallpox	0	100
glanders	0	2,000
Marburg	0	250

As shown in Tables 27.4 and 27.5, the USSR had an enormous BW research program with some 50 research centres and storage facilities (Alibek, 2000).

After WW2 the US also implemented a large BW research program, though not nearly as extensive as that of the USSR (see Tables 27.4 and 27.5). The US program was based mainly at one facility, Fort Detrick in Maryland.

In this massive arsenal the haemorrhagic filoviruses Ebola and Marburg are the most frightening because they are highly contagious and liquefy the body's organs.

At the main Russian BW research facility Vektor a scientist, Ustinov, was accidentally infected with Marburg virus. It took 15 days to kill him, developing into a new, more virulent strain that was called Marburg Variant U and weaponized for delivery by Soviet rockets.

Table 27.5. Other Russian BW agents (Alibek, 2000).

Argentinian haemorrhagic fever (Jinin)
Bolivian haemorrhagic fever (Machupo)
brucellosis
dengue fever
Ebola virus
epidemic typhus
Lassa fever
Russian spring-summer encephalitis

To date there have been no large scale BW attacks but in December 1943 news arrived in London that Germany intended to use a pilotless plane or rocket called the V-1 to deliver biological weapons. US intelligence learnt that they intended to use botulinum and the US had already developed an antidote to botulinum. By the summer of 1944 they had manufactured 4,000 gallons of this antidote, enough to immunize 700,000 troops (Regis, 1999).

In the spring of 1944 a worried Winston Churchill asked the US to provide him with 500,000 anthrax bombs. Churchill wrote in a memorandum, *"We should regard it as a first instalment."*

The Americans set up for production, aiming to produce a further 500,000 anthrax bombs for their own use. The task was never completed owing to the first atomic bomb test in July 1945, and then its use on Hiroshima and Nagasaki in August, ending the war a month later.

That Germany, the US and UK were preparing for massive BW warfare towards the end of WW2 suggests that there is a serious risk of BW warfare on a large scale at some time in the future.

In March 2013 the Syrian government, which has not joined a convention banning the use of chemical weapons, claimed that rebel forces had used chemical weapons in a rocket attack, a claim refuted by the rebels. Since then claims and counter-claims of the use of chemical weapons have continued in Syria.

Infrastructure warfare

A recent article in the *Far Eastern Economic Review* pointed out that US ports have only "superficial" security and that a terrorist attack on them using a weapon of mass destruction would bring the entire container system to a halt.

Information warfare (IW) is another threat to which the US is particularly vulnerable and it seems likely that some of the most sophisticated 'viruses' that have been let loose on the Internet may be deliberate IW.

Another example of IW, perhaps, recently the US has become concerned about Chinese hackers gaining access to banking and other information.

If hostile organizations can disrupt the banking systems or the stock exchanges of their major opponents such as the US and UK then serious damage could be done (Adams, 1998; Alexander, 1999).

IW is, of course, only a particular form of *infrastructure warfare* and poisoning water supplies, disrupting power and oil supplies, destroying bridges and hijacking aircraft are just a few of the many alternatives open to terrorists.

September 11, of course, was a spectacular example of such warfare. That numerous anthrax letters were posted around the country, resulting in the closure of public buildings for long periods, was perhaps another. Here there was, perhaps, no great aim to cause loss of life but, more important perhaps, to cause panic and disruption.

Another example of 'media spin', akin to brainwashing over time, the anthrax attacks were written off as having originated locally and being of little consequence. That seems unlikely indeed and it is only a matter of time before further attacks of this kind occur.

Economic warfare

During WW2 Churchill created a Ministry of Economic Warfare to help weaken Hitler's regime. Since that time economic sanctions have been targeted at dozens of countries, including South Africa and the USSR.

In September 1973 OPEC increased its oil price by 70%, increasing it a further 130% in December, thus quadrupling oil prices in just a few months (Batra, 1998).

There were further increases in 1975, 1977, 1979, and 1980, by which point the oil price had risen from about 3 dollars a barrel to about 35 dollars a barrel.

At the time the authors thought that this amounted to an economic war against the West and, indeed, it must have contributed to the present economic woes in Europe and the USA.

A concern now is that major oil-producing countries could destabilize the US by switching from US dollars to Euros as the currency in which oil is priced.

An article in the August 20-21, 2011 edition of *The Weekend Australia* reported on an economic war game conducted at the Warfare Analysis Laboratory in Maryland USA in 2009. There were 5 teams, America, Russia, China, Pacific Rim, and a 'grey' team representing criminal and terrorist organizations.

They were surrounded by an enormous array of screens normally used to simulate nuclear world war. The China team won and the article points out why China is a "huge threat." China is the biggest holder of US debt so that: "If China were to dump this debt it would totally screw with the [US] economy."

Conclusions

Enormous nuclear and biological arsenals having been established, all history suggests that they are likely to be used eventually.

In March 2013 the Syrian government claimed that rebel forces had carried out a rocket attack using chemical weapons, a claim which the rebels denied, saying that they did not have rockets. The rebels have had support from the US, which might have included short range rockets, whilst until now the Syrian government has not joined a UN convention banning the use of chemical weapons.

As usual, who did what is hard to know, and claims and counter-claims about chemical weapons usage in Syria have continued.

Economic warfare is now an added concern that could increase international tensions and hostility.

The growing pressures of excessive population and resource depletion are also likely to give rise to many future human conflicts around the world.

To sum it up, perhaps, an episode of the English comedy series *The Goons* called *The Bedsitting Room* took place on the first anniversary of World War 3 which had lasted a mere two minutes and twenty-eight seconds.

Initially, at least, nuclear and biological wars may be relatively quick as they are initiated simply by pushing buttons in a secure location. Their aftermath, however, will be felt for decades, if not centuries in the case of worldwide nuclear and biological warfare.

Chapter 28

REAL DEMOCRACY

The high contracting powers solemnly declare . . . that they condemn recourse to war and renounce it . . . as the instrument of their national policy towards each other . . . The settlement or the solution of all disputes or conflicts of whatever nature or of whatever origin they may be which may arise . . . shall never be sought by either side except by pacific means.
Aristide Briand, draft 20 June 1927, later incorporated into the Kellogg Pact, 1928, in *Le Temps* 13 April 1928.

Introduction

As most of the preceding chapters attest, conflict has dominated man's history. This is, no doubt, because we are, when all is said and done, just animals with an enlarged cerebral cortex for the semantic memory needed for our advanced languages. Many other animal species, including our close relatives gorillas, have dominant and aggressive alpha males who take charge of groups.

In humans we call this type A personality, a set of traits including ambition, competitiveness, impatience and hostility. Such people are often sociopathic psychopaths, the pathology of their condition also including lying and general delinquency (Davies, 1971), and in man's history many leaders have exhibited these characteristics.

Group conflict, whether tribal or imperialist, seems also to have become a habit in human societies. The Agricultural Revolution saw us establish not only towns and farms, but also armies to defend or to take new territory for growing populations.

Now with the exponentiating human population greatly excessive, and with resources, including arable land, being rapidly depleted, the prospects of conflict are increasing (Mohr, 2012b; Mohr et al., 2018a).

In the last century we had two world wars, the second involving circa 60 million dead. We also invented nuclear weapons and a range of potent biological ones, giving every reason to fear that future wars may far more devastating than any previous.

The Attitudinal Model of Conflict

This was introduced in Chapter 10, used to help conclude each of the chapters of Part 3, and extended in Chapter 24. In this section the model is reviewed and extended a little further.   By way of review, final comments on the simplified Attitudinal Model of Conflict, i.e. $A^{**} = A + B + C + D + S$ (Equation 10.2), are appropriate.

[1] Initial (previous history) attitude, *A.*
New opinions are always suspected, and usually opposed, without any other reason but because they are not already common, John Locke, *An Essay Concerning Common Human Understanding* (1990), Dedicatory epistle.

Humans have made a habit of the same group conflict that tribes of chimpanzees disillusioned Joan Goodall with (Goodall, 1971).

Worse still, however, we enshrine conflict in many sports such as boxing and fencing, as well as in many highly physical team sports that often involve both teams in a melee.

Similarly, for thousands of years we have laboured long and hard to invent and mass manufacture increasingly deadly weapons, keeping large armies at the ready to deal with the slightest provocation that some psychopathic leader might feel the need to start a war over.

If we are to avoid conflict our attitudes need to change and become those of:

➢ Equal status.

➢ Openness to discussion and negotiation.

➢ Cooperation (not competition).

➢ Having common interests and goals.

➢ Mutual understanding.

➢ Conciliatory nature.

[2] Behaviour, *B.*
People aren't inconsistent, but their behaviour is.
Mark McCormack, *What They Don't Teach You at Harvard Business School* (1984).

Humankind has a tragic and ongoing history of tribal and international war, now each nation having to have a large army equipped with increasingly sophisticated and deadly weapons. We need to settle all territorial disputes around the world, perhaps with the help of the UN, as suggested in point (10) of the following section.

We also need to force political and religious groups seeking greater power to accept democratic judgments by the people at large, and again UN support might be needed in some instances.

As for conflict on an individual level, for example in the areas discussed in Chapters 11 – 14, we need to behave with Equation 7.2 in mind, that is, make sure we adopt behaviours that are in line with proper social norms.

The bottom line, therefore, is that aggressive behaviour should be discouraged at all levels, and violent crimes, whether urban or international, should be penalized as heavily as possible. In addition, we need human societies to develop tolerance of all people, no matter what their colour, religion or ethnicity, and we need to focus not upon conflict, but upon tackling the common problems of mankind including overpopulation, resource depletion, climate change, and new diseases (Mohr, 2012b; Mohr et al., 2018a).

[3] Contact history, *C.*

Chief executives repeatedly fail to recognize that for communication to be effective, it must be two-way. Robert N. McMurry, 'Clear communication for executives', *Harvard Business Review* (1965).

Equation 24.2, that is,

$$C^* = C + d\,D, \text{ where } d = \text{scaling factor} \qquad (28.1)$$

shows that that 'positive differences' (i.e. similarities) increase positive contact.

[4] Differences, *D.*

If we cannot now end our differences, at least we can help make the world safe for diversity. John F. Kennedy, address, American University, Washington D.C. (June 10, 1963).

Equation 24.3, that is,

$$D^* = D + c\,C, \text{ where } c = \text{scaling factor} \qquad (28.2)$$

shows that positive contact increases 'positive differences' (i.e. similarities).

Equations 28.1 and 28.2 involve a 'positive feedback loop' which can be shown by writing

$$D^{**} = D^* + c\,C^* = (D + c\,C) + c\,(C + d\,D) \qquad (28.3)$$

Then if both scaling factors are 0.5 and the initial values of C and D were both scores of 5 (the range of possible scores being -10 to +10 as in Table 10.1), the result of Equation 28.3 is then

$$D^{**} = 5 + 5/2 + 5/2 + 5/4 = 11.25$$

and the outcome is 1.25 higher (i.e., the increase in D^{**} is 25% greater) than without the 'feedback' of increased D also increasing $C.$

Finally, note that, though a little confusing at first, the notion of 'positive differences' being similarities does help shift thinking from negative to positive.

[5] Societal attitude, *S.*

We call it a Society; and go about professing openly the totalest separation, isolation. Our life is not a mutual helpfulness; but rather, cloaked under due laws-of-war, named "fair competition" and so forth, it is a mutual hostility. Thomas Carlyle, *Past and Present,* bk 3, (1843).

This fifth term was included in the Attitudinal Model of Conflict to reflect the powerful effect of imitative or social learning in human society, its inclusion being comparable to the social norm term in the Theory of Reasoned Action in Equation 7.2.

Above all, more and better-reasoned action is what man needs. Indeed, it is increasingly imperative that all humankind must focus on the many common problems that threaten our survival such as overpopulation, resource depletion, climate change, and conflict (Mohr, 2012b; Mohr et al., 2018a).

[6] Responses, *R.*

War is not a continuation of policy, it is a breakdown of policy. Hans von Seeckt, *Thoughts of a Soldier* (1929).

If faced with conflict, in preference to the negative responses of Table 10.3, we should consider the more positive responses of Table 28.1.

Table 28.1. Attitudes towards measures to reduce conflict.

SCORE:	0	1	2	3	4
	Level of support for action				
Point out grievances					4
Peace negotiations			2		
Diplomatic visits			2		
Trade talks		1			
Financial aid	0				
Formal apologies	0				-
TOTAL SCORE:	9				

Table 28.1 shows an example of an assessment for a hypothetical individual concerning his or her views towards some external group currently in conflict with the individual's group or an ally thereof. The total score is a modest 9, or moderately supportive of negotiation etc., and this should be compared to the total obtained in Table 10.3.

The results of Tables 10.1 – 10.3 and 28.1 can be combined as:

$$A^{***} = A + B + C + D + S - (R_N - 12) + (R_P - 12)$$

where R_N is the score from Table 10.3, R_P is the score from table 28.1, and the last two terms are adjusted to allow for their different scale of measurement.

Reducing future conflict

Measures needed to reduce future conflict include:

[1] To reduce conflict in the world and, indeed, improve the overall quality of life for the general human population, the ***Attitudinal Model of Conflict*** presented in this book should be understood as widely as possible. Then it might be hoped that people will:
(a) Base their attitudes on rational thought, observations, and facts, not prejudice.
(b) Try to understand people of different backgrounds.
(c) Make 'positive' contact with other peoples to reduce, or at least understand their differences.
(d) Be more 'democratic' in their judgment of others, that is, consider the views of others when forming their own.

[2] **Education** of our children should not be the long drawn-out bore that it is now. Four or five years of incarceration in day care and kindergarten, and then twelve more at school is far too long. In the first few years home-based learning, perhaps in small groups with a special teacher gives much better results (Packard, 1978)

Then 10 years at school should be more than sufficient for the average child (Mohr, 2012a).

Indeed, because of growing public dissatisfaction with the US education system, many US children are home-schooled and often do much better as a result (Penn, 2007).

At school far more emphasis should be given to teaching life skills. They should, for example, be taught how to deal with bullying and bad bosses, how to develop realistic career goals, about consumerism, and about the 'time value of money'.

Finally, education at all levels should be less of a series of lectures by a 'parade of clowns' and, at least after the first few years, should more along the lines of 'here is the textbook, study this chapter this week and then we shall have a class discussion and question session on it'. A more mature, two-way, equal status approach such as this should be far more effective and much better preparation for life.

[3] A fair go for all. There needs to be a much fairer distribution of wealth in societies so that corrupt executives cannot make up to 1000 times more than those that do the actual work of producing saleable products.

[4] Ethnic harmony. Tolerance and understanding between different races, religions and ethnicities should be encouraged. Historically disadvantaged indigenous peoples such as the Australian aborigines should also be given a 'fair go' in society (Broom, 1980).

[5] Population control. As noted in the previous chapter, our population is exponentiating. It is now at least twice what it should be if everybody is to have a reasonably good standard of living. China's one-child policy, for example, has helped it advance greatly economically. Elsewhere, as Carlo Cipolla implored, there also needs to be more emphasis on 'quality not quantity' (Cipolla, 1974).

[6] Protect jobs. Globalization of trade should be reduced because, for example, shipping countless different makes and models of cars around the world cannot be economically sensible. In addition there should always be modest tariffs to protect local jobs.

A 4-day week, perhaps of 36 hours, should be made the norm. This could prove more efficient and would greatly improve quality of life.

Income splitting before tax should be allowed for married couples to allow one parent to stay at home to care for and oversee the crucial early education of children.

[7] Resource conservation. Resource scarcity is a likely source of future conflict. As of 1997, for example, in the 1500-mile expanse of the Japanese archipelago there wasn't a single major oil field and the rest of Northeast Asia was no better off with North Chinese and Indonesian fields approaching exhaustion (Calder, 1997).

More energy-efficient buildings and cities are needed to preserve crucial finite resources such as oil. Thus, growth of 'megacities' full of wasteful air- conditioned multistorey buildings and crowded freeways should be curtailed, and smaller regional towns encouraged instead.

[8] Control the arms industry. A highly excessive 8 million new small arms are sold each year, more than 60% to civilians (Thomas, 2007). The arms industry should be drastically reduced, land mines totally banned, and biochemical and nuclear weapons outlawed.

[9] Terrorism. Leaders of religions used as a justification for terrorism should be compelled to speak out openly and repeatedly against use of their religion as a *basis* for terrorism.

[10] Greater UN power. Every nation should contribute on a per capita basis, adjusted for their economic circumstances, towards a large UN armed force which could be used to deal with minor conflicts and deter larger ones.

Nations could save far more than this cost by greatly reducing the size of their armed forces to a level sufficient to deal with little more than domestic emergencies.

A UN court should also be established to judge grievances between countries and impose economic sanctions and heavy fines (c.f. Equation 24.5).

Finally, to make the UN more democratic, the power of veto given to a few countries should be removed.

There are, of course, many other measures besides the foregoing 10 'solutions' that might help reduce conflict and improve human life. To implement such measures large societies must be structured, however, and must have governance and, for this to have any hope of significantly reducing human conflict, it would need to be 'real democracy', and just what we mean by this is discussed in the following and final section of this book.

Real democracy

Relatively minor conflict between individuals in society cannot be avoided at times but can, with improvements in education and government be much reduced.

Larger scale conflict between groups of various sizes ranging from competing criminal gangs to competing nations is, however, a different matter as it is usually the leaders that instigate conflict.

In part, the problem here is that the 'meek do not inherit the earth', as the Christian Bible says. Far from it, for it has almost always been the most assertive and dishonest 'alpha types' with type A personalities that have led us by the nose to believe various and sometimes absurd religions and to fight for them if so directed.

Similarly, of course, political leaders use propaganda and lies to convince people to support them and, if need be, fight for whatever cause they see fit to fight for.

It would help, therefore, if we had *direct democracy* so that the populace can vote on major issues, hopefully preventing leadership groups from summarily committing nations to conflict.

One reason this is needed is seen in the Westminster system where parties have 'safe seats' that are given to people with more money and/or influence. Another problem is that party members must vote in unison as directed. A further problem is that ministers are chosen by the party leader, whereas they should be elected by the party.

Yet another is that in so-called democratic countries big business is able to make huge donations to political parties in return for more favourable treatment, for example, lower company taxes. The USA, for example, is effectively run by a higher echelon of long-established wealthy families who run large businesses. These businesses include the arms industry which makes massive profits from arms sales because, as long as even just a few minor wars are going at any one time, that encourages arms sales on a global basis. We have to be suspicious, therefore, about the motives of countries that have large arms industries and also a habit of almost always being involved in one war or another.

All this is not, of course, democratic. We should be represented by independent representatives in each electorate who have empathy for the concerns of people at the grass roots of society.

In addition, direct democratic voting should be allowed for all major issues to ensure 'government by consent.'

In situations of national emergencies that require rapid response, however, this is not practical.

The only solution, therefore, is to have what we will call *real democracy*, that is, truly representative democracy, features of which would include:

[1] Government should be by a parliament of elected representatives for each region of a state or country. These representatives should be elected as independent individuals not associated with any political party or group, and they should only be allowed one or two terms.

[2] People wishing to be selected for a pool of 20-30 prospective candidates for election would have to meet age and other criteria and pay a modest fee. As part of the selection process they would also be interviewed by electoral authorities to help assess their suitability. In Australia, for example, these interviews would be held at the Australian Electoral Commission offices in the federal electorate within which the prospective candidates resided.

[3] The candidates for election in each region should be chosen from the pool of prospective candidates by a panel of 15 – 20 people chosen randomly from the population of the region, but according to certain selection criteria such as age, selection of panel members thus being comparable to the way in which jury members are chosen.

As part of the selection process the prospective candidates would give a short public speech and be interviewed by the selection panel. Thus the selection process would be comparable to that used to 'preselect' candidates to represent a party at elections in the Westminster system, but would entail selecting circa six candidates.

[4] A new selection panel would be chosen for each election. The overall process is illustrated in Figure 28.1, the prospective candidates, of which there might be many, being interviewed to obtain a pool of 'prospective candidates' from which the candidates for election are chosen by the selection panel process.

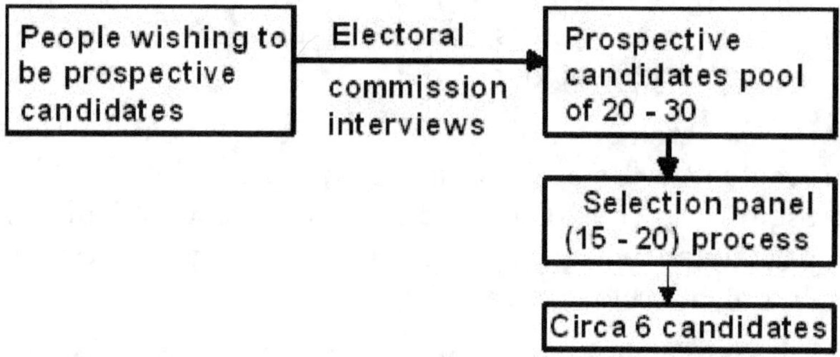

Figure 28.1. Selection of candidates for election.

[5] Members of parliament would elect a chairman and groups of members to deal with each of the main areas of government, for example finance, education and health. The chairpersons of each of these groups would be elected by the members of the groups.

[6] Elections of parliament would be every 3 – 4 years.

[7] The public at large would be allowed to vote on major issues such as taxation rates and foreign policy by referendum, and such referenda should also be able to be held when a certain number of people call for it.

[8] How members of parliament voted on each motion would be recorded in the newspapers etc. so that their electorate could judge whether their views were being represented appropriately.

[9] A record of how members of parliament had voted on all motions would be kept at the electoral offices of members and a copy made available to the public for inspection.

[10] Members of the public should be able to record how they wished the local member to vote on a particular issue at the member's electoral office.

A more truly democratic system of government such as this would be less open to control by a single leader and just a few of his or her friends.

It is this sort of oligarchical or 'clique' situation that has been at the heart of man's endless history of corruption and conflict, whether the form of government was ostensibly a monarchy or a so-called democracy.

It is only through 'real democracy', as outlined above, that the world might have any hope of lasting peace in the future. In addition, if we can always approach our dealings with people with the more logical and reasoned approach suggested by the Attitudinal Model of Conflict, then conflict at all levels of society might be reduced (Mohr et al., 2018c).

Having had plenty of opportunity to reach a bottom line myself, here are a few others from the last century:

> *We live under a system by which the many are exploited by the few, and war is the ultimate sanction of that exploitation.*
> Harold J. Lask, *Plan or Perish* (1945).
>
> *If the Third World War is fought with nuclear weapons, the fourth will be fought with bows and arrows.*
> Lord Louis Mountbatten, *Maclean's*, Nov. 17, 1975.
>
> *Mankind must put an end to war or war will put an end to mankind.*
> John F. Kennedy, speech to the UN 25th Sept. 1961.
>
> The first author:
> *Is the problem of the human race anthropology?*
> Answer: *Of course!* J.H. Argyris (1998).

REFERENCES

Aarons M, Loftus B, *The Secret War Against the Jews,* Mandarin Press, Melbourne (1999).

Alibek K. *Biohazard,* Arrow Books, London, 2000.

Allport GW, *The Nature of Prejudice,* Addison-Wesley, Reading MA (1954).

Baddeley AD, Thomson N, Buchanan M, World length and the structure of short-term memory, *Journal of Verbal Learning and Behaviour* 14(1975) 575-589.

Baddeley AD, *Human Memory, Theory and Practice,* Lawrence Erlbaum Associates, Hove, East Sussex (1990).

Batra R, *Surviving the Great Depression of 1990,* Bantam/Schartz, Sydney (1988).

Bell R, Hall R, *Impact: Contemporary Issues & Global Problems,* The Jacaranda Press, Brisbane (1991).

Ben-Menashe A, *Profits of War, The Sensational Story of the World-Wide Arms Conspiracy,* Allen & Unwin, Sydney (1992).

Bethe HA, *The Road from Los Alamos,* Touchstone Books, New York NY (1991).

Black E, *IBM and the Holocaust,* Little Brown, London (2001).

Blondel J, *Voters, Parties, and Leaders,* Penguin, Harmondsworth (1963).

REFERENCES

Brickman P, Redfield J, Harrison AA, Crandell R, Drive and predisposition as factors in the attitudinal effects of mere exposure, *Journal of Experimental Social Psychology* 8 (1972) 31-44.

Brook-Shepherd G, *Iron Maze, The Western Secret Services and the Bolsheviks,* Pan, London (1998).

Broom L, Jones FL, McDonnell P, Williams T, *The Inheritance of Inequality,* Routledge & Kegan Paul, London (1980).

Buchanan JM, Tullock G, *The Calculus of Consent,* The University of Michigan Press, Ann Arbor (1974).

Burrell A, Broker bastardization no laughing matter for juniors and "Jew Boys", *Australian Financial Review*, 7 Feb. 2001, p. MW16.

Burt C, The distribution of intelligence, *British Journal of Psychology* 48 (161-174) 1957.

Calder K, *Asia's Deadly Triangle, How Arms, Energy, and Growth Threaten to Destabilize Asia-Pacific*, Nicholas Brearley Publishing, London (1997).

Campos L, McCormick P, *Introduce Yourself to Transactional Analysis, A TA Primer,* 4th edn, Transactional Pubs, Berkeley CA (1974).

Carey J (ed.), *The Faber Book of Science,* Faber and Faber, London (1995).

Caselli F, Coleman WR, *On the Theory of Ethnic Conflict*, paper posted on the Internet (2012).

Cateora, PR, *International Marketing,* 9th edn, Irwin, Chicago (1996).

Chambers Dictionary of World History, Chambers Harrap, Edinburgh (1993).

Cipolla, CM, *The Economic History of World Population,* 6th edn, Penguin, London (1974).

Clark G, *In Fear of China*, Lansdowne Press, Melbourne (1967).

Clarkson W, *The Valkyrie Operation*, Blake Publishing, London (1998).

Cowie HR, Collins MB, Ryan DB, *Imperialism, Racism and Re-Assessments*, Nelson, Melbourne (1994).

Crough G, Wheelwright T, Wilshire T (eds), *Australia and World Capitalism*, Penguin (1980).

Dabscheck B, Niland J, *Industrial Relations in Australia*, George Allen & Unwin, Sydney (1981).

Davies, D, *An Introduction to Clinical Psychiatry*, Melbourne University Press, Melbourne (1971).

Davis JW, *An Introduction to Public Administration*, The Free Press, New York (1974).

Dees M, *Gathering Storm, America's Militia Threat*, Harper Perennial, New York (1996).

Doyle D, *Inside Espionage, A Memoir of True Men and Traitors*, St Ermin's Press, London (2000).

Dulany DE, Hypotheses and habits in verbal "operant conditioning," *J Abnormal & Social Psychology* 63 (1961) 251-263.

Dulany DE, *The place of hypothesis and intentions: An analysis of verbal control in verbal conditioning*, J of *Personality* 30 (1962) 102-129.

Eagly AH, Chaiken S, *The Psychology of Attitudes*, Harcourt Brace Jovanovich, Orlando FL (1993).

Fanteaux K, *Defusing Angry People, Practical Tools for Handling Bullying, Threats and Violence*, New Horizon Press, Far Hills NJ (2011).

Field EM, *Bully Busting, How to Help Children Deal With Teasing and Bullying*, Finch Publishing, Sydney (1999).

Fishbein M, Attitude and the prediction of behaviour, in M. Fishbein (ed.) *Readings In Attitude Theory and Measurement* (pp. 477-492), Wiley, New York (1967).

Fishbein M, Ajzen I, *Belief, Attitude, Intention, and Behaviour: An Introduction to the Theory and Research,* Addison-Wesley, Reading MA (1975).

Forbes HD, *Ethnic Conflict: Commerce, Culture, and the Contact Hypothesis,* Yale University Press, New Haven (1997).

Galton D, *In Our Own Image, Eugenics and the Genetic Modification of People,* Little Brown, London (2001).

Goodall (van Lawick-Goodall), Jane, *In the Shadow of Man,* Houghton Mifflin, Boston (1971).

Greer, Germaine, *The Female Eunuch* (1970). Reprinted by Farrar, Straus & Geraux, New York (2001).

Hamlyn (publisher), *The Sores of Civilization,* Marshall Cavendish, London (1970).

Healey J (ed.), *Issues in Society Vol. 330, 'Dealing With Bullying',* the Spinney Press, Thirroul NSW (2011).

Hughes-Wilson J, *Military Intelligence Blunders,* Carroll & Graf, New York (1999).

Jay P, *The Crisis of Western Political Economy,* The Australian Broadcasting Commission, Sydney (1981).

Jencks C, Smith M, Acland H, Bane MJ, Cohen D, Gintis H, Heyns B, Michelson S, *Inequality: A Reassessment of the Effect of Family and Schooling in America,* Penguin, Harmondsworth (1975).

Jones S, Israel P, *Others Unknown: The Oklahoma City Bombing Case and Conspiracy,* Public Affairs, New York (1998).

Kirchler E, Zani B, Why don't they stay at home? Prejudices against ethnic minorities in Italy, *Journal of Community and Applied Social Psychology* 5 (1995) 59-65.

REFERENCES

Knightly P, *Philby, KGB Masterspy,* André Deutsch, London (1988).

Larsen RJ, Buss DM, *Personality Psychology, Domains of Knowledge About Human Nature,* McGraw-Hill, NY (2002).

Lifton RJ, *Destroying the World to Save It: Aum Shinrikyo, Apocalyptic Violence, and the New Global Terrorism,* Metropolitan Books, New York (1999).

Lindzey G, Hall CS, Thompson RF, *Psychology,* 2nd edn, Worth, New York (1978).

Lynn J, Jay A, *Yes Prime Minister, The Diaries of the Right Hon. James Hacker,* vol. 1, BBC publications, London (1986).

Lynne R, Vanhanen T, *IQ and The Wealth of Nations,* Praeger, Westport CT (2002).

Mackenzie KR, *The English Parliament*, Penguin, Harmondsworth (1950).

Marcum D, Smith S, Khalsa M, *Business Think, 8 rules for Getting it Right – Now and No Matter What,* Wiley, NY (2002).

Marks B, Marks R, Spillane R, *The Management Contradictory,* Michelle Anderson Publishing, Melbourne (2006).

Masoff J, *Oh Yikes! History's Grossest, Wackiest Moments,* Workman Publishing, New York (2006).

Maxwell N, Yahuda M, Wheelwright T, Jayawardena C, The Chinese model: politics in command, in *Political Economy of Development,* Australian Broadcasting Commission, Sydney (1977).

McCormack MH, *What They Don't Teach You at Harvard Business School,* Fontana/Collins, London (1986).

McGuire WJ, Personality and susceptibility to social influence. In *Handbook of Personality Theory and Research* (eds. EF Borgatta & WW Lambert), pp. 1130-1187 (1968).

REFERENCES

McGuire WJ, The nature of attitudes and attitude change. In *Handbook of Social Psychology*, 2nd ed., Vol. 3 (eds. G Lindzey & E Aronson), pp. 136-314 (1969).

Miller J, Engelbert S, Broad W, *Germs, The Ultimate Weapon*, Simon & Schuster, New York (2001).

Mohr GA, *The Finite Element Method for Solids, Fluids, and Optimization*, Oxford University Press, Oxford (1992).

Mohr GA, *The Pretentious Persuaders, A Brief History & Science of Mass Persuasion*, Horizon Publishing Group, Sydney (2012a, 2014 – 2nd edition).

Mohr GA, *The Doomsday Calculation: The End of the Human Race*, Xlibris, Sydney (2012b).

Mohr GA, *The War of the Sexes, Women Are Getting On Top*, Xlibris, Sydney (2012c).

Mohr GA, Fear, Edwin, *World Religions, The History, Issues & Truth*, Xlibris, Sydney (2015).

Mohr GA, Fear E, Sinclair R, *World War 3: When & How Will It End?*, Inspiring Publishers, Canberra (2015).

Mohr GA, Fear E, *The Brainwashed, From Consumer Zombies to Islamism & Jihad*, Inspiring Publishers, Canberra (2016),

Mohr GA, *The War of the Sexes, The Problems & the Solutions*, Amazon-Kindle (2018).

Mohr, Geoff, *Mohr's Law of Hierarchies, and many other Mohr's Laws*, Amazon-Kindle (2018b).

Mohr GA, Mohr PE, Mohr RS, *The Population Explosion, The Problems, Solutions, and Predictions*, Amazon-Kindle (2018a).

Mohr GA, Mohr PE, Mohr RS, *World Religions, From Animism to Mohronism*, Amazon-Kindle (2018b).

Mohr GA, Mohr RS, Mohr PE, *The Psychology of Hope*, Balboa Press, Bloomington IN (2018c).

Mohr GA, Mohr PE, Mohr RS, *Brainwashed Zombies, Religious, Political and Consumer Persuasion,* Amazon-Kindle (2018d).

Natkeil R, *Atlas of 20th Century History,* Bison Books, Greenwich CT (1982).

Nojumi N, *The Rise of the Taliban in Afghanistan,* Palgrave, New York (2002).

Odle F, *The Picture Story of British Inventions,* World Distributors, Manchester (1966).

O'Guinn TC, Allen CT, Semenik RJ, *Advertising and Integrated Brand Promotion.* Thomson South-Western, Mason OH 2006.

Packard V, *The Waste Makers,* Pelican, Harmondsworth (1963).

Packard V, *The People Shapers,* Nelson, Melbourne (1978).

Panniker KM, *Asia and Western Dominance,* p. 116, Allen & Unwin, London (1959).

Penn, *Microtrends, The Small Forces Behind Today's Big Changes,* Allen Lane, London (2007).

Perlman D, Oskamp S, The effects of picture content and exposure frequency on evaluations of Negroes and whites, *Journal of Experimental Social Psychology* 7 (1971) 503-514.

Peter LJ, Hull R, *The Peter Principle,* Souvenir Press, London (1969).

Philby R, Lyubimov M, Peake H, *The Private Life of Kim Philby,* Fromm International, New York (2000).

Phillips L, Behaving badly, *HR Monthly,* Sept. 2000, pp/ 36-37.

Plowman D, Deery S, Fisher C, *Australian Industrial Relations,* McGraw-Hill, Sydney (1980).

Robertson TS, *Consumer Behaviour,* Scott Foresman, Glenview IL (1970).

REFERENCES

Sampson A, *The Arms Bazaar,* Coronet Books, London (1977).

Sargent M, *Drinking and Alcoholism in Australia: A Power Relations Theory,* Longman Cheshire, Melbourne (1979).

Sauerbruch F, *A Surgeon's Life,* André Deutsch, London (1953).

Schaefer TR, Contacts between immigrants and Englishmen: Road to tolerance or intolerance, *New Community* 2 (1973) 358-371.

Self P, *Administrative Theories and Policies,* 2nd edn, George Allen & Unwin, London (1977).

Snow RL, *Terrorists Amongst Us, The Militia Threat,* Perseus Publishing, Cambridge MA (1999).

Stone RJ, *Human Resource Management,* 4th edn, Wiley, Brisbane (2002).

Sweezy PM, *The Theory of Capitalist Development*, Dennis Dobson, London (1946).

Taylor L, Walton P, Industrial sabotage: motives and meanings, in *Images of Deviance,* S. Cohen, p. 219, Penguin, Harmondsworth (1971).

Thomas M, *As Used on the Famous Nelson Mandela, Underground Adventures in the Arms and Torture Trade,* Ebury Press, London (2006).

Vander AJ, Sherman JH, Luciano DS, *Human Physiology,* 6th edn, McGraw-Hill, New York (1994).

Vernon PE, *Intelligence and Attainment Tests,* University of London Press, London (1960).

Wheen F, *How Mumbo Jumbo Conquered The World,* Public Affairs, New York (2004).

Wolfe L, Brainwashing: How the British Use The Media For Mass Psychological Warfare Brainwashing. Posted on the Internet. Originally printed in *The American Almanac,* May 5, 1997.

Wolfe L, Americans Target Of Largest Media Brainwashing Campaign In History. Posted on the Internet and originally in *Executive Intelligence Review,* 16/10/01.

Wonnacott, P. and Wonnacott, R. Economics. McGraw-Hill, New York, 1979.

Yeltsin B, *Against The Grain, An Autobiography,* Summit Books, New York (1990).

Zajonc RB, Attitudinal effects of mere exposure, *Journal of Personality and Social Psychology,* 9, 1968 (no. 2, pt 2).

General reference sources

Chambers Dictionary of World History, Chambers Harrap, Edinburgh (1993).

Collins National Encyclopaedia, Collins, London (1966).

Egerton-Eastwick RW (ed.), *The Oracle Encyclopaedia,* George Newnes, London (1896).

Encarta Book of Quotations, Pan MacMillan, Sydney (2000).

Encarta Encyclopaedia 1999, Microsoft Corporation, 1998.

Encyclopaedia Britannica CD 99 (1999).

Encyclopaedia Britannica Ready Reference 2003.

Mindscape World Atlas & Almanac, The Learning Company Inc., Crawley, West Sussex (1999).

Natkeil R, *Atlas of 20th Century History,* Bison Books, Greenwich CT (1982).

The Oxford Dictionary of Quotations, 4th edn, Oxford University Press, Oxford, 1992.

The Oxford Interactive Encyclopaedia, The Learning Company, 1997.

Philips' New World Atlas, George Philip & Son, Ltd, London (1934).

Power Quotes, Daniel B. Baker, *The Business Library,* Information Australia (1992).

The SBS World Guide, 4th edn, Reed Reference Australia, Melbourne (1995).

The World Almanac and Book of Facts 1998, World Almanac Books, Mahwah NJ (1998),

1999 World Book Multimedia Encyclopaedia, World Book Inc. (1998).

Wikipedia.

HUMAN CONFLICT

This important book examines the history and psychology of human conflict concisely, its special features including:

> An overview of man's long history of conflict.
> The psychology of conflict including attitudinal psychology, contact theory, hierarchies, and personality types.
> A new six part Attitudinal Model of Conflict and discussion of this in relation to man's many areas of conflict.
> Conflict in marriage, schools, and workplaces.
> Urban crime and conflicting groups in society.
> Tribal, ethnic, religious and political conflict.
> Territorial and imperialist conflict.
> The two World Wars, terrorism and revolution.
> Democracy, socialism and the decline of the West.
> Future conflict: nuclear and biological warfare.
> How to reduce conflict and focus on the growing threats of overpopulation, resource depletion and pollution.
> *Real democracy* is proposed and detailed.

G. A. Mohr did his PhD at Churchill College, Cambridge. He published circa 60 papers for 20 international journals and more than 25 books, including:

A Microcomputer Introduction to the Finite Element Method
Finite Elements for Solids, Fluids, and Optimization
The Pretentious Persuaders, A Brief History & Science of Mass Persuasion
Curing Cancer & Heart Disease
The Variant Virus, Introducing Secret Agent Simon Sinclair
The Doomsday Calculation, The End Of The Human Race
Heart Disease, Cancer, & Ageing: Proven Neutraceutical & Lifestyle Solutions
2045: A Remote Town Survives Global Holocaust
The History & Psychology of Human Conflict;   The War of the Sexes
Elementary Thinking for the 21st Century
The 8-Week+ Program to Reverse Cardiovascular Disease
The Scientific MBA;   Mohr's Law of Hierarchies
The DIY Cardiovascular Cure;   Combating Cancer

Also with R.S. Mohr/Richard Sinclair & P.E. Mohr/Edwin Fear:

The Evolving Universe: Relativity, Redshift and Life from Space
World Religions: The History, Psychology, Issues & Truth
World War 3, When & How Will It End?
The Brainwashed, From Consumer Zombies to Islamic Jihad
Human Intelligence, Learning & Behaviour
New Theories of The Universe, Evolution, and Relativity
The Psychology of Hope;   The Population Explosion
Brainwashed Zombies: Religious, Political & Consumer Persuasion